# Billy & Bully

by David Instone

Thomas Publications

T P

Copyright © David Instone 2009

The right of David Instone to be identified as the Author of this Work has been asserted by him in accordance with the Copyright, Designs and Patents Act 1988.

First published in Great Britain in November 2009
by Thomas Publications

All rights reserved. No part of this publication may be reproduced, stored in a retrieval system, or transmitted, in any form or by any means, electronic, mechanical, photocopying, recording or otherwise, without the prior written permission of the publisher.

ISBN 978-0-9550585-3-0

Thomas Publications

Printed and bound by TJ International, Padstow, Cornwall

# Contents

Acknowledgements
Introduction
Chapter One:              Young Billy ..................................9
Chapter Two:              Cup Winner ................................21
Chapter Three:            Back With a Bang .....................32
Chapter Four:             A True Champion......................39
Chapter Five:             All Lit Up ....................................45
Chapter Six:              Glory, Glory Wolves...................56
Chapter Seven:            The Game's Up ..........................69
Chapter Eight:            What Next?.................................76
Chapter Nine:             Bully For Wolves.......................85
Chapter Ten:              Scoring Sensation .....................94
Chapter Eleven:           Miracle Man .............................102
Chapter Twelve:           England Calling ......................108
Chapter Thirteen:         Sky's The Limit .......................115
Chapter Fourteen:         Second Coming ......................128
Chapter Fifteen:          Record Breaker .......................133
Chapter Sixteen:          Deeply Devoted.......................136
Chapter Seventeen:        The Last Stand ........................142
Chapter Eighteen:         Saddest Passing ......................152
Chapter Nineteen:         Goals And Nearly Gone.........158
Chapter Twenty:           Born Again ..............................167
Chapter Twenty-One:      Last Chance Saloon ...............174
Chapter Twenty-Two:      The Final Curtain ...................186
Chapter Twenty-Three    All Over....................................195
Subscribers ................................................................206

Previous Wolves titles by Thomas Publications:

Wolves In Pictures
The Bully Years
Wolves: Exclusive!
Sir Jack
Forever Wolves
Running With Wolves
Wolves: The Glory Years

To check on the availability of the above,
please use the contact details below:

Thomas Publications
PO Box 17
Newport
TF10 7WT

Telephone: 07734 440095
email: info@thomaspublications.co.uk
www.thomaspublications.co.uk
www.wolvesheroes.com

# Acknowledgements

Many millions of words have already been written about Billy Wright and Steve Bull, in book form as well as in newspapers, so a few thank-yous are in order for making this account very different.

Our list of interviewees, some of whom patiently sat down long enough ago to have probably forgotten that there was ever going to be a book at the end of it, is an impressive 'cast,' containing Barry Fry, Eddie Stuart, Bert Williams, Ron Atkinson, Tony Cottee, Hugh Curran, Martin Swain, Steve Gordos, John Rudge, Neil Aspin, Barry Powell, Paul Darby, Derek Mountfield, John Harris, Roy Swinbourne, John Richards, Ted Farmer, Bobby Gould, Alan A'Court, Daz Hale, John Pike, Chris Brindley, Norman Giller, Micky Holmes, Nicky Clarke, Andy Mutch, Keith Downing and a certain Steve Bull.

We also spoke to Graham Taylor, alas all too briefly as he was away for several days just before our deadline, then we found ourselves timed out as he departed on reporting duty to England's World Cup qualifier in the Ukraine early in October. He was the only one of our targets we missed out on.

The comments of many other managers, players, team-mates and opponents are contained in the 224 pages of this definitive publication and we trust we have acknowledged where they were made in the cases in which they have previously appeared elsewhere, either in printed or broadcast form.

For our photographs, we have leaned on Mirrorpix, who have supplied some of the stirring front-cover material, Associated Newspapers, Thames TV, Peter Harrington, the Yorkshire Evening Post, Roy Swinbourne and Sue (Mutchy), who has been helpful and enormously supportive well beyond the call of regular duty.

The design work has again been left in the trusty hands of Tricia Mills and the author's wife, Liz, while Steve Gordos, himself a prolific writer on Wolves matters and the creator of a long-overdue tribute to Peter Knowles in 2009, spotted errors - grammatical as well as factual - in the proof-reading task he attacked with his normal urgency and diligence.

Most of all, though, we thank Billy and Bully for their fabulous deeds. This book is all about them and the Wolves and England teams they graced.

# Introduction

Billy Wright and Steve Bull are the two most important players in Wolverhampton Wanderers' history. Billy played 105 times for England and helped take the club's name all over the world; Bully scored 306 goals for Wolves, the first few dozen of them at least at a time when we were feared there might not be a Molineux for much longer or indeed a team in the town to support.

Their colossal imprints on the Wolves story are generations apart, their respective paths coming together only when Billy returned to the fold in his twilight years to serve on Sir Jack Hayward's board of directors while Bully was busy accumulating another 100 goals or so. But there's a surprising amount of common ground in the duo's football lives to fit snugly among happenings and facts that in other ways make them polar opposites.

One played all of his 541 League and cup games for Wolves while they were in the top division, for the most part while they were in and around the top of it. He won three League Championships and an FA Cup, had a celebrity marriage, was never booked or sent off and became the first player from any country to win 100 caps.

The other didn't make a single appearance for the club in the first grade, won nothing more than a couple of lower-division titles and a knock-out competition for Third and Fourth Division clubs, is married for the third time, was no stranger to red or yellow cards and, in these parts at least, is considered to be harshly represented by his record of 13 appearances for England, many of those as a substitute.

There are other big differences, the first of them purely positional. While Bully's goal tally for Wolves is 112 beyond his nearest challenger (John Richards) and stands as a magnificent statistical reminder of how he terrorised defences at one end of the pitch, Billy was largely content with supplying bullets rather than firing them and then, from when he moved from wing-half to centre-half in the mid-1950s, almost exclusively concerned with curbing the threat of opposing forwards.

And what of their playing styles? One was famous for his balance, timing, anticipation, elegant passing and no little eagerness in the tackle. The other was all about raw hunger, naked aggression, strength and an unfailing flair for getting on the end of whatever his team-mates could set up for him – or, indeed, he for himself. An on-pitch confrontation between the two would have been quite something.

The duo's post-playing opportunities are no less contrasting. Billy coached with England under-23s before managing Arsenal, Bully had to ask for some part-time work at Hereford and was then made to wait the best part of another decade to be given his break in the dug-out, at hard-up Stafford Rangers.

On the other hand, there are more than just the obvious similarities, such as both having their names adorning prestige stands at the stadium at which they are revered and both having letters alongside their names. Scratch beneath the surface and it becomes evident that Billy Wright CBE and Steve Bull MBE were both managed for many years by men born in the Cheshire town of Ellesmere Port (Stan Cullis and Graham Turner), each supported big clubs from outside the area (Arsenal and Liverpool) during boyhoods that were centred half an hour or so from Molineux and both sampled factory employment before football consumed them.

They also both had the potentially crushing disappointment of being told their careers might be over before they had properly begun. In his forthright way, Major Frank Buckley decided that the young Wright was too small to cut it and, 40-odd years later, a knee injury was initially deemed too serious to enable Bull to pursue a life in the professional game.

The two heroes also retired, unusually, during pre-season build-ups. Billy opted to go because he felt the combination of time and hungry young Wolves creeping up on him. Nature's wear-and-tear process left Bully with no choice other than to quit when he did; there's the coincidence/contrast thing again.

Most importantly, both are regarded as fabulously loyal one-club men, although they actually served two League clubs apiece. Billy, described by Sir Jack as 'England's finest footballer and gentleman,' played for Leicester during the war and it is to Albion's considerable pain that the striker who so spectacularly transformed the Molineux landscape in the late 1980s cut his teeth with a handful of matches while across the patch at The Hawthorns.

We trust that the entwined Billy & Bully tale is enriched in these pages for supporters by the memories of so many of their contemporaries and admirers, even by a few of their opponents. We are, after all, talking about possibly the two best-known players of any Molineux era and the occupants of third and fourth places in Wolverhampton Wanderers' all-time appearance-makers list.

I wasn't lucky enough to see Billy play, coming as I did from a generation who also missed out on Williams, Hancocks, Mullen and Slater, and caught only the very tail end of the Broadbent and Flowers years at Molineux. But I met him several times in his later years, once while interviewing him in his car for a chapter in a 1990 book, and never heard anyone say a bad word against him, nor he against them.

Conversely, no reporter saw more of Bully's goals and games than I did. The club wouldn't have been the same, even today, had it not been for him. And would there have been a Wolves that Sir Jack wanted to save if Bully hadn't started to stir the giant from a sleep that was close to becoming a coma?

So there is surely an inspiring story to be told. But why write it now, so long after the last of their magnificent, dramatic on-field deeds? Well, it's 70 years this year since Billy made his Wolves debut, 60 since he lifted the FA Cup and 50 since he played his last games for club and country. It also happens to be 20 years since Bully made his sensational goal-scoring England debut as a 50-plus-goals-a-season lower-division striker and ten since he was forced to quit. So many anniversaries. The time somehow seems right to celebrate the curiously coincidental and yet sharply contrasting careers of two of Wolverhampton Wanderers' very finest.

## Chapter One

# Young Billy

Like Steve Bull, Billy Wright is not only a Wolverhampton Wanderers legend but a home-grown legend. He was born on February 6, 1924, and lived at 33 Belmont Road, Ironbridge, where a plaque on the wall announces the fact. The club have had some wonderful performers down the decades but, of their top ten all-time appearance makers, only these two, plus full-back Geoff Palmer, took their first breath in what might be called the local area.

To think that one of them was born a few miles south of Molineux and the other half an hour or so to the west is yet more reason for Wolves fans to puff out their chest with pride at the thought of those 306 goals and 105 caps.

There was a bit of Bully about the young Billy. On his debut for Madeley School against Bewdley School, he more than compensated for his lack of inches by scoring ten times, the flow of goals soon starting to steer the blondest boy in the team towards a professional football career rather than one in the same iron foundry at which his father worked.

There are reports he was once given a couple of chocolate bars for scoring a hat-trick in one of his handful of games for Cradley Heath. But something a little more lasting soon came his way. He was still nearer his 14th birthday than his 15th when, having seen Wolves advertising in the Express & Star for young players, he joined the Molineux groundstaff in the summer of 1938.

Billy received £2 a week, of which 30 shillings (£1.50) went to the most famous landlay in Wolverhampton, Mrs Colley, his kindly but protective guardian for nearly two decades until he married a pop star. Five shillings went to his mother and the other five (25p) remained as his pocket money.

His pleasures were simple ones. He followed the fortunes of 'the Arsenal,' as they were then better known, grew to like rug-making in the digs on the edge of Tettenhall which he shared for a while with club colleagues Alan Steen and Cameron Buchanan and loved collecting players' autographs. No wonder he never refused a youngster's request for one of his in later years, when he sometimes displayed an amazing ambidexterity by signing left-handed.

It's astonishing to look back now and remember that the player who would win a century of caps for England was at one point considered not good enough to be kept on even by his club. Strictly speaking, that should read 'big enough' because it was on size grounds that Wolves manager Major Frank Buckley broke Billy's heart towards the end of his six-month trial by giving him the devastating news that he was being released.

The club, admittedly with some of England's top players already at their disposal and approaching true greatness as war neared, were *that* close to losing the lad who would go on to play 541 League and Cup games and lead them to three Championships and an FA Cup triumph.

"Wolves were a big strong side in those days," said Tommy Lawton in the authorised 2000 biography *'The Complete Centre-Forward'*. "Major Buckley wanted strapping lads who could plough through anything. It's no surprise he sent Billy home before he had even played a game. He was not really Wolves' type at all. What a loss he would have been, not just to them, but to England."

Where might Billy have gone? Kidderminster Harriers? Albion? A job in the iron foundry after all? Thankfully, there was a rapid reversal of the decision. Trainer Jack Davies had a valuable word in the manager's ear and the teenager, all 5ft 3in of him, was a picture of relief as the Major leaned over, jabbed a finger into his chest and said: "I have been persuaded to change my mind. I am assured that you are big here, where it really matters."

Billy, determined not to pass up the second chance, strove to make a good impression. He was promoted to the role of head kit boy and prepared the skip containing the playing gear, sometimes carrying it with help from Mullen, who had joined the club a few months before he had. It was a role he carried out in the build-up to Wolves' appearance in the 1939 FA Cup final, although it unfortunately didn't extend to travelling to unload it at Wembley.

Instead, he played in the A team, then tuned in his wireless to the big game, shedding tears at the shock of Wolves' 4-1 defeat against lowly Portsmouth. Almost 50 years later, a three-goal Cup exit of even greater improbability would cloud Steve Bull's early days at Molineux as well. It wasn't sadness that engulfed the striker after the humiliation by Chorley at Burnden Park, though – just disbelief and a little self-questioning of the career step he had just taken in moving from Second Division West Brom to Fourth Division Wolves.

# Young Billy

Wright didn't have to wait much longer for his big chance. With Hitler's march bringing about an early truncation of the 1939-40 League season, clubs relied instead on a hastily organised replacement competition and Wolves and Notts County found themselves in opposition on October 21, 1939, shortly before the launch of the Midland Regional League. Billy was as proud as punch as he played as a right-winger at Meadow Lane, more so as his side won 2-1.

He impressed sufficiently to keep his place for a month, his Regional League debut coming in a 3-2 defeat away to Birmingham. But his career soon took another detour from which it might not have fully recovered when the Major told him and fellow groundstaff lads Mullen and Steen they were being released as the lack of recognised competition curtailed their duties.

"For the second time, I returned to the Colley family at Tettenhall a very dispirited young man," Wright wrote in his 1957 *'Football Is My Passport'* book. Happily, Buckley relented once more and quickly informed the trio by telegram that they were required back; only so they could be told, though, that their football commitments would from now be restricted to weekends, with week-days to be spent labouring over damaged tyres at a nearby garage.

Billy also sampled life at Great Bridge Foundry in 'Bully country' – another acquaintance with a more regular existence that the striker, too, would have decades later. Interesting conclusions can be drawn. Maybe the Rooneys, Ferdinands and Ronaldos think they have missed nothing by sidestepping such brushes with everyday working folk but it's tempting to assume that Billy and Bully were driven on in their efforts to make the most of their second and even third chances by these humdrum experiences on the factory floor.

There was nothing like rejection to fire the passion these two legends of Wolverhampton carried through their playing careers – and nothing like a taste of a less privileged world to develop the more rounded personalities that helped make them such affable members of their dressing rooms.

Just as Bull's early Molineux months were played out against a background of doubt about the club's future, so uncertainty surrounded Billy's progress as more obstacles appeared in his path. Having played 20 times in the 1939-40 Midland Regional League or Cup, once with Yorkshire-born inside-forward Horace Wright, he saw his stage disappear when Wolves decided they didn't have the resources to participate in the same competitions 12 months on.

There must have been a danger that the club's talented youngsters would go to waste through inactivity and be snapped up by other clubs. The threat loomed larger in the case of Wright and Mullen when they were packed off across the East Midlands as guest players, the duo helping Leicester to win the 1940-41 Midland War Cup via a 2-0 success in the final over a Walsall side containing Johnny Hancocks.

"Jimmy and I scored 30 goals between us for Leicester and that helped my confidence when I returned," Billy said in a magazine article decades later. "I hadn't been able to score goals regularly beforehand despite being tried in various forward positions at Wolves." Mullen, who had made his senior Wolves debut at 16 and played in the 1939 FA Cup semi-final against Grimsby in front of Old Trafford's biggest-ever crowd, was a useful sounding board for his close friend. Wright was still playing on the opposite wing but had much to learn in the art of dribbling. And he could have had no-one better than the Geordie left-winger to teach him how to cross.

Billy's chances of making it as a centre-forward, meanwhile, were being stunted by his growth. Despite putting on the inches, he would not make it past 5ft 8in, so he was never going to climb above brawny defenders and head goals at the far post. But it wasn't just his skills and his frame that made him stand out in the Wolves pack.

His shock of blond hair was a strong distinguishing feature and earned him the nickname 'Snowy' from Hednesford-born wing-half Tom Galley among others. Mmmm, another contrast......while it was an abundance of distinctive coloured locks that helped make Billy easy to spot, Bully's most recognisable feature was his lack of them. He opted for a different look altogether on his frequent visits to the barber.

Unlike the 1980s and 1990s icon, who would make his Wolves debut at no 8 and then play his next 339 matches for them at no 9, Billy's football life, in the sense of which shirt he wore, was a nomadic one. As well as being used in all five forward roles, he was tried at both centre-half and left-half as the search to establish his best position continued. And here's another thing: the 'y' was rarely added when he was referred to by his Christian name in the early years, so this book might have been titled *'Bill and Bull'*.

Things still refused to run smoothly and the emphatic Midland War League Cup semi-final win over Albion in 1941-42 brought Billy a broken right ankle and fresh worries over his future. The Major, a war veteran and already a figure capable of striking fear into young players with his disciplinarian ways, did little to ease the anxiety. In what the player called a 'chilling' episode,' Buckley

# Young Billy

warned Mrs Colley the injury was bad enough to be career-threatening.

Billy, who said the wrenching of his joint from a perfectly normal tackle had made it feel like 'a million needles had been stuck in me,' put weight on in the weeks that followed the subsequent surgery, his depression added to by apprehension at how well he would recover. His biggest problem on the comeback trail was his reluctance to strike the ball flat out.

The Major, opting for something more demanding to test the joint, had the youngster in the Molineux goalmouth to strike first-time shots from crosses supplied from the wings by Cameron Buchanan and Mullen. It was only after several tentative shots that Mullen centred again and shouted 'Crack It!' that his team-mate hammered hard and low past Cyril Sidlow. "I had completed my greatest assignment – beating my own fears," Billy said.

Much later, Wright added: "From my early experiences in the game, I could never have hoped that I would be lucky to go on and have the career I did. It could all have ended for me once or twice and I often had to pinch myself later on to convince myself I wasn't dreaming when I was winning trophies with Wolves and captaining England in so many fabulous cities around the world."

It appears that revolutionary surgery had saved the day. More than 25 years later, journalist Mike Langley was at Highbury when Billy rolled down his sock, pointed to the legacy of the operation and said: "I've got a bone pin right through my ankle. Fortunately, it never gave me much bother."

It said much about the erratic availability of players during the hostilities – and the scope clubs had to use guests – that Wolves should win the cup semi-final against Albion 7-1 on aggregate, having lost 8-2 and 5-3 to them in the league a few months earlier. With Dennis Westcott at his peak and Wright a frustrated observer, they then overpowered Sunderland 6-3 in the two-leg final.

The massive loss of life in the war ensured that football injuries, even ones as potentially serious as Billy's, were kept in their proper perspective. And, thankfully, he was playing again anyway after a few weeks. Not that his routine was anything like back to normal.

He himself was having a taste of the Army, initially in Shrewsbury and then in Aldershot with the King's Shropshire Light Infantry, and became a regular in the Army side along with a host of big names that included his long-time Wolves colleagues Mullen and Hancocks, the latter of whom would move to Molineux from Walsall after the guns fell silent.

"I was able to play with such great players as Tommy Lawton, Billy Elliott,

# Billy & Bully

Willie Watson and Frank Swift," Billy recalled. "In their company, my game improved gradually and it was then that I moved to wing-half. And I soon realised how much happier I was having the game coming directly at me."

Billy, like many footballers, was a PT instructor and became a Private, then a Corporal and a Staff Sergeant. He was in the Combined Services side who took on the League of Ireland in Cliftonville, replacing Raich Carter in a team also containing Stanley Matthews, Frank Swift, Neil Franklin and Joe Mercer, but showed his nervousness with a misplaced pass aimed for left-winger Willie Watson in the first minute.

In response to the merciless howls of the crowd, Lawton kindly made a bee-line for the new boy and told him: "Don't take any notice of them. You can't call yourself a footballer until you've had a bit of that." Later, he said of him: "He was a great player, a fine captain and a great pal." It was mutual appreciation because Wright rated the Everton player one of the best centre-forwards he ever saw. But Lawton still believed there was one man Billy had to doff his cap to – a man he was lucky enough to have as his mentor for so long. In the biography *'The Complete Centre-Forward'*, Lawton said: "Stan Cullis was certainly the best centre-half I ever played against. Neil Franklin, Billy Wright, Bobby Moore, Franz Beckenbauer......Stan had them all beat."

With Billy's ankle mercifully recovered, Major Buckley, the man who had issued a gloomy bulletin on his chances of getting back to full fitness, shocked Molineux by leaving in 1944. Ted Vizard was in charge come the time of the return to Wolves action of a player who proceeded to hit a 17-minute hat-trick against Nottingham Forest – further food for thought in the debate over which role suited him best.

Wright, whose birthplace led to him acquiring the nickname The Iron Horse, fancied himself as an inside-left – and was not alone. Having travelled as a reserve to the England v Wales Victory International in October, 1945, he was picked in that same no 10 role for the follow-up game against Belgium at Wembley three months later.

His excitement at being selected for his country for the first time was compounded by his delight at the prospect of lining up closest to Mullen. But Frank Soo withdrew late through injury, so Wright moved to right-half and was satisfied with his performance as 85,000 peered through the fog for a view of Jesse Pye scoring one of the goals in a 2-0 victory a few weeks before he moved from Notts County to Wolves.

# Young Billy

The England team, captained by Joe Mercer, were smitten with the new boy in their midst. Wright was quiet, shy, polite, clean-living and utterly dedicated – qualities and good manners for which Mrs Colley and her husband can be at least partially thanked. It was she who had insisted he write home with news of his first international selection so his parents wouldn't be so taken aback when the paper dropped on the mat of their Shropshire home.

Column inches would soon follow, though, because his career was about to move on at a rare old pace. He played for Wolves in the Football League for the first time when recognised competition resumed in 1946-47, joining Bert Williams, Angus McLean, Johnny Hancocks, Pye and Fred Ramscar as debutants in an occasion that was as far removed as you can imagine from Steve Bull's debut 40 years later.

Whereas 5,252 would watch the 3-0 Fourth Division home defeat against Wrexham on November 22, 1986 that served as a painful introduction for Bully and Andy Thompson, Molineux was heaving under the weight of 50,845 spectators as Arsenal, Billy's boyhood favourites, were put to the sword 6-1 in those austere post-war days, Pye scoring a hat-trick.

"I couldn't have asked for a better start to my League career," Wright said. "The Arsenal had been a special club to me ever since I was a young lad and I always loved playing against them and regarded Highbury as a wonderful place. To beat them so well in the first League game at Molineux after the war made it a fabulous day for all of us."

Bully never played anywhere but at the head of Wolverhampton Wanderers' attack but Billy's versatility continued to be evident with club and country. Although playing at left-half to allow the well-established Tom Galley to play as Wolves' right-half, he continued to fill the Galley role (no 4) for England.

And, having kept his national jersey for the final three Victory Internationals – defeats in Scotland and France and a resounding home win over Switzerland – Wright won his first full cap on September 28, 1946, the day Wolves were beating Portsmouth at Molineux. There was no thought 63 years ago of ditching club fixtures while their best players were away on international duty.

Ironically, Billy had just missed two League games and been switched to inside-left for the next, a 2-0 home victory over Grimsby, by the time he proudly pulled on the three lions shirt during the short hop to Belfast. Only Raich Carter and Lawton of the line-up had previously played official games for their country and the lengthy series of firsts included the blooding of the

# Billy & Bully

former Manchester United centre-half Walter Winterbottom as manager.

Even the skipper George Hardwick was a debutant and the Middlesbrough left-back would lead the side out for each of Billy's first 13 caps, the Victory Internationals not having been marked by the presenting of such time-honoured keepsakes. Northern Ireland were no match for the visitors, crushed 7-2 as they were in front of 57,000 in the first full post-war meeting of two home countries.

Cap no 2 followed only two nights later in Dublin and came in a much closer contest. England won by the only goal and Billy returned to club duties by himself getting on the score-sheet in a 2-0 triumph at Everton. While Bully would hit the target 19 times in his debut Molineux season, Billy managed just this one appearance among the marksmen in his first year of League football with the club.

By coincidence, Billy and Bully would each contribute 37 outings to their breakthrough campaigns before both suffered crushing disappointment in the final Wolves game. That meant failure for the striker in 1986-87 in the Fourth Division play-off final and, on a furnace of a day on May 31, 1947, heartbreak in the climax to a thrilling League Championship race.

Billy had continued to play mainly at left-half for Vizard's Wolves, who set themselves up to lift the title for the first time in their 70-year history by winning at Huddersfield in their penultimate game. Two points, maybe even one, from their final match would see them crowned champions, so Football League officials transported the trophy to Molineux in anticipation. The sting, though, was that their visitors were Liverpool, who, along with Stoke, could also still finish top.

A Westcott-inspired Wolves had run amok at Anfield in the December to the tune of 5-1 and had led the table by 11 points at one stage, only for a severe freeze to restrict them to one League game between January 18 and March 1. All the postponements cost them momentum and their programme spilled over into its latest-ever finish. Consequently, the thermometers were showing so much red on the decisive day that officials and police were kept busy by fans in a 50,765 crowd fainting.

The occasion carried added poignancy as Stan Cullis had announced to his team-mates over lunch that this was to be his final game before retirement. Cullis, born a few miles from Merseyside in Ellesmere Port, had been an outstanding performer for club and country and made another famous imprint on Molineux principles that day after leading his side out into the sunshine,

# Young Billy

resisting the temptation to hold back Albert Stubbins and concede a free-kick when the forward broke away from his errant marking to score.

Cullis, intermittently troubled since wartime by concussion injuries, must have felt more despair that afternoon than anyone, knowing his last chance of playing honours had gone. Westcott, a sort of mid-century Steve Bull, was also entitled to feel extra pain. His 38 First Division goals in 1946-47 still stand as a record haul for a Wolves player in a League season.

But Wright and everyone else in an old gold shirt was bitterly disappointed at the 2-1 defeat that condemned them to third place and made Liverpool, once Stoke had lost an outstanding rearranged game at Sheffield United, champions.

The outgoing captain, who had also been part of the team who finished runners-up in both the League (for the second successive season) and the FA Cup in 1938-39 before his own career was ripped apart, knew many players would have hauled Stubbins to the ground. He famously said, though: "I didn't want to go down in history as the man who decided the destiny of a Championship with a professional foul."

With that act of sportsmanship, the Championship trophy was returned to its bag and taken back to League headquarters in Preston but Billy applauded his skipper's virtues. And Cullis's retreat into a backroom role at Molineux as he took up an offer to become Vizard's assistant had a major knock-on effect on the younger man's career.

When Wright reported for pre-season training a few weeks later, he was greeted by Vizard with the message: "I have some words I think will interest you. The directors have decided to make you skipper. Best of luck!" Cullis, already a powerful guiding light, would now be steering the 23-year-old in a different way.

By now, Billy had six England caps, one of them coming at Wembley in the April when he faced Scotland for the first time in a full international. Mullen added a first full cap to his one Victory and two wartime appearances as he lined up in front of a 98,250 crowd who saw England salvage a 1-1 draw with a second-half equaliser that ensured they won the Home (International) Championship. It was the first of the 13 outings Wright was given against the arch enemy – a figure equal to the number of senior caps Steve Bull would win in total.

All six of the home games Bully played for England were at the national stadium but, as when the venue was being spectacularly rebuilt at the start of the 21st century, games were often taken round the provinces when Billy was playing, particularly in his early days. Huddersfield's Leeds Road and Manchester City's Maine Road – at that time shared by Manchester United because of bomb damage at Old Trafford during the war – were among what might now seem unlikely ports of call.

"I was quite happy playing at club grounds but most players will tell you there's something really special about playing at Wembley," Billy told me as we sat in his car before a game at Molineux in 1990 for an interview towards my *'Wolverhampton Wanderers Greats'* book. "There was something magical when you walked out to play for your country at Wembley."

Billy didn't taste defeat in a full international until his country were beaten 1-0 by Switzerland on the occasion of Derby forward Raich Carter's final cap. Wright once said he found Blackpool's Bloomfield Road a challenging venue because of its tight pitch and surrounds, so it's perhaps no coincidence he fell below his usual standards in Zurich in a stadium described as cramped.

That seventh England appearance was quickly followed by an eighth as the side fulfilled the second leg of a summer tour that also took in Lisbon. And they clicked in a big way against the Portuguese with a stunning 10-0 victory which serves to show how much times have changed 60 years on.

Billy's satisfaction in featuring in one of the country's biggest victories of all time was soon compounded back at club level when, with the Molineux captaincy his, he proudly led Wolves out on the opening day of 1947-48 in their game against a Manchester City side containing his good pal Frank Swift.

A 4-3 defeat at Maine Road ensured the afternoon was less than perfect but Wolves responded spectacularly, beating Grimsby 8-1, Blackburn 5-1 and Grimsby, in the return, 4-0 in their next three games. Having been runners-up in two of the previous three completed seasons and third in the other, the club were determined to push hard again – and their new skipper played his part.

He scored five times for them in 1947-48, including home and away against Sheffield United, in compiling his record haul for a season in peacetime football and saw the goals fly in from those around him at international level, too. To make life easier for the debutant Tim Ward, Billy switched from right-half to his club position of left-half for the 5-2 England victory in Brussels early in 1947-48 and stayed there the following month when his caps total moved into double figures with a 3-0 victory over Wales at Ninian Park.

It wasn't long before the critics were suggesting Stan Mortensen was less effective without Billy supplying ammunition for him from the no 4 role but at least the Wolves man had more than one string to his bow. At the same time, his Molineux pal Bert Williams had good cause to reflect on the fact that goalkeepers have only one stab at a place and he might also have been in the team by now had it not been for the impact and popularity of a familiar figure at Wright's back.

Keepers are often eccentric – as in the case of the jocular Mark Kendall at the start of Bully's Wolves career – and Billy had an extrovert team-mate in the differently coloured jersey with England. Frank Swift was in goal for all of Wright's first 17 full matches for his country and became a firm friend, revered as he was by many for his personality.

Cap no 13 for Billy came at Hampden Park, where, by another quirk, Bully won the first of his 13 caps, and it was a memorable occasion as England silenced an astonishing 135,376 crowd by winning 2-0 to secure another Home Championship. Wright was back at no 4 and, yes, Mortensen scored. Not that too many conclusions should be drawn. The Blackpool player hit a hat-trick against Sweden in the previous game with Liverpool's Phil Taylor at right-half on the day Billy played for his country at Highbury for the second time.

Wright described the game at Hampden as one of the most bruising of his career and Swift and skipper George Hardwick presumably concurred. Swift was found to have two broken ribs after collapsing at the station as the team set off for home while Hardwick picked up a serious knee injury and didn't play for England again.

The captaincy consequently passed to Swift for the end-of-season clash with Italy in Turin, where England registered a somewhat flattering 4-0 victory. It's a macabre fact that both skippers from that day were to be killed in plane crashes, Swift when travelling as a journalist with Manchester United in Munich ten years later and Italy's Valentino Mazzola as ten players from then all-powerful Serie A champions Torino perished as they descended towards the city following a friendly in Portugal.

While life was successful with England, Billy was having his ups and downs at club level. Wolves struggled for consistency in their first season with Cullis on the coaching staff and, despite a Christmas double over Aston Villa in front of a combined 123,000 spectators, they trailed in only fifth, fully 12 points adrift of Arsenal.

The gap was then the equivalent of six victories and there was a feeling of déjà vu, although without the heartache, when they lost 2-1 to Liverpool in their final game, this time at Anfield. The similarity with the season before went a stage further when Vizard decided to quit soon afterwards. Cullis, who had made the retirement headlines 12 months earlier, was the natural choice as his successor and was duly appointed by the Molineux board.

"I had long been convinced that a great future in football still lay ahead of him," Wright wrote years later. "More than that, I was sure his future was at Molineux. He didn't take long to make his mark. Very soon, he called the whole playing staff together and said: 'I want us to see eye to eye right from the start. I want and am going to get 100 per cent effort from you all, on and off the field. If I get this support, you can take it from me that I will be 100 per cent behind you. Nothing else is going to be enough.'"

## Chapter Two

# Cup Winner

Under new management, Wolves hardly flew out of the blocks in 1948-49, winning only once in their first five matches (5-0 at Bolton) before a thrilling home victory over a Manchester United side of whom they would see much more that season, albeit some months after they promptly lost 2-0 at Old Trafford in the return.

Inconsistency was again a problem, as shown by results either side of a day that would define the life of their much-loved skipper for ever. Wright missed the 3-1 defeat at champions Arsenal in late September but was given a warm welcome home when leading Wolves to a crushing 7-1 win over Huddersfield – and not without good reason, events having moved on apace after he had won his 15th cap by playing in the 0-0 Sunday draw in Denmark.

In these days of glitzy cars and size 12 carbon footprints, the notion of an England footballer completing his journey back from a match in Copenhagen by catching the Wolverhampton to Tettenhall bus and walking the last bit to Claregate seems crazy. More remarkable still is the fact that the person collecting the fares, Helen Mearden, should be the one to tell him he had been named as captain of his country.

There, in the stop press section of the Express & Star the conductress was brandishing, was the news that Walter Winterbottom, having mutually decided with Frank Swift that goalkeeper wasn't the ideal position from which to skipper a team, had been backed by the selectors when proposing 24-year-old William Ambrose Wright as his successor.

Fifteen international matches and a season at the head of Wolves' side were all it had taken for him to graduate to English football's ultimate honour – a pedestal some journalists had been tipping him for in the previous few months. Never again would he be led out on to the international stage by a team-mate. Not by Swift, Hardwick, Joe Mercer or anyone else.

Winterbottom was happy to have the prestige position filled by a player in the midfield role that Billy effectively had at Wolves – and the player was so thrilled and shocked by his elevation that he nearly left his giant slab of ham (what else would he bring home from a game away to the Danish?) on the bus.

"I had no illusions about myself or the tremendous responsibility with which I had been entrusted," he said. "I had been chosen to lead a side containing such immortals of the game as Matthews, Mortensen, Swift and Finney, and realise it's an honour that falls to very, very few players."

Billy had demonstrated his quiet leadership on that trip by acting as a guiding hand to the uncapped Jackie Milburn. 'Wor Jackie,' uncle to World Cup winners Jack and Bobby Charlton, hadn't flown before and was grateful for a calming presence in the next seat. "He talked to me all the way there," said Milburn, who in the end didn't make it past the role of travelling reserve.

Billy had only a fortnight to wait before the first 90 minutes of his 90-cap reign as captain. He was back at Windsor Park, scene of his full international debut just over two years earlier, and accepted the best wishes of Swift, threw back his shoulders and walked out alongside Northern Ireland skipper Johnny Carey at the start of the proudest afternoon of his football life.

With Milburn scoring on his debut and making an impact substantial enough to ensure that Tommy Lawton's England career of 23 goals in 22 appearances went no further, the blooding was a fulfilling one, the visitors running out 6-2 winners as Mortensen netted three times.

Again, no matter how big the occasion, Billy made sure the minor detail was attended to. Milburn, as if to underline how things were done in those days, had also heard via the stop press on his return from Denmark – in his case in the Newcastle Chronicle – that he would be facing Northern Ireland. And he was thankful to be greeted by the new skipper with the words: "Just play your normal game and you'll be fine." Milburn subsequently described Wright in the biography *'A Man Of Two Halves'* as 'an awe-inspiring captain.'

It's a view Ronnie Clayton would have concurred with. When the Blackburn right-half was named for his senior debut in 1956, Billy travelled to Manchester City shortly before to watch him play for England under-23s against Yugoslavia to make the newcomer feel even more special. And he would often insist on sharing a room with debutants, so as to put anxious minds at ease.

"I learned that a captain is never off duty, that his personal game is not just a one-eleventh share of a team's effort but an example to all," Billy said. "I also learned not to bully or shout at a player on the field, not to demonstrate by waving my hands in the air and not to assume the mantle of a dictator. Captaincy is the art of leadership, not dictatorship."

The international in Belfast meant Wright missed Wolves' comprehensive defeat at home to Middlesbrough but he was back for a game at Newcastle that was played in front of almost 61,000 a week later. Milburn was there, too, and the man who stands as the Geordies' all-time record goalscorer showed how little sentiment there is in football by netting twice in a 3-1 home victory.

England had won 12 and drawn three of the games Billy had played and the success to which our fans were then accustomed continued in his first home match as skipper when the international circuit touched the Midlands for an odd-goal victory over the Welsh. Billy returned to left-half for the midweek game at Villa Park and performed heroically, especially after an injury to right-back Laurie Scott had left his side to soldier on with ten men.

Wright was still occupying the no 6 position a month and a half later when Wolves crashed 5-1 at the same ground in a League game that represented a rare turning of the tables. Two days earlier, Aston Villa had been crushed 4-0 in a Christmas Day fixture at Molineux.

Billy was perturbed by the dropping of Swift, Tim Ward and Len Shackleton following criticism hurled at England after the Welsh game, powerless as he was to influence the selectors. All three were on the sidelines at Highbury when he next led his country out but at least his disappointment was tempered by the chance thrown to his Wolves pal and fellow Salopian Johnny Hancocks.

The winger was born in Oakengates, a few miles from Ironbridge, and scored twice in a 6-0 victory over Switzerland in which Manchester United's Jack Rowley, having occasionally guested for Wolves during the war, keeper Ted Ditchburn, his Tottenham team-mate Alf Ramsey and the two-goal Jack Haines (Albion) also made their international debuts. Hancocks, famed for his own tiny boots, frequently had his hands on Billy's. The fact that the game at Highbury was postponed for 24 hours by fog did not prevent them adhering to the superstition they observed at club level, whereby Johnny would always do up his skipper's laces a few minutes prior to running out behind him.

As well as lace-tying beforehand, there was a danger of tongue-tying after the game because it was on this occasion Billy was called upon to deliver the first of his many speeches as England captain. But Neil Franklin advised him to keep it simple and brief – a maxim by which he stuck throughout his tenure.

# Billy & Bully

"When the toastmaster announced me, I did just as Neil had suggested," Wright later recalled. "I ended with a request for my colleagues to rise and give three cheers for our opponents. But I was relieved when it was all over." In time, Billy would deliver almost as many addresses as he would have stamps on his passport and his confidence for the task continued to be built by his on-field performances – at least most of them.

With revenge secured for the defeat in Zurich, England found the boot on the other foot when their next opponents got their own back on them. The Home Championship was a source of great interest, partly because top-flight players routinely shared dressing rooms with stars from other British countries. But whereas Steve Bull has nothing but good memories of facing Scotland 41 years later, Billy's hopes of defeating the old enemy at Wembley and so beating them to the title in his first season as captain were emphatically sunk.

For the first time, he tasted defeat as an international captain as one of his less celebrated displays on this stage was marked by a 3-1 early-April beating in which Tom Finney's return meant there was no place for Hancocks. At least, though, there was consolation – and lots of it – just around the corner.

Wolves, by their standards, were middling in the League as they headed for a final position of sixth in 1948-49, their lowest since 1935-36. But they were making outstanding progress in the FA Cup after two fallow seasons in the competition, hammering Chesterfield 6-0, winning 3-0 at Sheffield United, overpowering Liverpool 3-1 and squeezing past Albion at Molineux in front of 55,648. A semi-final epic with holders Manchester United awaited them.

Matt Busby's side were also en route for runners-up spot in the League for the third year running and represented a formidable obstacle; more so as Wolves were seriously handicapped in the tie at Hillsborough by injuries that reduced full-backs Roy Pritchard (from the sixth minute) and Lol Kelly to the 'limping passenger' status commonly referred to in those pre-substitute times.

For the second hour of a two-hour marathon in which Wolves led through Sammy Smyth's early goal, it was all about surviving to fight another day. Kelly's 65th minute departure on a stretcher and subsequent hobbling return came well after United's equaliser from Charlie Mitten but long before the whistle blew at the end of extra-time.

"Of all the matches I played for the club, the one that really stands out more than any other was the semi-final at Hillsborough," Billy told me in 1990. "United were an outstanding team with a lot of internationals and we had to

## Cup Winner

work even harder against them because of the misfortune we had with injuries to defenders.I went first to right-back and then to left-back and it was just a case of trying to hang on really. Bert Williams was fantastic and we were delighted to get away with a 1-1 draw. In the replay a week later, Sammy Smyth scored the only goal and we were on our way to Wembley."

Wright was described by Commentator in the Express & Star as having played 'like the world's best footballer' and continued to recover from the humbling he and his international colleagues had had against the Scots by leading his club out on to what truly is the hallowed turf and to a victory that put a broad smile on his and Wolverhampton's face.

Having caught a cold against Portsmouth a decade earlier, Wolves were in no mood to underestimate even a floundering Second Division side like Leicester and worked hard for their 3-1 win. But Billy's memories weren't all happy ones. He was told by Stan Cullis to announce the Wembley side en route and Laurie Kelly was so disappointed at the naming of Terry Springthorpe in his full-back slot that he got off the coach at Oxford and headed home.

The nasty shocks ended there and, by way of contrast with 1939, the match itself ran according to the form-book. Two goals by Jesse Pye and a tremendous solo effort from Sammy Smyth got the job done but the underdogs caused a few scares, notably by having a goal debatably disallowed at 2-1, before Billy was presented with the Cup by the young Princess Elizabeth.

He spotted Mrs Colley as he climbed the steps and therein lies another remarkable story. As well as 'mothering' Wolves' most famous player, she had also cared for Pye and Springthorpe; three members of the same victorious Wembley line-up being housed by one lady in Burland Avenue, Claregate!

Before leaving the Wembley pitch, the Cup cradled in his left arm, Billy was hoisted on to the shoulders of Pye and Bill Shorthouse for one of the more iconic pictures in Wolves' history. TV footage of the celebrations and homecoming have thankfully survived as well as that of the match itself, and it must tickle Steve Bull and his generation to hear the vocabulary.

Football was tougher then but the combatants rarely failed to display their best manners once the battle was won and lost. Thus Billy congratulated Leicester on 'a good sporting fight,' which is hardly a phrase we were reaching for when Bully and Steve Walsh were at each others' throats 40 years later.

Billy is said to have clutched the Cup all the way to the Café Royal, with Billy Crook entrusted with the base. In the Express & Star two days later,

Commentator said the match-day roars were no louder than the one which went up when the Mayor, Alderman Ted Lane, ushered Billy to the front of the Town Hall balcony during a victorious homecoming that packed out the streets.

"It's the greatest moment in my life to bring the Cup back to Wolverhampton," he told the masses. "It was grand to be in the wonderful team we had at Wembley." The 2007 *'Wolverhampton Wanderers Official History DVD'* captures the scene as Billy thanks the Mayor and Lady Mayoress before paying tribute to the tens of thousands below by referring to the 'most wonderful reception' given to the players. Such lovely manners – and already he was feeling more comfortable behind a microphone!

Billy, having introduced the players one by one with the apology that many would be too shy to make speeches, didn't have long to rest on his laurels. As well as hearing the following day that he had been named for England's summer tour, he had a match to prepare for – or four to be precise.

Much First Division football remained to be played following the FA Cup final that season, with Wolves beating Preston on the Monday, losing at Everton on the Wednesday, being beaten at Huddersfield on the Thursday and drawing with Chelsea on the Saturday. Billy played three of the four games and, with international commitments, would make exactly 50 appearances in the season in which he had taken over as England skipper and lifted the FA Cup.

Life soon became better still for three of the victorious Wolves line-up. Although England lost away to 1948 Olympic gold medallists Sweden on the occasion of Wright's 20th cap, his 21st brought a 4-1 win in Norway on the day Jimmy Mullen ended a wait of over two years for his second international outing. The winger was among the goals in Oslo and Dennis Wilshaw was in the party, too, as a reward for his scoring burst at the end of the season.

More Molineux satisfaction lay round the corner as England moved on to Paris. Bert Williams was given his debut in place of Frank Swift, whose international career ended there and then, and had the shock of conceding a goal inside 30 seconds. But Billy, of all people, equalised before the half-hour by emphatically finishing a fine move and so becoming the first non-forward to score for the team since the war.

His first international goal set him up for a contented close season and his mood remained bright when he embarked on the new season. Wolves' defence of the FA Cup was a reasonable effort, ended with a fifth-round replay defeat at Blackpool, but it was their League performance that was highly encouraging as they effectively said goodbye to the goal-machine side of their skipper.

Okay, that's stretching a point but Billy scored three times for the club to add to the two he managed the previous year and the bumper haul of five that showed against his name 12 months before that. Given that he would net only twice more in the nine Molineux seasons that remained for him, it was the end of an era of sorts, albeit not one that would make Steve Bull blink too hard.

Certainly, Wright was more prolific than one journalist led fans to believe, the writer describing his goals as being as rare as Sahara snow. Two of Billy's three in 1949-50 came in August, home and away against Charlton, by which time Wolves were already measuring up as title challengers. They won their opening six League fixtures and followed up what must have seemed the calamity of only drawing at Birmingham by winning at Everton and humiliating Huddersfield 7-1 for the second autumn running.

Three days before that Molineux slaughter, Wright, Williams and the uncapped Jesse Pye were in the England team beaten by the Republic of Ireland at Goodison Park – their first-ever home defeat against a non-British team. But pride was recovered by autumn victories, a month apart, in Home Championship clashes against Wales and Northern Ireland that doubled up as the country's first World Cup qualifying games. The latter victory was by a margin of 9-2 at Manchester City as Billy collected his 25th cap.

Wolves remained unbeaten in the League until late October and shared the Charity Shield with Portsmouth via a draw at Highbury. The fact Billy was out – nursing a thigh injury picked up when facing Wales in Cardiff – contributed to their 3-0 defeat at Manchester United as a run of nine wins and two draws in 11 games became one of eight draws and five defeats from 13 follow-up matches and proved Cullis's side weren't the finished article yet.

Nor were England. They were repeatedly bailed out by Bert Williams in the late-November friendly with Italy at Tottenham, the keeper performing heroics and earning the nickname Il Gattone (The Cat) from visiting journalists in a game settled by late goals from ex-Wolves trialist Jack Rowley, who had scored four against Northern Ireland, and Billy himself. "It was such a fluke, I felt embarrassed," he said of a cross from near the half-way line that swirled in the wind over the Italian keeper for the second of his three England goals.

Despite his scoring run, Billy wasn't in the greatest nick and discovered why when he had a check-up on his thigh problem and was found to have a blood clot that required a small operation. He quickly recovered his fitness and form but Wolves didn't find it so easy clawing back the ground they had lost to Liverpool in the Merseysiders' 19-match sequence without defeat.

In the end, it was Portsmouth who came storming through to overtake new pacesetters Sunderland and snatch the first of their two successive titles. But how Wolves ran them close in pursuit of their first crown! They finished by beating Arsenal 3-0, winning 4-2 at Bolton, where Billy was among the marksmen, and thrashing Birmingham 6-1, only to miss out because Pompey's goal average was 0.4 superior. The only game of their last five that they didn't win handsomely was at Chelsea, where they drew 0-0 on the day Williams and Wright were playing for England at a packed Hampden.

It was a heart-breaking end to an extraordinary season but at least there was much satisfaction, pride and hope to be taken from their challenge. The same couldn't be said when the Molineux contingent returned from World Cup duty in South America two months later with their tails between their legs.

England beat the Scots 1-0 in front of 133,000 in their last qualifying game but there was bombshell news even before the national side registered a pre-departure 5-3 friendly win in Portugal. Neil Franklin was described by Billy as the best centre-half he had ever seen and no less a figure than 1966 World Cup winner Jack Charlton revealed that in street football as a youngster, he was always Billy Wright or Franklin. Imagine the impact, then, when the Stoke man stunned his skipper and everybody else around him by choosing this as the time to defect in search of his fortune by playing in Bogota.

Colombia was outlawed in football terms, so Franklin had immediately ruled himself out of the World Cup. Well after England's ill-fated adventure in Brazil, Billy pondered how his own path in life might have changed had his team-mate not turned his back on the sport's ultimate tournament. "He would have played for England for at least another four years and I often wonder what difference that might have made to my career," said Wright of a man who was a guiding light to him in his early international months.

In Franklin's absence, the final warm-up game was momentous for Mullen, the Wolves winger who became England's first used substitute when replacing Jackie Milburn and scoring in a 4-1 victory in Belgium. He, Williams and Wright were subsequently handed seats for the plane to Rio de Janeiro but their stay was nothing to write home about.

With Laurie Hughes at centre-half and Mullen scoring one and making one, England papered over the cracks by beating Chile 2-0 in the Maracana Stadium

## Cup Winner

in their opening game. Then they suffered the most notorious defeat in their history, bar none, when the USA rode their luck to score the only goal from one of their few excursions anywhere near Williams's penalty area. That the game was played in Belo Horizonte – translation: Beautiful Horizon – was a sickening irony for a country shaken to the core. "If we'd won something like 10-1, it would have been a more accurate reflection of the play," said Williams. "We hit the post and bar more than once but nothing would go in. I hated losing at any time but that result really did hurt and took a lot of living down."

Billy was not exempt from the subsequent criticism and confessed to feeling lower than he ever had on a football field. Remarkable though it now appears, questions were asked as to whether he was the right man to lead England, one writer insisting he lacked the 'required fire and brimstone.' The safety net was the game against Spain in Rio – and the side slid through that as well by losing 1-0.

Mullen was sacrificed and there was little consolation in the fact England's display was improved. They were out of a tournament in which they had been expected to challenge strongly and Uruguay went on to beat the hosts in a final played in front of the small matter of 199,854 spectators. It had been an utterly miserable couple of weeks and Billy reflected: "The atmosphere was dead against us. I don't think we were comfortable in any match there. In Rio, they even had oxygen masks in the dressing room because of a lack of good air."

The skipper was renowned among the press for never changing his attitude to them, even on the rare occasions they pilloried him. And it might seem surprising that he wasn't above being booed, although it was only by vociferous opposition fans who picked on him as the most prominent player in Wolves' or England's side.

His tally of caps now well into the 30s, Wright, who had his name on a book for the first time in 1950 with the publishing of the 9s 6d (47.5p) *'Captain Of England'*, might have thought life could only get better back home. Wrong. Five wins in the first eight games, including the usual 7-1 victory (this time over Bolton), proved a false dawn early in 1950-51 for a Wolves side who won only two of their next eight matches.

Even the England outing Billy had in this spell was a mixed blessing as he and his side were largely unconvincing in a 4-1 triumph against Northern Ireland. He fondly remembered the game in Belfast for bringing him his third and last international goal – a low shot in a crowded area – but he was having more than a few self-doubts in the aftermath of the unhappy World Cup campaign.

The fact Wolves lost 4-3 to Middlesbrough on the day of his and Williams's appearance in Belfast underlined how his club still needed him and he had another record going – as the only British Isles player to have represented his country in every game they had played since the war. The run ended that November, though, thanks to a back injury suffered in a defeat at Burnley.

Billy missed the clash with Wales at Sunderland and also the follow-up draw against Yugoslavia a week later but Wolves clung to their proud boast of having at least one player in every England line-up since the war, Williams appearing in both games and Hancocks in the latter at Highbury.

In another deviation from today's protocol, Wright, having been considered unfit for England, turned out for Wolves in the meantime in a 4-0 slaughter of Everton. And the Molineux season continued to career along from the heights of slamming Bolton to the depths of a run-in that brought ten defeats and only one win in 13 League matches in the final two months.

Billy, shock horror, wasn't playing well. He confessed to some relief that injury had given him a breather after his 33 successive England outings and, to compound his darker than usual mood, he even failed his driving test. In the five-month gap between internationals, he set about finding form with Wolves, although the fact the club conceded 20 more League goals in 1950-51 than they did 12 months earlier suggests he was less than successful.

The FA Cup brought renewed hope. Wolves beat Plymouth, Aston Villa, Huddersfield and then Sunderland in a sixth-round tussle that attracted nearly 117,000 spectators across its two games. Another north-east club, Newcastle, barred the way to Wembley for Cullis's men, who nursed strong grievances after Roy Swinbourne had been denied by an offside flag when chesting down to 'score' from Billy's chipped pass in the first meeting at Hillsborough.

Newcastle won the replay at Huddersfield and then the final against a Blackpool side who included Bill Slater but Jackie Milburn never forgot an act of sportsmanship at the last-four stage. He was touched by how Wright looked beyond his own disappointment to seek out his England colleague at the end to shake his hand. A gentleman indeed.

Billy often talked out his troubles with Mrs Colley and her son Arthur – a virtual brother to him – and just how low he felt became apparent in his 1953 book *'The World's My Football Pitch'* when he wrote: "I shall always be grateful to my colleagues at Wolverhampton for never once reminding me of my poor play. They often carried me."

Wolves were sufficiently concerned as to prescribe a fresh-air cure aimed at clearing the captain's head. More than once, he was packed off to Blackpool with either Hancocks or Eddie Stuart and told to use the change of scenery to chase a change in fortunes. The ploy failed and Billy admitted: "I continued to serve up displays that could only be labelled fair. Try as I did, things wouldn't go smoothly for me. Just before the international with Scotland at Wembley, I regained a little of my form and was again chosen to captain the national side. Regrettably, however, I had my poorest ever international. The Scots beat us 3-2 and I thought my England appearances were at an end for that season."

Forty years later, Steve Bull found 27 goals a season insufficient to earn an England place. Here was Billy finding it just as hard to play his way out of the side. The selectors stayed loyal despite confidence levels he described as 'rock bottom' and retained him for Argentina's visit a month later but it was the same story as England won 2-1. This time there was no reprieve and Billy was dumped for the Festival of Britain celebration game against Portugal.

He had no truck with the idea he was being released for a summer club trip to South Africa rather than axed. Much though he appreciated such sensitivity, he decided he was better served in accepting the harsh truth and come to terms with it. This he emphatically did. In Johannesburg, Cape Town, Durban, Port Elizabeth and beyond, he found gentler opposition conducive to regaining his touch. He missed only four of Wolves' 12 games (all won) and had the bonus of scoring in a 13-0 romp against Eastern Transvaal in Benoni.

"That visit proved the turning point," he added. "Freed from the strain of competitive football, I began to regain the confidence I had been lacking. My passes began to find the right man again and, when I tackled, I did it with the knowledge I was going to win the ball. Football again became a joy instead of a headache."

## Chapter Three

# Back With A Bang

A club v country conflict today often revolves around a manager packing his players off for international duty on the understanding that they might be used by national bosses for only 45 minutes. In 1951-52, Wolves were at the centre of an altogether different dispute between their own interests and those of the national team.

Wright was now firmly established as a First Division left-half and had played nowhere for his club except wing-half since appearing at inside-left in a Boxing Day win over Huddersfield the previous season. So there was considerable disquiet at Molineux when it became known that England planned to use him in the latter no 10 role for the Wembley friendly against Austria.

This wasn't any old international. Austria might have become a football backwater by the time Steve Bull went on two pre-season tours there in the 1990s but, at the Alpine country's peak, their players formed possibly the top team in Europe; one considered to carry a threat of becoming the first overseas side to beat England in this country. So what was the controversial backcloth?

Well, imagine Jack Harris picking up the phone in the Molineux boardroom and ringing Bobby Robson in 1990 to say he thought Bully was being used too deep by England and reminding him his forte was having the ball knocked over the top to run on to. Well, in 1951, Wolves chairman James Baker rounded on the national selectors, who included his fellow Molineux director Arthur Oakley, for daring to deploy the skipper differently.

"I feel very strongly about selectors choosing men for a department of the team other than that in which they normally play for their clubs," Baker said. "These men are our players. We pay them, coach them and train them and feel we ought to have a say about the positions they occupy. We have tried Wright in the forward line several times and always come to the conclusion half-back is his proper place. It must be obvious that, if we considered him to be an inside-forward of international class, we'd have developed him on those lines."

In the event, the storm passed over on that damp November afternoon. An injury to Bill Nicholson meant England moved Billy back to right-half at the last minute for a game in which a penalty by stand-in taker Alf Ramsey helped earn a 2-2 draw. It was the second argument to be defused in the first half of 1951-52. The other was that Billy Wright was back in favour at international level and would never again be overlooked by his country's selectors.

Whereas Bully would often have to be content with morsels in his England career, Billy embarked in October, 1951, on a quite extraordinary sequence of 70 successive appearances – all in the starting line-up. The next time he didn't make the team was of his own choosing when he retired eight years later.

His comeback, if that's not an over-statement after he missed only the spring-time clash with Portugal, was against France at Highbury. The team's performance in a 2-2 draw was no great shakes and England would have been licking their wounds at a defeat had it not been for the excellence of Bert Williams. In front of him, the no 6 was back to something like no 1.

"The selectors watched me consistently from almost the opening day and when they announced the England XI against France, I found the name 'Wright, Capt' in the line-up once again," he wrote in *'The World's My Football Pitch.'* "I confess I nearly cried with joy and felt just as elated as on the first occasion that England had honoured me."

Wright, replaced as skipper against Portugal by Ramsey, found things up and down at club level, with another good start frittered away soon after he had been switched to no 4 for the game against Huddersfield – yep, you've guessed it, another 7-1 victory. He played 39 of Wolves' 42 League matches – as many as his England commitments would ever (apart from 1956-57) permit him to make. And there were further highlights like a 4-0 trouncing of Middlesbrough and a 3-0 eclipse of the Newcastle side who were on their way to lifting the FA Cup for the second successive year.

But Wolves failed to win any of their final nine matches and, having finished a disappointing 14th in 1950-51, actually took two steps backwards with a final placing of 16th. Furthermore, they went out of the FA Cup at Liverpool at only the second hurdle.

It presumably wasn't for what he achieved at Molineux, therefore, that Billy had the considerable consolation of being named Footballer of the Year at the season's end. More likely, he was hailed for proving wrong all those who had doubted him at international level. Twelve months on from the uncertainty he had harboured over his form, he was being feted. At 14, he had been told he was too small to make it. Fourteen years on, he was walking ten feet tall.

"It was a pleasant shock to be chosen as Footballer of the Year because Wolves had finished so low in the table," he later reflected, pointing out with typical modesty that Nat Lofthouse would probably have pipped him in becoming the fifth winner of the award had his Lion of Vienna heroics not come a couple of weeks after the decision had been announced.

Redemption had continued to come Billy's way with his part in Eddie Baily's equaliser in England's draw in Cardiff – a clash that brought Bert Williams into direct conflict with Trevor Ford. The Sunderland and Aston Villa battering ram caused the keeper more trouble than most forwards with his muscular presence in those more physical times and you wonder how many more goals Bully, for example, might have scored had he been allowed to terrify keepers by shoulder-charging them as well as bearing down on them with the ball at his feet.

Williams was then ruled out by a groin injury for the clash with Northern Ireland the following month, the selectors giving a debut at Villa Park to Birmingham's Gil Merrick in a match won 2-0 by the home side. The excellent impression made by Wright was underlined by his contribution in the draw against the Austrians a fortnight later as he played the second in a run of 14 internationals in which he was the only Molineux representative.

A shoulder injury meant Williams was an absentee at club level as well, Dennis Parsons taking his place for a two-month spell marked by only two defeats in 14 games in League and Cup. But the fact Bill Shorthouse, Roy Pritchard, Johnny Hancocks and Roy Swinbourne all had substantial exiles from the team was a factor behind the fact too many of the games were drawn.

Wolves' placing of 16th was their lowest since 1934-35 but Billy's spirits were lifted by England's spring victory away to Scotland in front of 130,000 spectators on the day he won his 40th cap. Bully would much later acquire his own special memory of Hampden Park but it was a source of great pride to Billy that he went through his England career without losing there in six visits.

England actually had to be content with sharing the Home Championship title with Wales on the occasion of the principality's 75th anniversary but fans across Europe could see that Billy, who unusually switched from left-half to no 4 for Wolves no fewer than 11 times in the season, was back to his best.

## Back With A Bang

He was a contented man again long before being crowned Footballer of the Year. England were having a good season and, despite his club's disappointing League results, he could see big things on the horizon as Stan Cullis adhered to the basics in his quest to elevate Wolves to the top of the football world.

"Stan put a great emphasis on fitness and I doubt if there has ever been a team in history to match us for stamina and strength," he said. "He thought it was so important that we were pushed hard in training, so we were in the best possible condition for matches that were often played on heavy pitches. We always felt as though we had an edge late in games because opponents were more likely to tire than we were."

There was still time before the summer for Billy to figure in a demanding three-match England tour that kicked off with him being mobbed by autograph hunters, reporters and photographers at Florence station. Fortunately, Wolves director Arthur Oakley realised the party had temporarily lost its star attraction and went to the rescue after spotting familiar blond locks amid the melee.

A 1-1 draw in Italy was followed by one of England's most famous wins of the era, Lofthouse scoring twice to set up a thrilling 3-2 victory over the formidable Austrians in Vienna – a scalp so treasured by England's players that they requested they be allowed to keep their shirts as souvenirs. Imagine, though, the surprise of keeper Gil Merrick when he went into hospital a decade and a half ago for his third hip operation and was told by a nurse caring for him that she had his jersey from the game, a member of Birmingham's back-room team having apparently passed it on to her.

Billy was thrilled to continue pulling on the Three Lions at a time when his form was so good. So was Lofthouse. The rampaging Bolton centre-forward added another brace when England made it an Alpine double by defeating Switzerland – no wonder modest Billy declared himself lucky to have beaten him in the voting by the country's football journalists.

The game in Zurich, in which Ronnie Allen won the first of his five caps, brought handsome revenge for the defeat suffered there in Billy's international infancy. Hard though it is to believe, it was also the occasion on which Wright became England's most capped player, a special presentation being made to mark his achievement in overtaking Bob Crompton's record of 42 international appearances, although record books later amended the Blackburn defender's tally to 41 by deciding a game against Germany in 1901 wasn't official.

Mrs Colley's sideboard was beginning to creak under the weight of her lodger's collection but the Sunday Express summed up the player's unchanging attitude by saying the head which sported cap no 43 was no bigger than the one on which cap no 1 had perched. And much more was to follow.

Wolves regrouped for 1952-53 with more pieces fitted in for the launch into their glorious era. The only way was up. In 1987, the club rallied spectacularly from the lowest point in their history by swapping life at the bottom with one at the top. In the Cullis reign, there wasn't the same scope for improvement but the club still achieved a 13-place climb in the season Ron Flowers and Bill Slater were blooded, a teenage Peter Broadbent became something like a regular and Roy Swinbourne hit a rich scoring vein for the first time.

By the time their skipper returned from his first England duty of the season, Wolves had won six and drawn two of their first ten games. The run included the spectacular overturning of a two-goal deficit in the 6-2 hammering of champions Manchester United at Molineux on the day of England's 2-2 draw in Northern Ireland. Wolves were having a taste of the pressure that comes with being League leaders and were starting to look the part.

Another demolition of a Manchester club followed in early November with a 7-3 mauling of City. This time Billy played. Many of the goals in the lift-off were coming, as they did under Graham Turner, from the boots and head of the man in the no 9 shirt, Swinbourne hitting hat-tricks against United and City.

The majority of his scoring was done in the first half of the season, then Dennis Wilshaw – in the no 10 jersey Andy Mutch took to so well alongside Steve Bull – seized the moment and netted 12 times in the final 16 League games, including one in a 3-0 triumph at Manchester United. Wright was his usual accomplished, inspirational self, missing only four matches, helping transform Wolves from distant also-rans to strong title challengers and even lining up at centre-half for the first time in a 3-0 home victory over Stoke.

Having had another spell as leaders, the side thumped Burnley 5-1 in their last home game to ensure they ended with more goals in a League season (86) than at any time since 1946-47, only to sign off by losing at Tottenham. Wolves pushed hard but Arsenal took the big prize on goal average, Preston squeezing into runners-up spot having also knocked Cullis's men out of the Cup.

Third place was nevertheless a platform Wolves weren't prepared to see go to waste and the club had another 'third' to show that they were a rising force. They made it three Central League title triumphs in a row, so the foundations were safely in place.

## Back With A Bang

Billy had appeared during the season in another prestige fixture that is no longer heard of – and at Molineux no less. Matches played by the Football League lasted just long enough for Bully to gain a further slice of international experience but they were pretty big business in the 1950s, so the 7-1 home success (there's that scoreline again) over the Irish League was something else for Wright and Co to be proud of.

With England, life went on pretty much as before. They needed a late goal to draw in front of a record 60,000 crowd in Belfast against a team who scored direct from a corner, then they made Wales' first trip to Wembley an unhappy one by beating them 5-2. The fact 93,000 turned up for the midweek afternoon clash showed what an attraction Home Championship games were.

Billy was still close to imperious and revealed another string to his bow against the Welsh by slotting in at centre-half for the first time for his country after Jack Froggatt had been carried off. He had to mark none other than Trevor Ford – a man he described as fearless, a friend and someone able to take the knocks as well as dish them out.

The Wolves skipper was back at right-half for the visit to an icy Wembley of Belgium, who were put to the sword 5-0 as Nat Lofthouse continued his scoring rampage. Then, five months later, came a 2-2 home draw against a Scotland side who struck with an equaliser in the dying moments to preserve their record of not having lost in England for 19 years.

England had been beaten only once in 17 matches since their 1950 World Cup nightmare and were becoming increasingly fancied for the 1954 staging of the tournament. To give them a close-up of some of the sides who were likely to stand in their way in Switzerland, the FA arranged a 1953 summer tour of the Americas that Billy described as the hardest he had been on.

Three games in three countries would be followed by a stop-off in New York for a match against the United States – a schedule which prompted him to write in *'The World's My Football Pitch'*: "Just to recite the details makes me realise how fortunate I have been to visit so many countries with the England team and to receive payment for the privileges of playing in many of the world's most colourful cities."

While his Wolves team-mates had their feet up at home or on holiday in resorts like Blackpool, Weston-Super-Mare and Cliftonville, Billy, the club's sole representative in an 18-man tour party, first led England into a game against Argentina in Buenos Aires that will be remembered only for the fact it

37

was abandoned mid-way through the first half because of water-logging.

Having spent a day or two hanging round in the hope it could be restaged – and meeting President Juan Peron in the process – England moved on to beat Chile 2-1 in Santiago before facing world champions Uruguay in Montevideo. The latter game was a red-letter one for Billy – his 50th cap – and he said: "All I wanted to make my happiness complete was a great England victory."

Alas, a match pushed back a day at the request of the visitors after they had been laid low with sickness and then experienced flight delays went the way of the impressive home team. With a performance that made England's 1954 task seem a little harder, Uruguay won 2-1 in a game that was commended for its sportsmanship – something very close to Billy's heart.

"When the coach moved off and the English players started to sing Land Of Hope And Glory, I could not have felt prouder had we beaten the world champions," he added. "I have no doubt the memory of our sportsmanship will remain with those who watched the match long after the result has been forgotten. Although I'm going to be criticised in some quarters for maintaining old-fashioned views, I insist it is better to leave behind a reputation as gentlemen footballers rather than as a team that will win at any price."

The tour was the longest in travelling time Billy would ever experience, the flight from Montevideo to New York taking 24 hours via Rio and Port of Spain. The trek was undertaken on the day of The Queen's coronation and there was enough patriotic fervour left to record a 6-3 revenge victory over the USA in the Yankee Stadium in the first game England had played under floodlights.

Revenge might be too strong a word for the bite they put on the home team in the Big Apple. The fact the crowd was below 8,000 – an attendance more in keeping with Bully's Wolves in 1987 – showed that the Americans still had little appetite for 'soccer' despite their famous World Cup win over England.

Again, the weather had intervened, heavy rain necessitating a day's further wait for a fixture that brought Billy into opposition with Shropshire-born Terry Springthorpe, the left-back in Wolves' 1949 Cup final win over Leicester and a lad with whom he had shared digs at Mrs Colley's. Springthorpe now played for New York Americans and had been selected for the national side after crossing the Atlantic to work in engineering. How he would have loved to sample a bit of what was coming the way of Billy and his Molineux colleagues.

Chapter Four

# A True Champion

The season in which Wolverhampton Wanderers made their big breakthrough as a world force in the game was also the one in which the Three Lions lost much of their growl. Glory and triumph at Molineux coincided with disbelief and recriminations on the international stage.

The start made by Stan Cullis's men was unusual and less than promising – a Wednesday evening defeat at Burnley, who hit back after a Roy Swinbourne goal in two minutes to hit four in the final 28 minutes. As impressive as Billy Wright was at soggy Turf Moor, he was down when Wolves lost again a week later at Sunderland but a 4-0 win at Manchester City in the meantime was a hint of what lay ahead in a season that started with three away games.

Then came five straight wins in an inspired run that contained the conquests of champions Arsenal in front of nearly 61,000 at Highbury and Liverpool two days later. Wolves were on the march, halted only partly by draws at Anfield and FA Cup holders Blackpool in which Billy switched to right-back because of Jack Short's absence through injury. By the time the skipper left on England duty for the first time that season – for a 4-1 win over Wales in Cardiff – Wolves had opened more eyes, handing Chelsea their heaviest defeat of all time (8-1) and drawing at Sheffield United. And their goal-laden early-season emergence was being recognised beyond the West Midlands.

From being Wolves' only England representative for the previous two years, Billy now had two Molineux mates for company when he pulled on the famous white shirt at Ninian Park. Dennis Wilshaw, combining football with his work as a teacher, had included a hat-trick against Portsmouth in an outstanding burst of 11 goals in the first 12 games and was rewarded with his first cap on the day Jimmy Mullen was recalled for the first time in four seasons.

Wilshaw maintained his excellent strike rate with two goals in the flattering triumph over the Welsh that took England the first step along the road to the

1954 World Cup finals in Switzerland. Not that his display was deemed good enough. He was left out of the 4-4 Wembley draw with the Rest of Europe 11 days later, Mullen keeping the gold flag flying by netting twice.

Wolves continued to shape up as title challengers on the day they were without their three England men, a 2-1 success bringing them their first victory at Newcastle for half a century and providing the springboard for a more decisive win over Manchester United next time out. And their unbeaten run stretched to a round dozen when they drew at Bolton in a game Billy sat out through injury before putting in another two-game shift at full-back.

It would be some months before Wolves fully appreciated the importance of their 1-0 November win over Albion in front of a Molineux crowd of nearly 57,000, the game coming three days after their captain's form had unusually been called into question when England struggled to beat Northern Ireland.

But the examination the national side had at Goodison Park was nothing compared with what awaited them after Billy had linked up following Wolves' comfortable win over Charlton in the capital. Only when the Republic of Ireland had beaten them at Everton in 1949 had England ever lost at home to a non-British country, so their 6-3 tanning by Hungary at Wembley on November 25, 1953, is a result burned painfully into the record books.

It's hard to equate the shock-waves with anything in Steve Bull's era, or anyone else's for that matter, because England could not claim in recent decades to have been the game's masters. But here, despite their lack of World Cup success, were a team considered to be worthy pretenders to that title being given a right going over in their own backyard. Hungary, operating a fluid, revolutionary 4-2-4 system, had won the previous year's Olympic crown and struck gold again in this friendly with a bewildering performance that had the 100,000 crowd rubbing their eyes in disbelief. It also convinced the game's administrators that we, the country who gave football to the world, had been caught and overtaken. How many times have we heard that?

It was the first time Billy got close up to the tubby genius that was Ferenc Puskas. He scored two that misty afternoon as part of a barely believable haul of 84 goals in 85 international games and so bewitched his markers that virtually everyone present marked the Hungarians down there and then as World Cup winners the following summer.

Billy was among that admiring majority and never failed to poke gentle fun at himself in later years after he was famously described by Geoffrey Green in

## A True Champion

The Times as being 'like a fire engine racing to the wrong fire' as he tried to prevent one of the goals. But he was hurt by the first defeat he had suffered against overseas visitors to Wembley in his six-year-old England career.

"Such was the brilliance of this Hungarian side, one of the finest of all time, that my main feeling is one of supreme gratefulness for having played against them," Billy wrote in *'One Hundred Caps And All That'*. "They produced some of the finest, most brilliantly applied football it has ever been my privilege to see. The ball did precisely what they wanted and they were relentless, superb."

Stunned though he was, Wright found solace in the only way he could – through Wolves success. Fortunately, none of his club colleagues played in the rout and the pick-me-up came in League wins over Sheffield Wednesday and Tottenham, the latter in a much happier trip to London that brought Wolves their first-ever win at White Hart Lane and took them top for the first time.

Wednesday forward Albert Quixall remarked after their 4-1 defeat at Molineux that it would be no bad thing if England selected the entire Wolves team. Well, they were all eligible at the time as Short was still at right-back before South African Eddie Stuart established himself.

Cullis's team may have been playing like champions but they weren't infallible. Another defeat against Burnley was the first of three they suddenly suffered at home and the sequence of 18 games without defeat was followed by a run in which they lost as many games (seven) as they won. A 6-1 slaughter of Sheffield United proved another highlight, though, as it featured a Johnny Hancocks brace towards the end of a season that would bring him no fewer than 24 goals.

On the debit side, there was an FA Cup exit against Division Two visitors Birmingham, one that preceded Billy's wearing of the no 5 shirt for only the second time. He lined up against Arsenal at centre-half in place of the injured Bill Shorthouse, then, on the day he turned 30 (February 6, 1954), he had the present he would have most wanted in the shape of a 4-1 win over Blackpool, Swinbourne contributing the club's third hat-trick of the season.

As Wolves' Molineux form improved, so they wavered a little on their travels. They didn't lose away between August and late January but then their setback at Portsmouth was followed by others at Chelsea and Manchester United before Preston, in the significant absence of Billy's England team-mate Tom Finney through injury, were beaten by Wilshaw's late goal.

Albion, of all clubs, were barring Wolves' way to a first League title triumph and still led the table, as they had for most of the season apart from a spell around the turn of the year when their fierce rivals took over. Going into April, the gap was two points – the reward for a victory in those days – but the Baggies had a match in hand which they blew by losing at Sunderland.

Then came the meeting of the big two at The Hawthorns and more of the outside intervention unheard of in the modern game. There were no two-week breaks for international fixtures, so the staging of Scotland v England on the same day at Hampden Park meant Wolves were without Wright and Mullen while Albion lost the services of Ronnie Allen and Johnny Nicholls.

It wasn't pretty – derbies very often aren't – but it proved to be the day the pendulum swung towards Molineux as Swinbourne's goal just before the hour left the teams level with five games to go. Albion fans had some consolation from the fact that Nicholls, a boyhood Wolves fan, and Allen scored in England's 4-2 taming of the old enemy, as did Mullen. Billy, prominent in what we would now term 'assists,' was just thankful England had taken the first step towards recovery following their mauling from the Magyars by qualifying as Home champions for the World Cup. Now for the League…..

Wolves welcomed Wright back by crushing Charlton 5-0, Albion's defeat at Cardiff the same day seeing the leadership change hands. But the two-point advantage was halved when Wolves' goalless draw at Sheffield Wednesday coincided with the Baggies wearing down Manchester City through Allen's penalty. A surprise feature of the tense run-in was that Billy, who had by now walked out as a captain at Wembley more than any other man, was employed not as a wing-half or centre-half but as left-back, Cullis deciding to keep faith with Bill Slater, Shorthouse and Ron Flowers as the powerhouse of the team after their strong showing at The Hawthorns.

Easter, as so often in key issues, was decisive. While Albion were held in their home derby with Villa, Wolves made it nine goals for and none conceded in two Molineux match-days by hammering Huddersfield 4-0 and could even afford the slip they made in the return 24 hours later as Bill McGarry's thunderous 25-yard shot gave the Terriers victory. What put 8,000 Wolves fans in such good heart on their way home was Albion's 6-1 crash at Villa on the same day. The Championship silverware, unless there was a freak combination of last-day results, was heading, eventually, to Molineux.

League officials had their fingers burned in 1947 when they took the trophy to Molineux in anticipation of Wolves gaining the point they needed against

## A True Champion

Liverpool to become champions. The plot didn't follow the script then but this time it did as Wolves overcame Spurs with a Swinbourne brace while Albion lost at Portsmouth. The margin was four points. Wolves had scored more goals and conceded fewer than any other Division One side – and Molineux partied.

"There was nothing complicated about our strategy," Wright later said. "It's just that we played attacking football and, if someone scored against us, we went chasing goals at the other end with even greater vigour. There was hardly a dull moment because we scored nearly 100. The club had waited for so long to be champions and it was a wonderful feeling, exhilarating."

It was 66 years since Wolves helped found the League but they were made to wait another 16 days to take delivery of their prize. Liverpool, the club who heartbreakingly pipped Vizard's Wanderers in 1947, were relegated this time by finishing bottom and the Civic Hall was packed to the rafters on May 10 to hear Alderman W J Harrop, the League's vice-president, tell the distinguished gathering that the Cup (Albion's share of the spoils in that epic West Midlands year) was for glamour and the title was 'the true test of the merits of any club.'

Celebration time was relatively short for the players who would soon be leaving Molineux and heading for the World Cup finals. Wilshaw, the club's 26-goal top scorer, was named alongside Wright in England's party and predictably found the skipper an inspiration. "Billy was the most consistent player I ever played with," he said. "He never boasted, never showed any conceit and loved to tell stories against himself."

Also in the Switzerland-bound party was Mullen, who had played a full part in Wolves' triumph as he and Hancocks reminded the football world why they were one of the best pairs of wingers of all time. Much of the team's attacking policy was based around them and morale at Molineux was sky-high. It was a promising launch pad for the World Cup trio but the final build-up to the tournament could hardly have been more deflating for England's players.

They headed first for a two-match tour behind the Iron Curtain, where Wright, Mullen and the Albion duo of Allen and Nicholls were in a side beaten 1-0 in Belgrade on the occasion of Tom Finney's 50th cap. That was bad enough. What followed was even more shocking. England were still bruised from the 6-3 hiding by Hungary six months earlier but that defeat looked respectable alongside the one inflicted now by the same nation in Budapest. The 7-1 thrashing was the heaviest in our history, the Daily Express famously describing Billy's face at the end as being as white as his shirt.

# Billy & Bully

Steve Bull's time as an international player appeared threatened when he was replaced in the second half of a 1990 friendly with Hungary that brought him his penultimate cap. Thirty-six years earlier, against a Magyar side who belonged in a quite different class, Sheffield Wednesday's Jackie Sewell and Chelsea's Peter Harris saw their England careers ended and it needed all of Billy Wright's gallantry and big-heartedness to coax even a half-decent showing from the players who survived for the World Cup.

The tournament was highly significant to him on a personal level. When Luton's Syd Owen was injured in the opening game (a 4-4 draw against Belgium in Basle), coach Walter Winterbottom turned to Wolves' skipper as the 12th centre-half tried since Neil Franklin's defection. And never again, in the 46 international appearances that still lay ahead of him, was Billy used by his country anywhere other than in the no 5 'pivot' role.

England immediately looked tighter as they beat the hosts in Berne on the sweltering day of Billy's 60th cap, his place at right-half going to none other than the debutant Bill McGarry. The fact Wilshaw and Mullen, both promoted from the reserve pool, scored the goals in a 2-0 victory made it another memorable day for Wolves supporters.

Mullen was promptly left out to accommodate Stanley Matthews's return, though, and an error-ridden performance by keeper Merrick contributed to a 4-2 defeat against defending champions Uruguay that ended our challenge in Basle in the quarter-final. The Birmingham man wouldn't play for his country again and Bert Williams had reason to believe his recall wasn't far away.

What was less predictable was the unfolding of the action in Switzerland following England's disappointing elimination. Billy delayed his return home so as to watch the rest of the tournament in the company of Winterbottom and Portsmouth's Jimmy Dickinson and described the semi-final collision between Hungary and Uruguay in Lausanne as an absolute classic, the best match he had ever seen.

He wasn't alone in thinking that the engraver would have been safe in carving Hungary's name on the World Cup trophy before a ball was kicked. They had, after all, been unbeaten for four years and 29 games but they still lost in the final to West Germany. Ferenc Puskas, not fully fit on the big day, wouldn't be quite as jaunty when he showed up at Molineux five months later.

Chapter Five

# All Lit Up

Goal-wise, it took Billy Wright eight years to do what Steve Bull did in five and a half months. The more recent hero scored for the 16th time for Wolves when he took the first step towards his hat-trick against Hartlepool in 1987. When Billy reached the same mark by notching at Tottenham in the second game of 1954-55, it was with the last goal he ever netted for the club. Stopping them rather than scoring them was now his preoccupation.

The new season was only three matches old when Billy made the latest and last of his positional changes as a Wolves player. Bill Shorthouse suffered a head injury in the champions' 0-0 draw on a stifling afternoon at Portsmouth and the skipper moved from left-half and stayed there, Molineux emergencies apart.

It was a change that appealed to him, although he certainly wasn't built in the brawny centre-half mould that struck fear into centre-forwards. Stan Cullis reckoned the retreat into defence would add several years to his playing span and Billy acknowledged: "I was beginning to lose just a little of my zip as a wing-half. Moved to centre-half, I suddenly found a new lease of life."

In his 1957 book, *'Football Is My Passport,'* he reasoned: "Almost every centre-forward I have to mark is several inches taller than I claim to be, so every time I climb into the air, it makes an extra demand on my strength. That's the reason I find heading duels the hardest part of the centre-half's job."

To build up the 'spring' for which he became famous, the teenage Billy would risk the giggles of bystanders by occasionally jumping as he went about every-day chores such as shopping and walking to the bus stop. Later, amid more refined methods, he would leap, both feet together, over hurdles spaced out on a track. As well as his slavish attention to hard work, he had a master of the craft to guide him in the shape of his club manager.

Four straight wins from the end of August again had Cullis's Wolves in the thick of the battle at the top of the table, although two defeats followed before the side played out a midweek Charity Shield classic with Albion at Molineux, the rivals sharing the spoils following a 4-4 draw watched by 45,000.

Wolves, helped by a first goal of the season for Broadbent and Hancocks, then beat Manchester United 4-2 on the day their skipper undertook his first England duty of 1954-55. Amid the fall-out of another World Cup failure, seven players, including goalscorers Johnny Haynes and Don Revie, made debuts in the 2-0 victory in Northern Ireland, the scattergun selection policy being underlined when both were omitted for the visit of Wales a month later.

Billy had company from Molineux in the 3-2 win over the Welsh, for whom the two-goal John Charles gave the new centre-half an exacting examination. But it wasn't Mullen, whose England career ended at 12 caps with the World Cup, Wilshaw or Bert Williams. It was Bill Slater, the wing-half who had played for the club as an amateur prior to turning professional in 1953-54.

The Charity Shield clash launched Wolves into a ten-game unbeaten run that amply demonstrated the desire to hang on to their League title. The fact it included a 4-0 trouncing of Albion and a 5-0 slaughter of a Burnley side who had been a thorn in their side the previous season went a long way to explaining why they were three points clear at the top in early November.

No sooner had England packed their bags in Switzerland a few months earlier than they learned they would be welcoming the newly-crowned world champions West Germany to Wembley in December. It was a game Billy couldn't wait for and he prepared for it in the capital by helping Wolves to a 1-1 draw on the previous Saturday away to his boyhood favourites Arsenal.

Slater kept his England place and was delighted when Williams joined him in the side. It was more than three years since the keeper had last been named by the selectors but here he was ousting Manchester United's Ray Wood and winning his 19th cap on a beguiling Wednesday afternoon on which a 100,000 crowd generated record receipts for the stadium.

England's 3-1 win, albeit against a weakened side, was a reminder of what might have been six months earlier and confirmed that Billy was adjusting to his centre-half role with aplomb. Positional changes or not, it was accepted he would deliver high-class displays; how well the team would fare depended on the ability of the constantly changing players around him to gel.

Not until April would the international side reconvene but a huge patriotic blow was struck by Wolves in the meantime. Floodlights were still a new phenomenon, Wolves having made a big thing of beating a South Africa XI at an illuminated Molineux the previous season and displayed their renowned stamina by hitting four second-half goals against Moscow Spartak.

More than one member of the old Wolves school has chided me over the years for not including these prestige games in players' appearance records. My argument is that, amid the bigger picture, they were friendlies, accepted as it is that there were no points nor cup progress at stake. And if you include these fixtures in the official stats, why not add summer tours, testimonials and the like? Steve Bull once scored two terrific goals against Moscow Dynamo but they aren't part of his haul of 306. They came in a pre-season match.

What can't be disputed is what big business the 1950s floodlit games were. A crowd of 44,055 had seen Wolves beat Tottenham to lift the League Championship in April, 1954. There were over 11,000 more present for the win over Spartak, then 54,998 turned up on a dismal December night for the visit of a Honved side containing the bulk of the Hungarian team who had so humiliated England home and away. I've looked pretty hard at Billy Wright's various books in search of his thoughts all those decades ago about Wolves becoming League champions. They aren't easy to find. His delight at a Molineux 'friendly' victory that restored some national pride after England's bruisings is much easier to read up on.

Obviously, the fact Wolves hit back from apparent impending defeat goes some way to explaining the euphoria, although younger fans, indeed Bully as well, might find it hard to comprehend why Billy should call this 'the greatest moment in my club career.' It wasn't a sentiment confined to the skipper either. Cullis, the man whose vision had initiated the installation of the lights, chipped in: "It was without any question the most exciting match I ever saw."

Wolves were two down at half-time on a sodden pitch and still trailing with 15 minutes left, then Roy Swinbourne struck two goals in two minutes after a Johnny Hancocks penalty had started the fightback. As Wolves' players trooped off in their specially-for-floodlights fluorescent gold shirts, the fans rejoiced as if England had at last beaten Hungary. Even journalists in the cramped press box became caught up in the euphoria as they penned their eulogies, one paper suggesting Wolves' team en masse should be picked for their country.

That option wasn't quite possible as Eddie Stuart was now playing but the writer named Roy Pritchard an alternative to the South African, who remains fulsome in his own memories of the night. And he is unequivocal in his praise of the skipper. "Billy wasn't great on the ball like Peter Broadbent, Johnny Hancocks, Roy Swinbourne or Jimmy Mullen but he played it simple," he said. "If he had one bad game a year, that was it. He was consistently outstanding."

Hungarian FA chairman Sandor Barcs was gracious enough to hail Wolves as deserved winners, saying: "They are a great team and I have never seen a greater centre-half than Billy Wright." Rich praise indeed for a man still fairly new to the role. And Puskas himself called his team's conquerors the best club side they had ever faced. Bert Williams said: "The player I was most pleased for was Billy. "He had played against them when I was a substitute and watched us lose so heavily. He had a bit of a rough time at Wembley and was then in the team who lost 7-1 in Budapest, so to play against many of the same players who had run him around and to get the right result this time was great."

Ron Atkinson is a central character to the plot of this book, his lifetime in football having spanned the prime of Billy and Bully. He was among the groundstaff lads ordered by Cullis to water the Molineux pitch the day Honved first visited in the hope that Wolves' supreme fitness levels might become a factor. He, too, was a huge Wright fan.

"He was a phenomenal footballer, absolutely phenomenal," he said. "I don't recall trying to copy his style but what we could all take from him was the example he set with his great love of the game. One of the first commercial ventures I was ever involved with was with Billy in an advert. I think it was for Bic biros and we were pictured queuing for his autograph, which was easy because he was our big hero. We got ten bob each, which seemed a fortune."

Generally, players were much lower-profile. Even many of those at their peak in the 1950s were down-to-earth, not that far removed from the fans who flocked to watch them. So much so that the two factions often sat side-by-side on public transport on the way to games. But players weren't above enjoying the occasional perk. "I used to be in digs seven or eight doors away from where Billy lived with Mrs Colley and I made sure I walked down to the bottom of Burland Avenue, close to Aldersley Stadium, and hopped on the bus with him," said Stuart. "He could get on for free as captain of Wolves and England and it would save me threepence if I was with him.

"It was the same at the cinema where he often went – and there would be some tickets for our games in return for them. I don't remember feeling embarrassed about it either! Footballers weren't on that much at the time. Billy would take me under his wing as he was obviously older and more established than me and he knew I was trying to settle in a foreign country. I'm glad to say we became very close friends."

If Billy led a somewhat privileged life, he wasn't above redistributing some of his earnings. "Just imagine today, a lodging house where three or four multi-million players might live together," recalled Leon Hickman, the long-time former head of sport at the Evening Mail, in filming for the *'Wolverhampton Wanderers Official History DVD'*. "Billy basically stayed there for almost 20 years, bed and breakfast.

"Our family have been Wolves supporters for around 120 years and lived in the next street, so I knew Billy and he was a very gentle character. Christmas was wonderful and about six of the local ruffians, myself included, used to carol-sing at the age of seven or eight and Billy and the other players invited us into Mrs Colley's front room. We sang away and, at the end, they gave us all half a crown, which was a lot of money to a young boy. Billy used to go to the Fieldhouse pub and chat away for three hours or play dominoes and never a drop of alcohol would touch his lips. He only ever drank orange juice."

Down to earth Billy though was, everyone knew him, as South African Des Horne found out in his early weeks in Wolverhampton. "I hadn't long joined Wolves when I went out for a walk one night and got lost," the winger said. "I couldn't even remember the name of the road my digs were in, so I just asked this woman where Billy lived. I was okay then because I knew my way back from his house."

Maybe the floodlit exertions took something out of Wolves in 1954-55. The minimum 44-game season they were committed to before a ball was kicked became one of 47 in League and FA Cup because they reached the sixth round of the latter. Eleven players, including Halesowen-born left-winger Leslie Smith, contributed 36 appearances or more to the effort and on top of all that came a series of gruelling extra fixtures against some of Europe's finest.

First Vienna and Maccabi visited Molineux as well as the more powerful Moscow Spartak and Honved and, although the games were by and large won in front of big, bewitched audiences, you wonder in hindsight whether the additional workload was damaging on the home front.

Wolves, having just lost 4-3 at home to Chelsea, didn't win any of their four League games straight after the Honved epic and caved in 6-1 at Bolton the other side of two reviving victories. But their response was spectacular. In a prolonged snowy spell, they skidded to a 6-4 win over Huddersfield, beat

## Billy & Bully

Charlton 4-1 in the FA Cup, overpowered Manchester United 4-2 in front of only 15,679 at Old Trafford and crushed Leicester 5-0.

Cup elimination came on a white carpet at Sunderland, where an injury to Shorthouse led to young wing-half Eddie Clamp gaining a foothold in the side as Billy moved for a couple of games to left-back. The two matches brought Wolves a solitary point, the latest downturn stretching to four games by the time Williams, Wright and Wilshaw faced Scotland at Wembley in April.

By way of a tonic, the trio couldn't have asked for more. Wilshaw especially found the occasion of his captain's 65th cap a memorable one as he became the first and still only England player to score four times in a game against the Scots. Three decades before Tipton was to unleash something special on to the football world, Dudley's finest, Duncan Edwards, was seen for the first time on the international stage as a 7-2 win proved a memorable way for Billy to celebrate his 50th game as England captain.

Faltering Wolves drew at home to Preston on the same day, then set off for the season's decisive fixture at leaders Chelsea. Incredibly, the 75,043 attendance was all of 27,000 above the 1954-55 average at Stamford Bridge, where Billy was thankful to keep Roy Bentley – a prolific England scorer earlier in that campaign – fairly quiet. But here's a scandal! Remember that England's finest footballer and gentleman was never booked or sent off in a career of 541 League and Cup matches, 105 internationals and dozens of representative or so-called friendly games. Well, on this sunny afternoon, he was pictured diving across the line to save a goal-bound Chelsea effort with his hand. So Billy Wright did have a dark side!

Today, without question, his intervention would have brought a red card but the subsequent 75th minute penalty seemed a severe enough punishment for Wolves when it was converted by Peter Sillett for the only goal. By winning three and losing three during the run-in, the visitors finished second to the Londoners, four points adrift. A little more consistency from the side and Billy would have had his hands on the League crown for the second year running.

Hancocks and Wilshaw deserved another medal, having scored 28 and 25 League and Cup goals respectively, and the tiny winger would surely have won more than three England caps had it not been for an acute fear. His dread of flying left him grounded from several Wolves trips and no doubt made his task of dislodging the likes of Stan Matthews and Tom Finney at international level all the more difficult.

## All Lit Up

Wilshaw, who overcame his part-time status at Molineux by achieving amazing results, still had no fewer than three Wolves colleagues as company when he next travelled with England – for a defeat in Paris that brought Ron Flowers his first cap. It wasn't a good tour for the side, who added a draw in Madrid and a defeat in Oporto – their first against Portugal. Williams, Wright (inevitably) and Wilshaw played in all three games but Flowers was cast aside and bizarrely didn't reappear in the starting line-up for three years.

Results-wise, the quartet were no more successful when packing their bags at club level shortly afterwards for Russia, Wolves breaking more new ground with their two-match trip to Moscow and being soundly beaten in both. The summer rest that followed was welcome.

The 43 League and Cup games Wolves played in the following season (1955-56) added up to 18 fewer than the 61 Steve Bull would light up with his 52 goals 32 years later but there was little let-up for those who also represented their country. Although there were four years, rather than two, between major tournaments, there was little time for a breather for the best players.

Much though Stan Cullis had his hang-ups about how some players were asked to play in international games, he would never have dreamt of telling Walter Winterbottom to use Bert Williams for only 45 minutes or not play Dennis Wilshaw in a friendly. And Billy Wright, as skipper, was always the first name on the team-sheet.

There was a minor concession for the trip to Denmark in October, 1955, though, in the shape of the FA's agreement to take only one player from each club as the Sunday game was considered disruptive to the previous day's League fixtures. Wright was therefore Wolves' sole representative in a capital in which Bull would later appear for both club and country in friendlies – and the 5-1 victory was as one-sided as some of those Wolves had already chalked up that late summer and autumn.

Manchester City were buried beneath four goals by Swinbourne in a 7-2 Molineux thrashing, Huddersfield caved in 4-0 as he hit three a fortnight later and in between came Wolves' biggest away win of all time, a 9-1 romp at Cardiff, where he and Hancocks rattled in hat-tricks. It seemed inevitable Swinbourne would be capped by England as he produced a Bully-like blitz in which he scored 17 times in the first 11 games, only for a fall among youngsters sitting round the pitch at Luton in November to cause severe knee damage. A brilliant career of 114 goals in 230 games effectively ended there.

## Billy & Bully

Happily, there were no such problems for Billy, although a second trip to Ninian Park brought a furrow to his brow as England suffered their first defeat against Wales for 17 years. On the day of the defender's 70th cap, Williams played his 24th and final England game and Wilshaw was also present, the forward then scoring twice a week and a half later when normal service was resumed with a comfortable home win over Northern Ireland.

Billy used the latter game to regain colours lowered slightly and, having played more floodlit football than most thanks to Wolves' far-sightedness, was little troubled when he played for the first time under Wembley's new lights in a 4-1 late-November taming of Spain. Not that everyone concurred with his sky-high reputation.

Manchester City and Swansea star Roy Paul said in his autobiography *'A Red Dragon Of Wales'* in 1956 that he didn't think Billy would have been an international at all if he had been born in Wales, suggesting he would not have ousted Ronnie Burgess, Ray Daniel, John Charles and himself. He conceded that the Wolves man was a 'great-hearted player' but his praise for the way in which, as skipper, he could 'hand over bouquets of flowers before an England match in so charming a manner' appears less than unequivocal. Paul insisted he didn't mean any disrespect with his comments, which should make us glad Billy didn't cop for a few thoughts on one of his grouchy days.

The seven hat-tricks Swinbourne had scored stood as a post-war Wolves record until Bully came along but the goals that suddenly went out of the side in 1955-56 were one handicap too many for a team with their eyes on another title. Although Jimmy Murray started well after his promotion and Wolves won thrillingly at champions Chelsea, they stumbled by losing five home games out of six after going unbeaten at Molineux for a year.

Come the spring, Billy clung to his proud boast of never being on the losing side at Hampden thanks to Johnny Haynes's last minute equaliser for a side who followed up by beating Brazil 4-2 at Wembley. But Wolves were chasing only the minor placings. Manchester United had an unshakable grip on the title race and Blackpool edged second place on goal average, with Cullis's men third despite winning their last three home games.

It was a season of unfulfilled promise and the skipper, in seeing his caps tally click past 75, had the familiar frustration of England peaking in another non World Cup year. They recorded a win and a draw on a two-match trip to Scandinavia, where Wilshaw's goal-scoring return against Finland ended a run of four internationals in which Wright was the only Molineux representative.

Nat Lofthouse hit a brace in Helsinki, where Billy had never previously played, and the Bolton man was a confirmed devotee of the man who led him out. "I had the highest respect for Billy, who was captain in just about every game I played," he said. "He was a great player but, above all, a great captain. A true leader. He might have been having a stinker but that didn't stop him encouraging the others. He never let his own performance affect his captaincy."

England dropped off on the way home to beat World Cup holders West Germany thanks to a terrific performance by Duncan Edwards in the country where he died 21 months later. The Black Country colossus scored in Berlin and underlined the excellent understanding he was developing with Billy. Not that Cullis was able to watch his thrilling emergence without tinges of regret.

It is well known that Wolves were hot on his trail before United stepped in and persuaded him to change tack northwards. And Matt Busby once revealed how he had had to placate his Molineux counterpart after a United visit to the West Midlands in which the player stood head and shoulders above all others. "I remember the inquest in the boardroom afterwards," Busby wrote in his 1957 book *'My Story'*. "Stan Cullis said: 'Matt, I'd like to know how you managed to sign Edwards. We thought he was lined up to join Wolves.' I said: 'I got Duncan in the same way you got Colin Booth.' Young Colin is a Manchester boy and I was with his parents the night before he joined Wolves. I didn't hold that against Stan. The boy just wanted to join Wolves."

Billy was too diplomatic to make waves and happy anyway to have Slater, Flowers and Clamp as his club's wing-halves. Helping beat Germany in front of 100,000 was a terrific end to the season for him and he had a new challenge in 1956-57. No longer would England be able to seek World Cup qualification through the Home Championship. Their path to the finals took them overseas for the first time but there was a familiar start to the international season with a trip to Belfast that ended in a draw, the door subsequently closing on Wilshaw despite his record of close on a goal per game from his 12 appearances. Shades of Bully perhaps in being discarded so soon……

The overlooking of the forward, who had a Bull-like ratio of better than one goal in every two games for the club – 112 in 219 matches in his case – meant Billy would play ten more internationals before having a Wolves player by his side. In the meantime, though, he had not only the company of Edwards but also that, on occasions, of Albion's Derek Kevan and Don Howe.

## Billy & Bully

And more bids for places were built as Wolves remained great entertainers. Broadbent kicked on thrillingly with 18 goals while Jimmy Murray was only one behind and Slater, Clamp and Flowers vied for the right to play alongside Wright. A game against them was no picnic. While Billy's strengths were his anticipation, timing and clean tackling rather than physical presence, he had robust specimens around him, Stuart's performance at Anfield once prompting Billy Liddell to ask Billy: "What do they feed him on, raw meat?"

Bill Shorthouse, also able to mix it when necessary, played his last senior game in 1956 but opposition forwards saw another barrier going up as Clamp was used more and more. Competition was fierce and there were some good players in the Molineux reserves who rarely had a look-in because the senior men were so strong, formidable and fit. But results didn't always reflect the promise. Wolves had a self-destructive streak as well, so spectacular wins over Manchester City (5-1), Luton (5-4), Portsmouth (6-0), Arsenal (5-2), Blackpool (4-1), Charlton (7-3) and Albion (5-2) were accompanied by sufficient setbacks as to keep the club looking in from the outside on a title race that was again won by a distance by Manchester United.

The season in which Bert Williams, like Shorthouse, played his final match was also the one when Bournemouth rocked Molineux to its foundations. The Cherries' 1-0 Cup win did not spell humiliation of Chorley dimensions but the memory of defeat by a Third Division South side put Billy and Bert in mind of the shock KO England had suffered against the USA in 1950.

Cullis's men scored 94 League goals and let in 70, making this the club's most goal-filled season since 1934-35. They managed only one against United, though, and the fact they finished a distant sixth while Busby's side took three points out of four off them demonstrated that the balance of power remained at Old Trafford for a while longer.

United were predictably well represented in an England team who followed their 3-1 home win over Wales with an eighth successive Wembley triumph, Yugoslavia this time falling by the wayside as Billy's monumental collection of caps reached 80. Then came a very special stopping-off point in his tour of the world's football hot-beds with a rare England outing at Molineux.

The opening game of the country's World Cup qualifying programme was not only the usual story of excellence as far as his display was concerned, it was also a triumph for United's contingent as Tommy Taylor scored three and Edwards the other two. Denmark were the hapless victims in a game that was watched by 54,000 supporters on a Wednesday night shortly before Christmas.

Wright, so proud to be leading his country out in his spiritual home, had again displayed his ambassadorial side the day before by dashing back from a training match at Albion to meet the Danish captain in the company of Stanley Matthews at the Mayor's Parlour in Wolverhampton.

Molineux's main dressing room was obviously an inspirational place as Wolves were in a run of 11 wins in front of their own fans and the success Billy was having with England continued when Edwards retained the goal knack by thumping a late winner in the Scots' visit to Wembley. The impetus was maintained with a 5-1 home win against the Republic of Ireland, the other side in a World Cup qualifying group featuring England and Denmark. Taylor used the game to rattle in another hat-trick and so re-raise the spirits of Manchester United after their surprise Cup final defeat against Aston Villa.

England duly won the group by adding to a 4-1 win in Copenhagen they recorded in the last of Matthews's 54 caps. The mercurial 42-year-old winger had joined the spectator ranks by the time the country gained the single point they still needed by drawing in Dublin, where Billy produced an outstanding performance to emphasise why he was named runner-up to Real Madrid's Alfred di Stefano in the European Footballer of the Year voting.

There being no England tour that summer, Billy had the opportunity to make a belated entrance on Wolves' return visit to Southern Africa, the setting for his precious rediscovery of form six years earlier. He joined up with his team-mates for games in Northern and Southern Rhodesia after they had shown off their talents all over the republic and helped ensure they again achieved a 100 per cent win record. "He was an outstanding player as well as a wonderful team-mate and friend," says Stuart, the captain on that tour in his absence. "There was a right way to tackle and a wrong way to tackle and Billy had the art mastered perfectly. When he went into a challenge, his whole body weight was right behind the ball. For a relatively small man, he had very sturdy legs and he had brilliant sense of timing, whether he was making interceptions or climbing for headers."

Great times were awaiting Billy at club level in the shape of a second League title but Wolves' triumph was clouded by tragedy – one that effectively binned any hopes he had of ever leading England to World Cup glory.

Chapter Six

# Glory, Glory Wolves

Wolves, with Malcolm Finlayson keeping goal in succession to Bert Williams while Gerry Harris established himself as Bill Shorthouse's replacement at left-back, lost at Everton in their opening game of 1957-58 but did little else wrong in the next eight months.

Crushing wins over Bolton (6-1) and Sunderland (5-0) got them moving and just round the corner lay a brilliant nine-game run containing a draw at Leeds and eight victories, among them one at Molineux against champions United, another over runners-up Tottenham (4-0) four days later and then one at St Andrew's over Birmingham by the small matter of 5-1. Happy days indeed. For Billy, now approaching the twilight of his glorious career, it was a particularly exciting time. When the no 5 shirt was taken off the peg by George Showell instead for the mid-October home victory over Chelsea, Wright was pulling on the three lions and inspiring his country to a 4-0 win in Cardiff while keeping a fatherly eye on a trio of debutants including Wolverhampton-born Don Howe.

Totally out of character, England lost a game in early November, 1957, when Northern Ireland recorded their first victory over them since 1927 and their first in this country since 13 years before that. Shock horror, Billy conceded a penalty as his side's unbeaten sequence ended after 16 games. The incident had spectators blinking and doubting what they had just seen because many would rarely even remember him giving away a free-kick.

Normal service was restored when England hammered France 4-0, Bobby Robson scoring twice on his debut. But it wasn't only on the international stage that Billy was crossing swords with some of the Continent's biggest names. The continuing success of his club was opening doors as well.

European tournament football hadn't yet arrived in Wolverhampton but there was a strong hint as to how close it was when Stan Cullis took his men for a prestige friendly at Real Madrid a few weeks after they had beaten them in Billy's absence at Molineux. Interestingly, the 2-2 away draw came to be regarded by the skipper as one of his fondest memories – another sign that such so-called friendlies carried a highly competitive and significant ring to them.

"It was probably the greatest moment for British football at the time," he recalled. "Real were the top side in Europe, with players like Di Stefano and Gento in their fabulous line-up and the football Wolves played that night was a credit to the British game. I rate Di Stefano as the finest centre-forward of all time. He was quite brilliant."

So buoyed were they by their performance in the rainy Spanish capital that many Wolves players unusually defied their manager's orders and treated themselves to some 'down time' on the town before retiring to their rooms. Unfortunately for them, their high-spiritedness was clocked by Cullis but Billy, who frequently used the story when speaking at dinner engagements, revealed: "He was only angry because he said he would like to have come with us!"

The side went 18 League games without defeat up to Christmas, losing again for the first time at Tottenham on Boxing Day, being beaten at Blackpool in January and then from the start of February building another magnificent sequence of nine wins and a draw from ten First Division fixtures. It was after the first of those victories, though, with the title on the way to Molineux, that disaster struck the English game.

Although Wolves had lost at Blackpool just before, they were back there to prepare for their big game at Manchester United in early February. "We often went to the Norbreck Hotel before matches even as far away as Manchester and were there in that dreadful week in 1958," said Eddie Stuart, who choked back tears relating the story on the *'Wolverhampton Wanderers Official History DVD'*. "About eight of us were in a restaurant near the tower when this guy rushed in and said: 'Bill, you won't be playing at Old Trafford on Saturday. There has been an horrendous air crash involving the United players.'

"We thought and hoped he was kidding. But, an hour or two later, going back on the tram to the hotel, people were openly crying. There was no TV but the news had got round by radio and word of mouth and we were very upset. The disaster was on Billy's 34th birthday and, instead of preparing to face United on the Saturday, we got ready to go back early to Wolverhampton to pay our respects because, by then, we knew there had been fatalities."

Billy, among others, cried his eyes out when learning seven players had lost their lives after the aircraft carrying them home from a European Cup game against Partisan Belgrade had crashed on its third attempt at take-off following a refuelling call at Munich. He shed more tears a fortnight later when Duncan Edwards was added to a casualty list already including Tommy Taylor, red-hot for England in preceding games, and fellow international Roger Byrne. Geoff Bent, Eddie Colman, Mark Jones, David Pegg and Liam Whelan also perished.

The grief increased with the loss at the same time of Frank Swift, Billy's great friend going back to his nervous early England years, and seven other members of the press corps whom he regarded as friends. The former keeper by then wrote for the News of the World, who had taken out an advert on the centre pages of the already-printed United v Wolves programme to say he would be present to report on the game.

In all, 23 people died when that Elizabethan airliner failed to climb off the snowy tarmac. It was one of the gravest tragedies ever to envelop British sport; a fantastic young team decimated – and a big hole also driven through the English team.

Instead of running out at a packed Old Trafford two days later, Wolves' players were called into Molineux by Cullis for that day's Central League home fixture and lined up on the pitch in their overcoats to observe three minutes' silence. "Although United were big rivals of ours, we all felt their loss very badly," Stuart added. "We had good friends, close friends, on that plane. Billy was as upset as anybody. He knew several of the players through England as well as from playing against them in big club games and he and Stan were very keen that we should all pay our respects. It was a very sad time."

The crash prevented United from challenging Wolves' supremacy at the end of that decade and caused a vacuum in which one or two of Cullis's men gained footholds in the England team. What shouldn't be argued, though, is that Wolves won the League in 1957-58 on the back of the reigning champions' horrific misfortune. They did it on their own merits.

They already headed United by eight points – the equivalent of four wins – and their six-point lead over Albion in December was the biggest mid-way lead by any club since the war. The fact that the first point they dropped after the February 8 tragedy was on March 22 proved that United would have found it nigh on impossible to catch them.

Jimmy Murray and winger Norman Deeley were to finish the campaign with 55 goals between them, the centre-forward's claim of the lion's share persuading Cullis that he was able to let Dennis Wilshaw join his home-city club Stoke. Wolves could even afford the tremors caused by Wright conceding penalties home and away against Arsenal over Easter.

A triumph that had looked probable for many, many weeks became fact on April 19, when Wolves defeated their nearest challengers Preston 2-0 at Molineux. It would have been fitting for Billy to climb the steps into the directors' box and lead the celebrations after this final home game of the season. As was sometimes the case in that bygone era, though, he and the recalled Bill Slater were away playing in a victorious England team at Hampden, the visitors losing Tom Finney and Scotland skipper Tommy Docherty to the same fixture.

United had fresh representation in the side in Bobby Charlton, a fortunate Munich survivor who was part of the guard of honour two days later as the home players welcomed the new champions for an emotional rearranged date at Old Trafford. Wolves were up against a much-weakened side and won easily; 4-0 against the Scots, 4-0 away to United – these were dizzy days for Billy.

Despite defeat in the academic last game at Sheffield Wednesday, Wolves had topped 100 goals in a Division One season for the first time and had as many points as any top-flight side had managed since the war. The club also won the Central League, Birmingham League, Worcestershire Combination, Worcestershire Combination Cup and FA Youth Cup; not a bad season's work.

"We played fast, attacking football that gave little thought to defence," recalled Wright, who was described by Commentator in the Express & Star as having led his team on rather than driven them on. In other words, his captaincy was understated and thoughtful rather than of the chest-beating variety.

There was little respite for him. On FA Cup final eve, he and Slater played in an England side at Chelsea against an under-23 team including Eddie Clamp and Peter Broadbent. Further down the international tree was a young hopeful from well outside the Midlands who held a big torch to Wolves' title-winning side and one man in particular. Barry Fry, an England schoolboy international and one-time Manchester United youngster, was hooked on Molineux thanks to the screening of the floodlit games and says now: "We didn't have a TV but I used to go to a neighbour's at the age of nine to watch these matches in black and white and I fell in love with the club and particularly Billy.

"He was my idol. I still have two scrapbooks, one just on him and the other about Wolves. I also have a huge scarf my mum knitted, with all the players' surnames on. But Billy was given his full name. The stitching says Billy Wright. When they played at Luton or in London, I'd jump on the train after playing on a Saturday morning and go and watch them."

Billy got his hands on silverware before even departing for the World Cup – the League title. Civic banquets were a way of 1950s life for Wolverhampton Wanderers and there was more to celebrate this time, with the club having swept the board through their various teams. Blown-up pictures of players hung all over the Civic Hall on the evening Barnsley chairman Joe Richards, also the Football League president, handed the trophy over. It was the third time the Wolves skipper had taken receipt of a major honour and Molineux had a big-time feel. So much so that Richards, looking round at a room full of 500 guests, quipped: "This would be a big gate at Barnsley."

Richards told the gathering that Billy's distinguished record was one that would take a lot of beating yet, amid all the back-slapping, Cullis found a way of ensuring egos wouldn't be allowed to over-inflate. "I hope all the players will commit this occasion to history for we can't carry into next season any of the points we have gained this season," he said.

Before England set foot in Scandinavia on their latest World Cup adventure, there was time for Billy to take his tally of caps into the 90s, their countdown beginning with a 2-1 victory at home to Portugal. Bobby Charlton was the hero with both goals a few days after playing in a Manchester United side beaten in the FA Cup final by Wolves' sixth-round conquerors Bolton.

The follow-up was ominous, though – a 5-0 hiding against Yugoslavia in Belgrade. The game caused doubts among Winterbottom's squad, who still included Billy's Molineux half-back colleague Slater, and was poignant for Charlton. He was back in the city where eight of his United mates had played their final games three months earlier and there was even a stop-off in Munich in a trip that showed how far England had gone back since the crash.

Whereas Steve Bull had Andy Mutch with him in England's under-21 and B teams before going solo to the World Cup, Billy was falling over players he shared a dressing room with every day. Clamp and Broadbent were on the scene as well, Clamp forming an all-Wolves half-back line with Wright and Slater for the final pre-tournament friendly, a 1-1 draw in Moscow.

USSR were also the first opponents in Sweden and the same trio played in another draw, this one salvaged from the position of two down. England, who must also have thought hard about including Ron Flowers in their squad, remained in Gothenburg for their next game – a more than satisfactory 0-0 draw with Brazil in which Billy's performance was described as 'magnificent.'

England would have reached the quarter-final with a win over Austria in their next game, only to find themselves chasing their tails again and thankful to twice hit back for a draw in Boras. Bobby Robson's 1990 vintage, Bully and all, matured from a poor start to flourish in Italy. In Sweden, a similar lift-off was needed, with the young Robson a playing member of a party who returned to Gothenburg to see their hopes sunk by the USSR in a play-off.

The third meeting of the countries in a month brought Broadbent a surprise debut at Robson's expense after a season in which he had scored 21 League and cup goals for Wolves. But the World Cup had been a disappointment and Billy knew his lingering chances of the ultimate glory had died. What he probably didn't know was that his career had only one more year to run.

He was now 34, twice the age of a Brazilian lad called Pele who lit the tournament up and did much to take the cup back to South America. The clock was ticking but Billy's own form in the face of national letdown and criticism had been excellent. His personal peace of mind was further improved as serious romance was in the air for him for the first time.

"Everybody knows that Billy's devotion to Wolves and the sport as a whole was unbelievable and I'm not sure Mrs Colley ever allowed him to have a girlfriend," said Eddie Stuart. "Then Joy Beverley came on the scene and things changed. I had met the Beverley Sisters some time earlier after I was hit in the eye by the ball near the end of our second title-winning season. They were appearing at the Grand and kindly came to visit me in the Infirmary, although Joy and Billy weren't together at the time."

The two stars of stage and soccer were soon what would now be termed an item and, to use a tired cliché, yes, they were the Posh and Becks of their day. Wolverhampton's showbiz circuit may not have been one to rival the big cities but it helped none other than John Rudge to meet the happy couple when he was still an impressionable boy with hopes of a career at his beloved Molineux.

"Billy was a big favourite of everybody's but I was in awe of him when I met him for the first time," Rudge recalls. "I was Wolves daft and used to take a box from my mom's fruit and veg stall on Wolverhampton market to stand on at Molineux. That's how I watched the Honved and Spartak games and I was also fanatical about getting the players' autographs.

"Me and my cousin were walking in Dudley Street one day when two chaps asked if we wanted to earn some extra pocket money. They were from a magician's act called Benson Dulay and wanted us to go to the Gaumont that night and the rest of the week to be part of the act. We'd sit in the audience and, when they asked for volunteers, put our hands up and be called on.

"We got a pound for the week but what really mattered was that we met Billy and Joy one night. I was too awe-struck to say anything but it was very special just to see him. Fortunately, I met him another three or four times when he was a Wolves director in the 1990s and I'd got over my shyness. He was still a great star and I'm so pleased I had the chance to speak to him properly."

As a schoolboy, Rudge trained at Molineux under the tutelage of Bill Shorthouse and Jack Dowen, his brother-in-law Peter Clark taking him to sessions often staged in the shooting pen under the main Waterloo Road Stand. Rudge's career took him elsewhere, notably to the Potteries as the long-serving and successful Port Vale manager, and is still going strong on the other side of the city. But the idolatry he felt for Wolves' skipper half a century ago was something he had in common with thousands of teenagers in the town.

The man at the centre of such hero worship now had eyes for something and someone other than Wolverhampton Wanderers and England. Mr Wright had waited years to commit himself to Miss Right but, having found her, delayed the big step into marriage only until later that summer. Within a month and a half of the World Cup KO, he and Joy were wed in Dorset.

As big a step as he was taking from the cosy world of sewing blankets and listening to gramophone records at Mrs Colley's to a celebrity union of national football captain and star singer, he struck no deals with magazines. Nor were there marquees, thrones or a Maldives honeymoon. The couple sought secrecy over their big date of July 27 and their chosen location of Poole Register Office, a few miles from where Joy was appearing with the Beverleys. But a not so small circle of friends were treated as 'insiders' and one Black Country girl had a surprise visit during lessons at Grange Hill Infants' School in Coseley.

"I remember being in class and the headmaster coming in to say there was someone to see me," said Paula Morris, the daughter of Albion's long-time captain Len Millard. "I soon discovered it was Billy but wasn't in awe of him. Although he was the captain of Wolves and England, our two families knew each other well, so I regarded it as a meeting with a friend rather than anything else. Billy, I think, was just about to set off for Dorset and wanted my dad to know from him that he was getting married rather than read about it in the paper. I'd be nine or ten and he asked me to pass on the news, which I did."

As they are inclined to do, the details leaked out anyway via a freelance reporter and the couple made a very public appearance before a cast of thousands on their happy day. Whatever their surprise, they showed with their warm smiles how comfortable they both felt in front of the cameras.

As a result of their alliance, Billy had a special spring in his step as he prepared for 1958-59, a season that kicked off spectacularly for Wolves with a 5-1 mauling of Nottingham Forest and then two sobering defeats, 2-0 at West Ham and 6-2 at Chelsea. They were back on a more familiar footing, though, with four successive wins, including a high-scoring double over Aston Villa.

They were still going well when Billy reported with his country for the 97th time, as was amply underlined by their 4-0 crushing of Manchester United on the day England drew 3-3 with Northern Ireland in Belfast. Peter Broadbent's reward for a prolific start to the campaign was retention in the national side and maybe there was a shade of tiredness when the duo returned two days later for a Wolves team who were well beaten at Bolton in the Charity Shield.

When Broadbent was omitted for the visit of the USSR three weeks later, Slater stepped into a team who gained a modicum of revenge for World Cup elimination by winning handsomely. Charlton scored once and Johnny Haynes three times but the game was also notable on one other score. The 5-0 success proved to be the international swansong of Tom Finney, who was the last surviving link in the chain stretching right back to the England line-up into which Billy had nervously stepped for the first time over 12 years earlier. The Preston Plumber was stood down reluctantly by the selectors after winning 76 caps but his good pal had a little further to travel.

In his final competitive outing at Highbury, Wright helped Wolves to a 1-1 draw with Arsenal and another title challenge was well under way. He was in good heart as he departed for England's 2-2 Villa Park draw with Wales, only to produce a less than convincing performance on the occasion of another farewell – that of Nat Lofthouse after a terrific return of 30 goals in 33 caps.

Although Broadbent scored twice, these were trying times for the country. In 11 games up to the Munich disaster, England had won eight, drawn two and lost one. In 11 matches since, they had won three, drawn six and lost two. The tragic void caused by the loss of some of Manchester United's finest was proving hard to fill, especially as other big names were ageing.

Billy was still making a decent impression, though, particularly on the younger element of the side. "He was deceptively good in the air and no slouch on the ground," said Liverpool winger Alan A'Court. "And he was great with the other players. He always made you welcome and I remember him giving me the thumbs-up when I scored against Ireland in my first game. When you look back, it's remarkable how well Wolves were represented in the team. There was the famous time when they provided the entire half-back line at the World Cup and, when we went to Russia just before that, I remember Tommy Banks rushing past Bill Slater to receive a short corner in the first minute and Bill saying in a very polite voice to Billy Wright: 'Where is he going?'"

Many a cricketer stuck on 99 has gone through agonies waiting for his first delivery and first run next morning. Billy couldn't allow himself any such butterflies when marooned on that figure for nearly five months! He had Wolves' bid for a second successive League title to spearhead in the meantime, their hopes boosted by three consecutive wins over Christmas. The latter two were a magnificent 5-3/7-0 double over Portsmouth – conquests on successive days to which Broadbent, Colin Booth and Deeley contributed hat-tricks.

Billy's final FA Cup tie ended in disappointment and defeat against a Bolton side whom Wolves failed to beat in four meetings in 1958-59. And their fortunes in another knockout had been no better when their first appearance in the European Cup was terminated as Schalke edged past them. But the impetus in the League was being maintained in an eye-opening fashion.

They took heavy toll of Blackburn (5-0), Newcastle (4-3) and Leeds (6-2) and, had they not lost narrowly at Manchester United, the title race would have been over even earlier than it was. Wolves were a highly formidable unit as they rattled on with the sort of victory margins unheard of on such a regular basis until Steve Bull came crashing along almost three decades later.

With emerging forwards Micky Lill and Bobby Mason well into double figures in the goal charts in the slipstream of Jimmy Murray, Broadbent and Deeley, the side ran up a staggering 110 goals in League matches alone – their highest since their Second Division title-winning campaign of 1931-32. It was also the third of four seasons in a row in which they would score more than a hundred goals in all competitions.

Billy's last game against Arsenal was marked by a 6-1 Wolves win at Molineux (just like his first had been) and his final meeting with Albion was a 5-2 success. There was barely time to breathe. Wolves won 13 of the 17 matches in their run-in, including all of the last four, and were champions again

Billy Wright exchanges pleasantries with the Duke of Gloucester after being presented with the FA Cup by Princess Elizabeth following Wolves' comfortable 3-1 final victory over Leicester in 1949. It was the first of the skipper's major honours in the game - and possibly his proudest - and came ten years after he, as a young groundstaff lad, had been left in tears by the club's shock Wembley defeat against Portsmouth.

Wolverhampton's streets were packed with tens of thousands of ecstatic townspeople when Wolves returned with the FA Cup in April, 1949, more than three decades on from when they had last won it. Billy is seen here with the silverware safely in his grip at the front of the bus.

Did David Beckham ever do this? Young Billy dutifully lays the table at the digs run by the woman Eamonn Andrews described as England's most famous landlady, Mrs Colley. The player stayed there for almost two decades - 'basically bed and breakfast' as journalist Leon Hickman put it.

A proud day for Wolves and their supporters as Billy leads England out for their game at Tottenham against Italy in November, 1949. It was the day the captain scored the second of the three goals he netted for his country but the star on this occasion was the also-pictured Bert Williams, who produced a magnificent performance that earned him his nickname The Cat.

An exciting place to go to work......Billy Wright makes his way out in front of Molineux's eager masses for a friendly against Racing Club of Argentina in March, 1954. In his career, the skipper met counterparts from all over the globe - and hoped they spoke at least a few words of English!

On the other side of the camera for a change. Billy sees to it that forward Roy Swinbourne's photo album has a nice snap from the sight-seeing time the Wolves squad had on their trip to Russia in the close season of 1955.

Above: Billy and Mrs Colley compare musical tastes with a flick through a gramophone record collection at her home in Burland Avenue, Claregate, on Wolverhampton's outskirts.

Right: For all his travels with Wolves and England, this was the only competitive European tie Billy played in - a surprise 4-3 defeat on aggregate in the European Cup first round in the November of 1958. Inflicting the damage were Schalke, who followed up this 2-2 Molineux draw by winning at home.

Okay, time for a little reflection and appreciation......Billy has a sort through his England caps (above) in the year that he said his Wolves and international farewells. It was in this particular spring (1959) that he brought up his famous century of official England appearances. On the left, wife Joy is at his side as he receives the CBE.

Three nostalgic images from the day Billy Wright bowed out as a professional footballer. He finds himself flanked by schoolboys as he makes his way to Molineux on the day of his farewell appearance - for Stan Cullis's colours against the whites. The guard of honour afforded him by his applauding team-mates left him more than a little embarrassed but it was work as usual once the game kicked off, with his eyes firmly fixed on the ball as he headed away this cross (below). And, with that, one of the sport's very finest called it a day.

No-one could ever accuse Steve Bull of ever giving less than 100 per cent to the cause in the colours of Wolverhampton Wanderers. Left: He is all effort as he holds off a defender and shoots at goal away to Newport on the 1987-88 night that his brace took his goal tally for the season to 50 and ensured promotion for the club from the Fourth Division. Below: George Foster, later to serve at Molineux as chief scout, is the man in pursuit as the striker, again in a change all white strip, rushes towards goal in a Third Division game at Mansfield near the end of 1988-89.

Having shared the goal-scoring burden, Andy Mutch and Steve Bull were happy to share the Third Division title spoils for a few precious moments after Wolves' draw at home to Sheffield United in May, 1989, had made them champions for the second season running.

Bully watches Paul Cook, Mark Venus and Gary Bellamy repel a Leeds attack in March of 1990, the first season Wolves had spent back in the Second Division.

## Glory, Glory Wolves

after beating Luton 5-0 on April 18, the same date on which Bully sat next to Andy Thompson in the Billy Wright Stand and celebrated the club's promotion to the Premier League in 2009.

Technically, Wolves could still have been caught by United but a telegram of congratulation from Old Trafford within half an hour of full time confirmed that the pursuers had given up the ghost and accepted that Billy would have his hands on the League Championship trophy for the third time. With two points against Leicester four nights later, the formalities were addressed, the side thus becoming only the eighth in the 20th century to successfully defend the Championship crown. Cue more photos of Billy with one hand on the trophy and the other acknowledging the cheers of the crowd.

Maybe one or two on the inside suspected that, 20 years on from his Wolves debut, the end was close. But no-one knew at the time that Billy had just made his final appearance for the club, by coincidence two years to the day after Bert Williams played his last game. At Everton on the following Saturday, Cullis opted to give another chance at no 5 to the emerging George Showell and the club's future appeared to be in safe hands as a fourth successive clean sheet paved the way for a 1-0 win, Wolves finishing six points clear.

It was a fantastic time for the club, who, much to Billy's delight, had lifted the Youth Cup the previous year by beating United in the semis and Chelsea in a spectacular turnaround in the final. For the skipper, it was a particularly blissful phase. Baby Vicky had arrived to add to the marital delights and, on the day she took her first breath, he received the call-up for his 100th cap.

With fitting sense of occasion, the landmark was reached at Wembley and against none other than Scotland. Apart from a World Cup final, there could have been no grander stage for Wright to savour becoming the first man on the planet to complete a century of games for his country. Mother (minus baby but with her twin sisters and fellow Beverleys) sat in the crowd at Wembley as her beaming husband led England out.

It seems pre-ordained that England would win, which they did thanks to a Bobby Charlton header. Broadbent and Flowers were also in the line-up. Whereas Bully had to make a bee-line for the pocket of England fans in Hampden when he scored there on his international debut, Billy was surrounded by friendly faces and back-slappers at football headquarters on April 11, 1959 – in the crowd as well as among his team-mates.

The photo of him being chaired off by Ronnie Clayton and Don Howe is one of the iconic images of his unbelievable career and he wrote: "I wouldn't have exchanged the noise and buffeting of that happy little journey for all the travelling comforts of the modern world. A victory was the best centenary present I could have had and we won more easily than the score might suggest.

"Of all the years I enjoyed as a player, 1959 has to be the most memorable. Wolves won the Championship, I was awarded my 100th cap and Joy and I had our first child, Vicky. On top of all that, I was awarded the CBE for services to football." Renowned cartoonist Roy Ullyett superbly captured the moment in the Daily Express with a drawing of Billy holding a ball in one hand and his one-day-old daughter in the other, with 100 caps stacked on his head. The caption read: 'Congratulations Billy Wright, the Daddy of them all!'

It was celebration time wherever he turned. About 1,000 letters or telegrams poured in, among them ones from FIFA, Real Madrid and many of Europe's national football associations. Then, on April 29, came a banquet at the Civic Hall, Wolverhampton, where Joe Mercer kept a date to speak in his honour, although it meant him leaving before the end of his Villa side's draw with Albion that condemned them to relegation.

Billy's arm ached by the end of the evening from all the hand-shaking with various dignitaries who stepped forward to make presentations. From Cliff Everall, on behalf of Wolves supporters, there was a huge piece of silver, from the FA a silver salver, from the Mayor, Councillor J C Homer, on behalf of the Wolverhampton people, there was a silver rose bowl, from the FA of Ireland and Football League of Ireland, other keepsakes.

"He is our champion of champions," the Mayor said of Billy. "We can be sure that every Wolves supporter is here tonight in spirit. They, above all, have come to be grateful to him for the pleasure he has given them over the years. There's no doubt he's far and away Wolverhampton's best-known citizen and I can tell them there's no-one in the town who would wish it otherwise."

The plaudits rolled on……"It's trite but true to say that he has been an ambassador wherever he has travelled," said Joe Mears, chairman of the FA's international committee. And Wolves chairman James Baker followed up by calling him 'the greatest sporting personality of this generation' and relating a pledge from a Honved official, who had once said: "If you want to play a benefit match for Billy, I will bring every great player in Europe to play."

Stan Cullis, his own stock sky-high following Wolves' lifting of the League Championship for the second consecutive year, was no less praising, pointing to Billy's dedication, professionalism, integrity and consistency. "He has done as much as any player to raise the status of the professional footballer," the manager said. "It may be that we shall see better players but I'm certain of one thing: there will never be a name that will grace the annals of association football better than that of Billy Wright."

Mercer cast aside his worries at the opposite end of the table to Wolves by describing his former England team-mate as a 'man of 100 caps and a million friends.' "Congratulations on this fantastic run of internationals," he said. "You can take it from me that your international colleagues, the toughest critics who never give praise lightly, are 100 per cent in agreement that you are a great player, a greater captain and an even greater man."

Even with a third Championship and a 100th cap under safe keeping, Billy's work wasn't quite done. Bizarrely, the same issue of the Express & Star that carried a long report of his big night at the Civic also had a story on its back page bearing the heading: 'Billy Wright Put On Transfer List.' Happily, this was not the national captain but the Newcastle left-winger of the same name who had been signed from Leicester the previous summer.

As the celebrations died down for the real Billy, he went off with Flowers and Broadbent to play in England's home draw against Italy and then packed his bags for the longest of the many international tours he undertook. Deeley and a young Jimmy Greaves were on board, too, as the country's finest departed for Rio de Janeiro, then Lima, Mexico City and Los Angeles.

More than 150,000 packed the Maracana Stadium, which was alive inside three minutes when Jimmy Armfield, like Deeley a debutant, got into a tangle with Wright and saw Julinho put Brazil ahead. A side containing seven of the players who had won the World Cup the previous year beat England 2-0.

The game was disappointing but the stay in Brazil contained a personal highlight. It was there Billy learned via a telegram from Joy that he had been chosen for 'a very great honour.' A follow-up message from his mother-in-law was cryptically signed off: 'Congratulations. See Be E' and the penny dropped. He was down for a CBE on the Queen's Birthday Honours List.

Billy broke the news to his team-mates on the coach and begged them not to threaten the protocol by saying anything out of turn before the matter was made official. They didn't. But the happiness didn't extend to the pitch, where the skipper's fortunes grew no better after his trying time in Rio when England were hammered 4-1 by Peru. Again, he didn't play well.

He was nevertheless still making a big impression. "Whenever I went on tour with England, the one man everyone wanted to see was Billy Wright," wrote Ronnie Clayton in his 1960 book *'A Slave To Soccer'*. "In Brazil, the kids loved him and the foreigners just flocked to see him. Without him, it didn't seem like an England team. When we went on the field, it was Billy the photographers made for and, off the field, it was Billy who was called on to say a few words here, make a formal speech there or do a TV appearance. He took it all in his stride. Just before his century of games for England, the Brazilians came to our hotel to present him with a beautiful carved candlestick about two feet high. And, when we were on tour in South America, they presented him with a handsome bronze statuette."

Another defeat followed in the challenging altitude of Mexico, then came two goals by Flowers that contributed to an 8-1 spanking of the Yanks. Despite that victory, it had been a difficult two and a bit weeks for the skipper as well as for his side and he did some serious thinking on the long homeward run.

## Chapter Seven

# The Game's Up

Billy didn't simply step off the plane bringing England's players home from the Americas and realise the game was up. Instead, he took a few weeks' break, then reported for training with Wolves for the 1959-60 season. It was only well into that punishing push for fitness that he made his big decision to retire, one that was heavily influenced by a meeting he had in the June with the then Home Secretary 'Rab' Butler.

The player and his wife had been invited to the Essex home of this senior member of the Harold Macmillan Government after receiving confirmation of his CBE. Butler related how his fourth year as Chancellor of the Exchequer had proved one too many following three successful ones and he pulled no punches in urging Billy to heed the danger of going on too long.

As well as marital bliss, other factors were now turning the head that sported that famous blond hair. One was the emergence at Wolves of George Showell, the Black Country boy who had been restricted to 42 appearances in five years as a first-team challenger. Billy was told by Stan Cullis that the younger man, who had excelled in Wright's absence on that summer's tour of West Germany and Switzerland, would not be so easily satisfied with stand-in duty in future and was likely to become his first-choice no 5 at some point in 1959-60.

It's well documented, too, that Wright felt all of his 35 years when pounding the hills of Cannock Chase some weeks later and found himself unable to prevent the wannabes in the group surging past him. His struggles might have gone undetected at other clubs but this was Cullis's Wolves and he recognised it as another reminder that time waits for no man.

Clubs very rarely undertook pre-season tours in those days – 'bonding' wasn't part of the football vocabulary – and Wolves' warm-up programme before facing FA Cup holders Nottingham Forest in the Charity Shield was essentially the annual Colours v Whites run-out at Molineux; a game between the probables and the possibles, a chance for the lesser lights to ruffle the feathers of the established men by staking their own claims to places.

The 1959 staging of the fixture was a couple of days away when Billy went back on his decision to pull on the gold jersey for a 22nd season by breaking the news of his momentous decision to Cullis and then to the Express & Star's Wolves correspondent Phil Morgan, known in his earlier years in the press box as 'Commentator.' It was clean and uncomplicated, just as he wanted it to be.

"Many stars hung grimly on to their playing days," Billy wrote in his 1962 book *'One Hundred Caps And All That'*. "I saw players whose ability and achievements had given them household names refusing to accept the fact that this is a game for the young man. I made up my young mind that, if ever I achieved stardom, I would take both my health and my reputation into retirement. I never changed my mind."

Billy's retirement merited only two paragraphs on the front of the E & S on August 6, 1959 – admittedly a day on which it had to compete for space with the disclosure that The Queen and Prince Philip were expecting their third child. It was, of course, the lead story on the back page but it was all rather understated given his colossal status and considering how Steve Bull's demise would be reported 40 years later. "Yes, this is it," Billy was quoted as saying. "I've had a wonderful run with a wonderful club and I want to finish while I'm still at the top."

There was no question of Wolves standing in his way or of Cullis insisting he spent a year on the fringes of the side to help groom his successor. "Under no circumstances would I ask Billy to play in the Central League team," the manager said. "He will finish as a first-team player."

So where did the rethink come? "I told you last April I thought I was good for another season at least but, since I got my England 100 and the CBE, I have thought it over and decided now is the time to quit," Wright continued. "After all, the Wolves policy is based on the development of young players and I feel the time has come to make way for George Showell to take my place."

Billy, who had faced 28 different opponents as a full England player, was turning his back on Wolves' European Cup campaign as well by hanging up those well-worn boots, the club having already been drawn against Vorwaerts from the old East Germany. He made it clear he was not planning to play elsewhere and didn't have a manager's job lined up.

Cullis added of his already-made decision to effectively install Showell as his first-choice centre-half and risk marginalising a genuine giant of the game: "It's the most difficult thing I've had to do in my 11 years in the job." He was losing him as a player but he was keen to retain him for the good of Wolverhampton Wanderers in another capacity.

Lurking in the background was the possibility that Billy might choose to work for the FA and not stick around with Wolves. After all, how could he not be highly coveted by the organisation he had so wonderfully represented as ambassador as well as player? Cullis said, though, that he wanted him as his chief coach, with special responsibility for bringing on youngsters who nursed the same aspirations he had two decades earlier. A lot of dust, gold dust of course, still had to settle.

It's fair to say the big announcement was greeted with something less than shock among Billy's international colleagues. "It came as no surprise," wrote Jimmy Greaves. "The rumours had been circulating for weeks but it signalled the end of an era for English football." Only 21 of Billy's 105 internationals had ended in defeat; a ratio of one loss every five matches and a fitting record for a man of whom Walter Winterbottom said: "English football has not had a better servant."

The phenomenal Greaves, part of the Chelsea team sensationally beaten in the Youth Cup final at Molineux the previous year and sufficiently outspoken as a TV pundit to appear in a 1990 World Cup studio in a shirt bearing the message 'Let The Bull Loose,' had been the catalyst for a few self doubts when leading Billy a merry dance while scoring five of the goals in the Londoners' 6-2 taming of Wolves at Stamford Bridge on the second Saturday of 1958-59.

He was also proved correct in another hunch; that Wolves, with or without their most famous player, would push very hard in 1959-60 to emulate the achievements of Arsenal and Huddersfield in challenging for three League Championships in a row.

What a thing it must have been for Billy to slip into retirement having, only a few weeks earlier, lifted the League Championship. That highlight came at the end of his final game for what was, other than a few wartime matches for Leicester, his only club. Notwithstanding the contention of some that you are a long time retired so you should play as long as possible, he had beautifully observed the alternative theory that it's best to quit at the top.

In compiling what was then a record 541 League and cup appearances for Wolves – over 50 more than his nearest challenger Jimmy Mullen – Wright had never appeared anywhere but the club's first team since making his League debut. So it was a lovely touch by the so-called Iron Manager to take him out of the Whites (reserves) team at the last moment and grant him his usual place in the Colours (seniors) side for the Saturday afternoon curtain-raiser.

Among the 20,000 attendance that was about double the normal turn-out for the game and which produced record charity proceeds of £1,205 was a Wolves supporter from Finland's third largest city, Turku. Before it was too late, 22-year-old Matti Kaitila, who by then had a posting at Salford Town Hall, was determined to travel from Manchester to see in the flesh a player he had admired from afar for several years.

Billy was photographed hiding his face as he walked down the guard of honour before kick-off looking suitably embarrassed. He wasn't booked, he was in the first team and it was business as usual, except Wolves lost 4-2 after leading 2-0 in the first half. So was his retirement decision the correct one?

"Stan Cullis knew he couldn't hold George Showell back any longer and that could only mean that Billy was going to have to make way," said Ted Farmer, the rampaging young centre-forward Wright marked in that game. "And it just wouldn't have seemed right for him to be out of the side. Like Steve Bull was for many years, he was never injured, so the only way George used to get in the side for ages was when England were playing.

"George was a very good centre-half as well and really needed to be playing. When you consider that he marked Albert di Stefano off the park on the night Wolves faced Real Madrid, you can see why Stan felt he needed to play him. Billy thought Di Stefano was the best forward he ever faced.

"George had to be very patient but he had a wonderful player to follow. Billy is the greatest footballer of all time for me, the perfect role model for everybody because of his professionalism and dedication. The game was much more physical then than it is now and he could have been devoured by rough centre-forwards if he hadn't been so clever in knowing when to go in and when to hold back. I played against him many times in practice matches and was four inches taller than him and several yards faster but I didn't get near the ball. He knew where it was going before it was delivered, so you rarely had chance to judge your pace against his – or to capitalise on your extra height. He was pure class. I'd say the nearest to him since has been Franz Beckenbauer and I'd put him above Bobby Moore.

"I'm sure Bully would have scored plenty of goals playing with the likes

## The Game's Up

of Hancocks and Mullen but there would have been plenty of days when he wouldn't have had a sniff if he had been playing against a side containing Billy Wright. Billy's performances never faltered."

It is customary to describe retiring players as hanging their boots up. In this case, it's not strictly true because Billy presented the pair he wore in 1958-59 to George Garland, a cobbler with shops in Blakenhall and Penn who, having worked as a PT instructor in the Army when he first met Cullis, was appointed as the club's official cobbler and was even invited to sit next to physio George Palmer on the touchline at the 1960 FA Cup final.

Billy, back in his civvies, was pictured with his rarely photographed father Tom as he left the ground after the game, his own step-son Vincent at their side. It had been a low-key departure, the sort of which would hardly be permitted in today's media-frenzy society. "There were no speeches or demonstrations," wrote Commentator. "It was a finale with dignity."

The public reaction to Steve Bull's enforced retirement would prove enormously different and my slow trawl through the back copies of the Express & Star from August, 1959 revealed only one letter on the subject of Billy's going – and that in an era when we were supposedly a nation of letter writers.

The only 'extras' the paper carried were two picture stories, the first showing Wright shaking hands with Showell to wish him all the best – a piece in which the younger contender confirmed he was taken on one side on the day of the announcement and given the news by the man himself. The other photo captured Billy and Cullis striding down the first fairway together at South Staffs Golf Club and was intended to allay any suggestions of a fall-out between them, although the manager was quoted as saying he intended taking half a crown off him by winning their game.

Joy Beverley also did a little fire-fighting. So perturbed was she by a report alleging she didn't wish to stay in the West Midlands that she rang the Express & Star from Llandudno, where she was performing with her sisters, to say: "We lived in Wolverhampton from the time we were married and everybody there was more than kind. Wherever Billy wants to go, I will go. To suggest I don't want to live in Wolverhampton is downright vicious."

Predictably, there weren't many negative stories and the tributes flooded in. Stan Mortensen called Wright 'a captain who led by marvellous example' and Bill Kaye reflected on Moscow Radio on the dismay the news had caused Wolves' friends behind the Iron Curtain. "Of all the players to visit this country," he said, "Billy can be proud that he won the heart of the Moscow crowd. His battle cry when Wolves were three goals down (against Dynamo in 1955) stirred his mates on to reduce the margin to 3-2 and had the crowd on their toes. No-one came in for a bigger ovation than Billy Wright and we're all very sorry he's leaving. It's a loss not only to England but to international football in general. We all wish him success and luck in his new life."

Nat Lofthouse, Bert Trautmann and Bill Slater subsequently named Billy in their Dream Team, with Slater interestingly selecting him as a wing-half rather than centre-half. And, from the same international dressing room but the other side of the Black Country divide, Albion's Don Howe said in later years: "He was a nice bloke but when he stepped into that arena, he wanted to win."

Tommy Docherty had no hesitation naming Billy in his all-time best English XI and wrote in his 1960 book *'Soccer From The Shoulder'*: "When I think of Wolves, I think of Billy Wright. I don't think I ever saw him commit a deliberate foul. He was tough enough but scrupulously fair with it."

When briefly serving Wolves as manager in the mid-1980s, The Doc found Molineux a much more miserable place than Billy ever did but no doubt took inspiration from the showcased trophies his predecessor had helped to win. And he added: "He became one of the greatest players the game has known. He has had praise heaped on his head and few men have earned it more."

Eddie Stuart was immediately named captain in succession to the man who had held the job, England duties apart, for 12 years. In 200 or more games, the South African had added a little of the brawn alongside Billy's acknowledged brain and has no doubts the timing of his friend's retirement decision was like so much of his on-field work; perfect. "He wanted to end at the top and decided it was time to go," he said. "It would have been a shame if he'd gone on too long and found himself out of the side. It was the right decision in my opinion. I've always been an emotional person and think I was more upset than Billy!

"I was his vice-captain for five or six years and he hardly missed a game. He never got injured. It was great for the club but I admit I wish I'd been able to lead the side out more. When Stan made me captain, I was so proud but it was also a big burden because it was impossible for anyone to replace Billy."

The club's last link with their pre-war years was broken when Billy's teenage pal and lifelong friend Mullen also quit. Between them, they totalled 1,027 competitive Wolves matches and 117 England games, and were even team-mates at Leicester during the war. Mullen stayed in the town to run a successful sports shop business up to his sudden death in 1987 but the strongest indication yet that Billy wouldn't be taking up Wolves' coaching offer came when he and Joy announced they were moving to live in London.

It was an arrangement that allowed him to drop in on their autumn clash at Tottenham and he travelled with the squad as a special guest for their European Cup assignment in Barcelona. In between, he was present for the visit of Blackpool as he became only the second Wolves player after Mullen to receive a third benefit cheque of £1,000 for long Molineux service. He was the perfect team man and a dream for a manager to have in his side.

Chapter Eight

# What Next?

And so the lad who grew up in Ironbridge, loved a good Western on TV and lived for almost two decades with a landlady who taught him how to sew rugs, retreated into the sunset with more than 100 England caps. Others have since reached the mark, although some with their tally devalued in the eyes of traditionalists by the number of substitutions now permitted.

Furthermore, Billy Wright, although undeniably a national hero and celebrity, had no millionaire lifestyle. He couldn't have had on his wages. Only after he had skippered Wolves to the League Championship for the second time in 1957-58 was he deemed worthy of receiving as much as £20 a week from his club. And it wasn't that the fingers controlling the Molineux coffers were unduly tight. Football was still in its maximum wage straitjacket and even star turns like the long-time England captain had to chug along accordingly.

I am again indebted to Norman Giller's affectionate *'A Hero For All Seasons'* biography for telling us Billy was on £10 a week at Molineux (but only £7 in the summer) when he broke into the national side – recognition that brought him £20 appearance money a time. Even by the time his club salary had doubled, he was only due £17 a week in the close season.

We're reliably informed he earned around £15,000 in total out of Wolves, including win bonuses – and there were an awful lot of those. As reward for his long service to the club, he had two benefit cheques of £750 and the third one for £1,000, as well as £2,000 for winning the League three times.

Norman also pointed out Billy had a £1,500 Provident Fund pay-out on his retirement in 1959, earned a maximum of £50 for any of his England appearances and therefore grossed less than £4,000 for winning 105 caps for his country. Sponsorships did boost his income and he made sure he had sound advice when he went to negotiate a deal with a soft drinks company to have his face on coasters. He took Mrs Colley with him!

## What Next?

Football provided a very good living for him compared with the every-day working man but his earnings were small change when stacked up alongside those of today's top players. As for comparisons with Cristiano Ronaldo, we won't even go there. One thing is for sure, though, the pouting Portuguese forward could not be enjoying his career any more than did the man who was both proud adopted Wulfrunian and patriotic Englishman.

"He absolutely loved Wolves," said his team-mate Roy Swinbourne. "He was brilliant with the younger members of the side like myself and you just couldn't think of him going off to sign for any other club. I'm sure he had gold and black in his blood. We were so lucky to have him here." In terms of sharing a dressing room, Bobby Robson knew him only as an England player, although he had a few years of Wolves-Albion combat with him. "He loves those three lions," he said of him. "Prior to the game, he would go round individually to all the players and say little things. He was inspirational."

Such selflessness was also recognised by Ronnie Clayton, the Blackburn wing-half who succeeded him as England skipper. "He was one of the wisest footballers I have ever known," he said. "When I became captain, I vowed I'd try to keep a level head and tackle my problems as Billy tackled and overcame his. There were no cliques when he was around. Everyone was part of a team."

Journalist Leon Hickman added: "I knew him like an uncle, so I wouldn't hear a bad word against him. He was just the greatest guy. No player I ever saw made more of what he had, no player. What a great player he was. He set standards in fitness and behaviour and he was a great organiser."

Bert Williams echoed the same theme and clearly believes there was never anyone better at setting the right example: "He played every game as if it was a cup final," he said. "He incorporated everything you wanted to see in your own son or idol. He obeyed the rules and I don't recall him ever being spoken to by a referee, let alone booked. He was a 100 per cent club man."

On the face of it, Wolverhampton Wanderers didn't immediately miss their most famous ever player. In the months that followed his decision to call a sudden halt to what had been his way of life for over half of the 35 years he had spent on the planet, they were still a highly formidable unit. In the first season in 20 in which Billy had not been on the club's books, Cullis's side went within a goal of becoming the first club since Aston Villa in 1897 to win the coveted League and FA Cup double. That they failed, though, inevitably sparked questions of whether Billy's presence for just one more year might have turned runners-up place into the joy of a third successive title triumph.

Much though everyone knew the skipper had to go some time and understood the need to give George Showell his head, it was tempting to wonder whether even ten or a dozen appearances from the senior man might have made the difference in 1959-60. Wolves topped 100 League goals for the third season running but the going was tougher at the other end, where they conceded 67 compared with 49 in 1958-59 and 47 in 1957-58. "Unfortunately, George was slightly past his best by the time he got in regularly," recalls Ted Farmer, the forward who would soon become a colleague. "It wasn't long before he was switched to full-back because he had lost a bit of his pace."

A year on from Billy's final game, Wolves completed their League programme with a stunning 5-1 victory at Chelsea and were at home with their feet up by the time the destination of the crown was resolved. In another reminder of how the game's rulers did things differently decades ago, the decisive rearranged First Division match was allowed to be played two nights later between Manchester City and Burnley at Maine Road. In 1988, Bully's Wolves used the Sherpa Van Trophy final against Burnley to confirm their relaunch. Twenty-eight years earlier, the Clarets were less easily overshadowed and, in Cullis's nervous presence, recorded a 2-1 win that meant the title switched to Turf Moor after two years on the Molineux mantelpiece.

A season in which Wolves also won through two rounds of the European Cup before being mauled by Barcelona was a big triumph for Bill Slater. He followed Billy's lead by being named Footballer of the Year and was moved to his ex-skipper's no 5 role after Christmas while Showell went to right-back.

The reshuffle spelled huge disappointment for Eddie Stuart, who had been a regular for two and a half seasons but lost his place after appearing in the first four games of the club's victorious FA Cup run. The Johannesburg-born defender blamed hate mail and the booing he received from a small minority of Wolves fans following racial atrocities in South Africa for Cullis's decision to leave him out – a sidelining that would cost him his place at Wembley. So Showell had effectively ousted not one but two Wolves captains in the space of a few months.

And there was a South Africa link for Billy while the team he left behind were winning 6-4 at Manchester City and 9-0 at home to Fulham in their first few weeks without him. To be strictly accurate, his playing career didn't end with his retirement announcement at Molineux because he agreed to go to

## What Next?

South Africa to play four matches early in September, 1959 at a time when he said he was mulling over two job offers – one on the coaching staff at Wolves, the other with the Football Association. Not that England coach Walter Winterbottom was completely sure about the latter.

He made plans to speak urgently to Billy and Cullis, sensitive as he was to the fact his long-time skipper didn't have even his preliminary coaching certificates – qualifications other candidates possessed: "I know there has been a lot of talk about Wright being given a job by the FA," Winterbottom said. "Frankly, I know nothing about it. I am going to talk to him and Stan to try to discover what the situation is. As far as I know, the coaching appointments for this year have been filled and we aren't looking for anyone else."

A personal visit from a representative of Johannesburg Rangers, the club for whom Stuart played prior to his migration to the West Midlands, led to the 'substantial and wonderful' offer of three weeks' work in what was then commonly called the Union. News of Billy's impending 12,000-mile round trip to a country he had twice visited with Wolves broke while he was spending a week in Llandudno, where the Beverleys were playing a summer season.

He had to ask for Wolves' permission to go as they still held his playing registration but he was delighted to follow the lead of Stanley Matthews a couple of years earlier and play in a series of exhibition matches, although he had to go off with a cut head when appearing in Durban for Natal Professionals against Transvaal Professionals.

Amid talk that he might make a lucrative switch to Inter Milan, Billy's three-week stay stretched to four, with some coaching thrown in, before he was met off the plane at London Airport by Joy. Also there to greet him were a posse of reporters who, presumably mindful of the fact Wolves had conceded 15 goals in eight games in September, were eager to put to him reports that the club were to ask him to consider lacing his boots up once more.

As would be the case with Steve Bull almost three decades later, though, talk of a comeback died almost as soon as it began. "I can tell you that I won't be playing again," Billy said. "That's definite." In also confirming he wouldn't be going back to Africa, he reiterated that he was retired and hinted that he wouldn't be doing much for a while, which suggested he wasn't in a rush to take the coaching job on hold for him at Molineux.

Cullis was quoted in Norman Giller's book *'A Hero For All Seasons'* as saying that Billy's endearing personality – quiet and well-mannered – made him too nice to be a successful manager, lacking as he was in ruthlessness. But one of the youngsters coming through in his slipstream later played under him at international level and has a theory why the great man's career on the touchline was nothing like as successful as the one on the pitch.

Ted Farmer, like Steve Bull, scored around 300 goals for Wolves – in his case many of them coming in the junior teams as his time in the senior side was restricted first by fierce competition for places and then by a serious knee injury that ended his career the day before his 26th birthday. But he believes things could have been different for his all-time hero. "Billy was fine as a coach, the same fella as far as I'm concerned," Farmer says. "I suppose it did me no harm that he knew me from Wolves and I scored eight goals in three under-23 matches for him and got a hat-trick in Holland in Bobby Moore's first game as captain of the team.

"I believe that Billy, like Stan Cullis, was done no favours by the scrapping of the maximum wage. When Billy went to Arsenal, he signed Ian Ure for big money from Scotland and players like George Eastham and Joe Baker were becoming very powerful as pay went up. I think he lost some of his control as a result – the same problem Stan had because he thought players were being overpaid if they received even £20 a week!"

Billy trod Molineux's hallowed turf once more when he and Jimmy Mullen were given a joint testimonial in April, 1962 and faced an International XI containing Tom Finney, Derek Kevan, Bobby Collins and Terry Hennessey, the latter a distant relative of latter-day Wolves keeper Wayne Hennessey. Seven of the duo's former team-mates played in an entertaining 4-4 draw.

For all the suggestions Billy would walk into a coaching job at Molineux, Arsenal proved to be the only club he served following his playing retirement, although in 1961 he is said to have turned down a £2,200 annual salary to coach them under George Swindin. Instead, he chose to cut his teeth for a while with the England youth and under-23 teams.

There was nevertheless a strong pull for him towards Highbury, his love for the Gunners having been established from the day when, as an 11-year-old, he watched Herbert Chapman's side draw at Wolves in 1935. His pride at striding through the Marble Halls to play for England against France in 1947 and winning 3-0 can easily be imagined. It was after all the ground which he said 'had the best facilities in the League' and it came to be lucky for him with England. He led the team to big subsequent wins there over Sweden and

## What Next?

Switzerland, although the Yugoslavs escaped with a fortunate draw in 1950.

Billy had seemed settled in his FA role, using Chelsea as a training base before an under-23 game against Turkey at Southampton, until the call to manage Arsenal came in the summer of 1962. He had a doubly tough act to follow, both in as much as his predecessor Swindin had been a relative success and because arch-rivals Tottenham were blazing a glorious trail at the peak of the English game, Spurs winning the double in 1961 after Wolves had narrowly missed out a year earlier. Then they became the first English side to lift a major European trophy when they got their hands on the Cup Winners Cup. So there was considerable pressure from within for the Gunners to fire a few headlines of their own across the back pages.

Seventh place in his first season, in which Wolves' spectacular 5-4 defeat in North London was balanced by a 1-0 win at Molineux, was no disaster and the club also reached the fifth round of the FA Cup before losing to Liverpool, their run launched by a big victory over Oxford at the opening stage in a tie that left a sizeable impression on the visitors' Ron Atkinson.

"I remember arriving at Highbury and seeing Billy talking to some reporters in the foyer," he said. "Three or four of us had been youngsters at Wolves without making it; lads like Maurice Kyle, Cyril Beavon and myself, who had been seeing to all the menial tasks at Molineux among those legends. Not only did Billy recognise us, he broke off with who he was talking to and came over to say hello and ask how we were getting on. He was a top bloke."

When Arsenal scored 92 goals in Billy's second season, optimism grew. The problem was that, despite signing Ure for what was reported to be a world record £62,500 fee for a centre-half, his side conceded 80 and finished a place lower than 12 months earlier. "Billy wasn't a good manager," Ure was later quoted as saying. "He was not hard enough and didn't have the willpower to get the players to work together. Some players simply played for themselves."

One of the most notorious defeats in Gunners history blighted the manager's attempts to kick on, an FA Cup exit at Peterborough coming in a 1964-65 campaign in which they trailed in a disappointing 13th. The day before Stephen George Bull arrived in this world on March 28, 1965, Arsenal's run without a win was taken to four games by a defeat at West Ham – while Wolves bizarrely lost 7-4 at Tottenham.

By today's standards, the three years Billy had already been given may seem generous but he recalled Major Buckley reigning for 17 years at Molineux and

Cullis ruling the roost for more than 16 seasons. Indeed, Bully's first and favourite Wolves manager, Graham Turner, occupied the same not-so-hot seat for a few months short of eight years, so maybe it wasn't so unusual. But Billy, whose second daughter Babette was born in 1964, was deeply upset when the end came after his stay had stretched to a fourth full year, one in which Arsenal dropped even further to a final placing of 14th. It wasn't just results that brought about his downfall. Fans seemed to be losing faith with him as well.

Difficult though it now is to believe, a paltry 4,554 watched the home game against Leeds near the end of 1965-66, with Highbury's North Bank so sparsely populated that some spectators lit a fire and danced around it. Although the shock at the attendance – the lowest for a top-flight game in this country since the war – was lessened by the fact the European Cup Winners Cup final between Liverpool and Borussia Dortmund was being shown live on TV at the same time, Arsenal's 3-0 defeat was another nail in his coffin.

Billy, who had been forced to endure chants of 'Wright Out,' the like of which were seldom heard at the time, was on holiday with Joy when he took the call from his coach Les Shannon that warned him the end was nigh. And where should they be at the time but Sweden, the country in which Bully was training with Wolves 33 years later when he had to admit defeat. It's somewhat ironic that England should enjoy its finest football hour with the winning of the World Cup a few weeks after Billy – the holder of 105 caps – had seen his last full-time posting in the game ended by the sack.

History has not been kind when the various factions have sat in judgement on his reign. A variety of players spoke of him being overly nice to be a successful manager and Frank McLintock said he was too inclined to go for big-name players, although Peter Simpson slightly muddied the waters by saying in an article in a Charlie Buchan magazine: "Some days he was too soft, others he was too hard. We didn't understand him."

But there was an interesting legacy. Just as Wright had been influenced by the grooming of the Buckley Babes and then seen Cullis set up a conveyor belt of hungry young talent, so he put solid building blocks in place. As well as signing proven performers like Joe Baker from Torino, Wolverhampton-born Don Howe from Albion and McLintock from Leicester for a bargain price, he oversaw the formation of a thrilling youth team.

Keeper Bob Wilson, whom Billy had taken to Highbury for £4,000 from under Wolves' noses, Pat Rice, Sammy Nelson, Peter Storey, Jon Sammels,

## What Next?

John Radford and Simpson had all played in Arsenal's junior teams during his reign and formed the backbone of the side who beat Sunderland to win the FA Youth Cup in 1966 after the club had lost the previous year's final to Everton.

Just before being relieved of his duties, Billy also signed Charlie George, the man who struck a spectacular winning goal in the 1971 FA Cup final against Liverpool and so clinch Arsenal's double. Wilson, Rice, Storey, McLintock (as skipper) and Simpson were also in the side at Wembley, with Howe pulling the strings as coach to Bertie Mee, so was Wright's time in the Marble Halls really such a wash-out? Clearly, he had an eye for a player.

Sadly, he was damaged by the experience. Norman Giller told us in print in 2002 that Billy would sometimes be in tears of despair at a club where he was initially stirred by the bust of the great Gunners manager Herbert Chapman and later haunted by it. The author also pointed out, in his own delicate way, that it was the time Billy started to find solace in alcohol.

The keys he held to the cocktail cabinet made the occasional sherry easy to come by and he developed a weakness, too, for gin and tonic as results on the field refused to improve. It's a sad coincidence that Wright went into decline around the time that Wolves did. Having totalled 876 League goals in nine seasons from 1952-53, including 100 or more in four campaigns in a row from 1957-58, they languished in a final 16th place in 1964 and went down the year after in the wake of Cullis's departure.

Despite promotion at the second attempt, the club weren't the star turn Billy had known as a player when, some years later, regional TV took hold with him at the forefront. His marriage to a showbiz star had broadened his horizons and he had been such a convivial interviewee in his playing days that media doors were always likely to swing ajar. His phone was never quiet for long.

Billy was not new to TV when appointed as a sports producer by Lew Grade at ATV (the forerunner to Central TV and in turn Carlton) in 1966. As far back as 1955-56, he had worked, mainly in an advisory role behind the scenes, on programmes about the coaching of young footballers. Then he was appointed to a 12-strong committee chosen by the Postmaster General to report to the Government on the future of TV and radio in Britain – a project that culminated in the publication of the Pilkington Report in 1962.

Once employed full-time, he regarded himself as privileged to be working in an 'exciting and expanding' industry that still brought him into close contact with the game he loved. He became Head of Sports and Outside Broadcasts and enjoyed other sports as well, although it soon became clear that he was no wordsmith at the microphone. A magazine programme called 'Sport – You Are Tomorrow' that he hosted was not a success and he was better utilised elsewhere in the organisation.

"I can't stress enough how good he was at opening doors for the station," said his long-time friend and work colleague John Pike. "I joined the ATV sales team in 1968 and Billy was brought round the departments some time after and introduced to us, which was ironic really as everybody instantly recognised him. As a Wolves fan from Devon who had seen him play when I first watched the team beat Birmingham 6-1 in 1950, I was in my element.

"He was a brilliant PR man, as you can imagine, and because he had been round the world with Wolves and England and befriended players like Puskas and Di Stefano, he had no end of contacts. Obviously, he was very useful as well when meeting advertisers. Everybody wanted to talk to him.

"He worked extensively on Star Soccer, the Sunday afternoon highlights programme, and at Molineux he would call me to sit with him in one of those big light blue vans that the cameras were transported in. He and the programme director Tony Parker would be studying a number of different screens and deciding which picture they should zoom in on.

"Much later, I also worked with Billy at Telewest, so we were friends for a long time and I'm proud to say I was given his club blazer by Joy after he died."

Wright retired from Central in 1989, having given his former England colleague Jimmy Greaves an important leg-up in the TV world, but there was soon to be another important calling. What had been the comatose form of Wolverhampton Wanderers was stirring again and Billy wanted to be part of it, especially as there was a local boy just like him making a name for himself.

## Chapter Nine

# Bully For Wolves

Watching Wolverhampton Wanderers rise from the ashes on the back of all those Steve Bull goals in the late 1980s was something special. The club had been to the very brink and the swashbuckling manner of their march back from the abyss prompted many thousands of the fans who had turned their backs to fall in love with them all over again.

Within two or three years, Wolves had respectability again but it's easy to forget now, more than a couple of decades on and from a Premier League perch overseen by the club's second successive mega-rich owner, how low they sunk. They certainly weren't seen as a prize catch for ambitious players. They had become such an embarrassment in the mid-1980s that one individual, who later had a good career with them, confided in me that a training session at his previous club had contained the put-down to an errant team-mate: "Any more wild shots like that and Wolves will be in for you."

Players came and went in the 1980s at a frightening rate. Where once Billy Wright had played 541 matches, to be followed by the Richardses, Hibbitts and Parkins, other men with a fraction of their ability passed through briefly, maybe seduced by the club's reputation and then forced to retreat, tails between legs, after accepting that the slide was too just deep for them to do anything about.

Remember these names? Michael Coady, Ray Hankin, Keith Lockhart, Willie Raynes, Darren Wright. And there were others, many others, like Lomax, Rosario, Wassell and North. In those one-substitute days, Wolves used 34 players in League games alone in 1985-86 as they became only the second club after Bristol City to hurtle through the divisions in consecutive seasons. Their nosedive came with them finishing bottom of each table except the Third, in which they escaped the wooden spoon on goal difference on the last day.

Two years on from playing in the top flight, Wolves were contemplating trips to Aldershot and Halifax and weren't even sure they would be performing at Molineux for much longer. There was talk of them ground-sharing with Birmingham and Walsall, and didn't Jimmy Greaves once mischievously suggest he thought they should consider moving in with Willenhall?

More alarmingly, after they had been relegated in 1986 for the fourth time in five years and received what now almost seemed to be their annual summer visit from the Receiver, some were suggesting they would swap places with Enfield and drop into non-League football just to ensure they stayed alive. They had fallen an awful long way.

We'll never know whether Brian Little would have lifted Wolves up the divisions. He wasn't given the chance to build on the impact he made in three months as acting manager because, having inspired the side to two successive wins, he was sacked by the new Dick Homden-Jack Harris alliance on the board and replaced by recently fired Aston Villa boss Graham Turner.

It was said that Little, who had been taken to Wolves by Sammy Chapman, would have been happy to remain as a coach and work under a new manager. Unfortunately, he had served with Turner at Villa, where their parting of the ways was less than amicable, so this was a liaison that wasn't going to be resurrected in WV1.

The team Little handed over in better shape were still losing more games at home than they were winning – a blight on four of the previous five Molineux seasons – with such luminaries as Cambridge and Lincoln coming and conquering. Early in the Turner reign came a 2-1 loss at home to Halifax and there was a damaging quartet of 3-0 defeats, the first on a Friday night at Colchester. Before the second of them, though, came the day that changed the course of Wolverhampton Wanderers' history. Steve Bull was signed.

Turner had spent some weeks knocking without success on the door of Albion chairman Sid Lucas, his eye caught by a raw, goal-hungry striker who, on the day Wolves drew at Crewe in September, 1986, scored a couple of goals in a League defeat at home to Ipswich – an impact he followed up by netting in a losing cause at Derby's Baseball Ground in the League Cup.

Ron Saunders was happy to entrust the striking duties at the Second Division Baggies to Bobby Williamson and Stewart Evans, with Craig Madden and Garth Crooks in the wings. A year later, only Williamson was still playing there and Saunders was on his way, too. The manager who had won the League title at Villa had not shown Albion fans the same sound judgement.

## Bully For Wolves

Not that he gave in easily when the rivals from across the Black Country went calling for a player who had initially turned out for the third team on Saturday mornings or at night in the reserves after a day's work - either in the Vono bed factory, stacking boxes of fasteners in a warehouse or at the wheel of a forklift truck he drove at a local building supplies company.

"We tried three or four times to get him before we succeeded," recalled Turner's loyal, long-time scout Ron Jukes, who described the player as having the 'heart of a lion when it came to chasing goals.' The hunt was continued in earnest and, eventually, Albion relented, packaging Bully with the diminutive Andy Thompson in a deal that would result in a total of £96,000 changing hands between the clubs.

"When I had seen Steve at West Brom, he was just impressive in that he had raw aggression and the ability to get in scoring positions and get shots in," Turner said when interviewed for the *'Official History of Wolves dvd'*. "Nothing stood in his way between him and the goal. But it took a lot of persuading before West Brom let us take him. It was on the very day that I was going over to do the Thompson deal that Ron Saunders wavered and agreed to sell Bull as well."

Albion, in particular Bully's first Hawthorns coach Nobby Stiles, had seen glimpses of the goal-grabbing potential they were kissing goodbye to – and not everyone was happy. "I remember seeing Carlton Palmer outside The Hawthorns the day after the deal and he said he was bloody furious," said the former head of sport at the Birmingham-based Evening Mail, Leon Hickman. "He said his club had just sold the best striker he had ever played with."

Turner was convinced it was fine business for Wolves, at a cost. "It's a big investment but we'll get a long-term return – there's no doubt about that," he said then. "They are two bright young players with a lot of potential and they will prove a wise investment. The deals will also prove to supporters that the people who have taken over the club mean business."

Wolves were hammered at home by Wrexham on the day Bull and Thompson were handed their debuts, making their introductions a little less memorable than when Ted Vizard's team had embarrassed Arsenal 6-1 on the day Billy Wright, Bert Williams, Johnny Hancocks and Jesse Pye had played a Division One match for the club for the first time just over 40 years earlier. And things grew worse before they picked up. It's now well documented that the ineligible duo looked at each other and wondered what they had let themselves in for when they sat side by side in the stand at Bolton to see Wolves lose 3-0 to Chorley in an FA Cup first-round second replay. Billy's Wolves may once have been humbled by Bournemouth but, in terms of upsets, this one on November 24, 1986 was off the Richter scale.

The switch from no 8 to the no 9 shirt that came to be seen as Bully's personal property for well over a decade was accompanied by a follow-up hiding, again by 3-0, in the fog at Lincoln and there seemed no obvious reason to assume the club's fortunes were about to go into a 180-degree turn. In the gloom of Sincil Bank, could supporters really foresee that this guy would acquire a priceless ability to flick a switch and light up their lives?

"I think we could all see a lot of hunger in Steve and a fierce determination to succeed," said midfielder Micky Holmes. "He gave it absolutely everything but there were plenty of rough edges as well. It's not as though he came in and immediately looked in a different class to everybody else. We hoped he would click in a big way but it took him a few matches to get going."

Bully got off the mark next time out with a scruffy winner at Cardiff in the Freight Rover Trophy and did the same in the League at Hartlepool the following weekend. He was moving and Wolves, depressingly familiar with life at the bottom of divisions for the previous three years, were at least keeping their heads above water in their first ever season at the League basement.

His first Molineux goals, two of them, came from close-range finishes in the Freight Rover Trophy against Bournemouth. The fact that Wolves were playing in a competition designed only for clubs in the bottom two divisions showed just what and where they were. Only 1,923 were present – and that was a near 20 per cent improvement on the 1,618 who watched the home tie with Torquay the previous season.

By Christmas, the striker had chipped in with another three goals and boldly revealed he had taken a couple of bets on himself ending 1986-87 with 25 or more for the club – a confidence that started to look more justified when he netted again 24 hours after a Boxing Day defeat at Hereford. A month into his Wolves career, he had scored home and away in both League and cup football.

At 21, he wasn't so much hungry to succeed as ravenous. He had stepped into the pro game off a huge council estate in the Ocker Hill area of Tipton known locally as the Lost City, his skills displayed initially in the school team at Willingsworth Junior, then with Princes End Colts and Bustleholme Boys. The combination of his humble background and the jobs he had undertaken in local factories made him even more determined to seize this special chance.

He had already inspired a Wolves revival of sorts, although not one built on firm foundations. Whereas Billy Wright had been part of a Wanderers team hewn out of home-grown talent, Bull and Thompson had to listen hard for familiar accents in a changing room populated by the likes of northerners Holmes and Steve Stoutt, Scouser Andy Mutch, Welshman Mark Kendall, Scot Alistair Robertson and any number of waifs and strays. Nicky Clarke and the sparingly used Chris Brindley were local lads but Wolves' youth system had gone the way of so many of the club's other functions during the downward spiral. Turner and Jukes had to start from scratch and it's just as well they had two solid football men at their shoulder in the boardroom.

Homden and Harris had been directors at Walsall for many years together but were Wolves supporters. Following the abhorrent Bhatti reign, here were two men intent on putting them back on a firm footing. The man in overall control, though, was a builder and rugby follower by the name of Tony Gallagher, who didn't try to kid anyone that he had any great love for or knowledge of football.

He made no pretence of the fact his involvement in the complicated 1986 takeover of the club in a deal brokered by Wolverhampton Council was based on his hopes of being given permission to construct the giant Asda complex that now sits next door. Wolves, more a street corner grocer by the mid-1980s than a luxury department store, were in effect saved by a supermarket.

When the first of the sizeable bids came in for Bull, Homden and Harris had to work hard to convince Gallagher not to cash in on the prize asset. "Tony was a decent fella but knew little about the players and couldn't even remember Steve's name," Homden once told me. "At one meeting, as the goals were flying in, he referred to him just as 'the guy with the same name as an animal.'"

The businessman in Gallagher initially made him a little twitchy about whether Wolves should capitalise on a player in whom they would already be able to display a big profit. Thank heavens he had the good sense to be guided by the wise men around him – and they were of one voice; that the focal point of their discussions had a lot of goals left in him and Wolves would be blundering by parting with him so hastily.

So what did Steve Bull cost? And how was it paid to Albion, a club in such a descent of their own as to lead them to the Third Division within four years? The deal signed by popular Wolves secretary Keith Pearson shows the Baggies received just £39,000 straight off, with a further £15,000 due at the end of that season, which just happened to be four days after the first of the striker's Wolves hat-tricks. By then, Albion had received another £5,000 tranche after Bully played his 20th League game for Wolves – and the same amount would follow after a second 20 matches. And that's it. The total price of 306 goals, 13 years of service and a lifetime of legend was £64,000 plus VAT. His close pal Thompson set Wolves back £32,000 – hardly a fortune either for a player who would make 451 appearances in ten and a half years at Molineux.

It further pained the Hawthorns regime of the time and subsequent boards that Bull not only delivered big time for Wolves but stayed with them. Such heroics at a club outside the top flight would lead to a transfer to a bigger stage nine times out of ten. This case was the odd one out. As we now know, Wolves resisted any number of offers and Albion missed out on their loot.

If Bully had chosen to chase the lira after Italia 90 or Wolves had lacked the clout to withstand big-money approaches, Albion could have trousered something like £2m under a clause that entitled them to a third of any profit their neighbours made on him. It didn't happen, though, and the glee Wolves fans felt at their neighbours' loss was compounded by the excellent impacts of Robertson and Robbie Dennison after they made the same move.

While Wolves were climbing the divisions a year or two later, Albion – the club Billy Wright's mother supported – were heading the other way. Relegated from the top flight with their record low number of points in the spring Bully made his debut for them (1986), the Baggies flirted with the drop in three of the following four seasons as well.

Most of the banter came complete with gold and black wrapping but wasn't totally one-way. When Wolves scout and former headmaster Jukes took his Hawthorns seat for an Albion reserve game a couple of years after helping sign the striker, one of his former pupils, who was working as a steward, greeted him with the words: 'Here's the bastard who took Bully from us.' Ron, who died in 2008, recalled in his autobiography *'Super Scout'*: "I felt proud not only to have signed Steve Bull but also to have given one of my pupils such appropriate command of the English language."

Some of the comment from the navy blue and white side of the divide was more measured. "I was at school with Bully and he wasn't even the best player in our side," said Albion fan Neil Burns. "I played at right-back or centre-half and was in the same team as him from 13 to 15. He was very keen on football because he hadn't got that much interest in academic subjects but there was a player on the left wing called Steve Cooke who I'd have thought had more chance of making it. Bully didn't have much technical ability and I could never have predicted that he'd go on to achieve what he did. It shows what can be done with a lot of application and the right breaks. I'm delighted for him, although I'd have been much happier of course if he'd done it at Albion."

Thankfully, from their darkest hours – and there were plenty of those in the 1980s – Wolves recovered. Bully did more than anyone to stir what had appeared to be the comatose giant, his steady output of goals at one end being accompanied by the meaner streak Turner developed around Robertson, Floyd Streete and Kendall at the other.

Beating Halifax and Rochdale was small beer for a club who had won the League Cup only seven years earlier but some filthy water had flowed under the bridge since and it felt good to have them challenging again for promotion. Crowds rose sharply as well following the gloom of having no fewer than 17 Molineux attendances of below 4,000 in the 1985-86 campaign.

If there's one game seen as the turning point in Wolves' climb back from the pit, it's the one played on February 7, 1987, a day after Billy Wright's 63rd birthday. Stockport were 91st in the League and stood within 11 minutes of a win that would have mirrored what so many other languishing sides managed in the mid-1980s. Then the tide turned spectacularly with three goals, the last of them a lob by Bull, and an improbable three points that turned into the launch-pad for a sustained surge up the table. Victories suddenly came easily, although Bully underlined the fact he was still an erratic finisher as he failed to score any of the five that brought a win at Burnley, nor any of the four that saw Swansea off.

Andy Mutch was on target at Turf Moor – not in itself an exceptional shred of information, except it was his first goal in 17 games since the signing of the man who was to become his favourite and famous strike partner. The Liverpudlian, having quit his job as a refrigerator engineer when signed by Chapman the previous March, did not immediately hit it off with the new boy.

Mutch had lost his place and his no 9 shirt to Bull for the trip to Lincoln in late November. He was immediately re-promoted from the bench, wearing no 10, but his personal duck would stretch to almost three months despite the presence of a partner who was a year his junior. Then it just seemed to happen.

Billy's Wolves were no strangers to substantial runs of successive wins in their title-winning seasons. Now, three divisions lower, Bully's Wolves were doing the same, reeling off a club-record-equalling eight in a row which also brought them seven clean sheets as they pushed late and hard for promotion. A Friday night defeat at Southend ultimately prevented them going straight up but they proved their new-found confidence remained intact by winning their final three League games, their place in the play-offs secured by a 4-1 home win over Hartlepool on a sun-filled afternoon that brought a statistical landmark and a quirky issue for the anoraks to debate.

It was the day Bully scored the first of his 18 Wolves hat-tricks and begged the question of whether any player had ever scored three goals in a match for the club while wearing two differently numbered shirts, his no 9 one being ripped from his back in an invasion of celebrating fans in mid-game and having to be replaced, between his second and third goals, by a no 12. Remarkably, it was also the first hat-trick by a Wolves player since John Richards's treble at home to Leicester in the autumn of 1977.

"I remember being interviewed for either the Express & Star or Sporting Star after Bully had played his first few matches for Wolves," said early 1960s sensation Ted Farmer. "He hadn't scored many but what was already apparent was how outstanding he was at getting into scoring positions. I said he'd score an unbelievable number if his finishing improved. Obviously it did and we were all thrilled because there was a time not too long beforehand that Wolves weren't even the best team in Waterloo Road. Wasn't there one season when the top scorer was Mel Eves with six? That hurts anyone with Wolves' interests at heart but Steve came along and the supporters had a new hero."

Like Billy Wright, his name was just made for headline writers. Instead of 'Wolves Are All Wright,' 'Billy Whizz' and 'The Wright Stuff,' fans were now picking up papers to read about 'The Raging Bull' or 'Bull Fight,' with the team, in particular their star turn, portrayed as unstopabull, irresistibull or irrepresibull. Unfortunately, the striker wasn't able to get the club across the finishing line in the promotion race. His 19th Wolves goal came in the away first leg of the play-off semi-final against Colchester, only for the side to then fail to score in their next three matches, including the last two-leg play-off final. Wolves had twice beaten Aldershot in the League and finished nine points ahead of them but the long climb back was on hold for 12 months.

The despair was felt deeply by players whose careers were generally too short to have suffered many peaks and troughs. Robertson had spent the best part of two decades at Albion and Barry Powell, at Molineux for a second spell as a player, possessed an abundance of experience. But most were youngsters, a little bewildered how their tremendous run had still left them short.

The wounds ran deep enough as to last until Wolves took a firm grip on the top of the table the following autumn. And, by the next May, play-off final failure in 1986-87 was something to be thankful for, because, without it, the club and Bully wouldn't have had a record-breaking follow-up season.

"I joined in the summer of 1987 and sensed Wolves were a club on the up again," said midfielder Keith Downing. "I'd just been released at Notts County, although John Barnwell wanted to re-sign me there, and had talks in the meantime with Weymouth, who were actually prepared to offer me much more – £220 a week as against £150 at Molineux. And I'd been on £280 at County.

"I was single, though, and had feelings for Wolves from being a supporter, so I joined them and never regretted it. My first impressions of Bully were that he was a nice guy who laughed easily and who was very single-minded. He wasn't necessarily the best finisher but, purely on the chances he got himself on the end of, he was likely to score a lot of goals. Word quickly spread among other teams that they mustn't give Bully and Mutchy the chance to use their pace by running behind them on to balls we clipped through. But it was one thing saying it and another doing it. I don't remember Graham Turner working that much on just finishing but Steve was so competitive. Even in six-a-sides on the car park behind the North Bank, he wanted to score and win.

"I soon detected this excellent team spirit. There was always lots of fun and pranks and the gaffer fed off that. I recall him sending Jackie Gallagher off running round West Park after missing the photo call and David Barnes having these plastic ears which he hung round his peg for when he came in."

We suspected Wolverhampton Wanderers might not be hanging round at the basement for much longer but we didn't know just how dramatic a swathe they and Steve Bull were to cut through lower-division football. It was time for haircuts, heroics and some slices of history.

## Chapter Ten

# Scoring Sensation

The first day of Steve Bull's first full season as a Wolves player was by no means perfect. True to form, he scored but his side could do no better than draw 2-2 with Scarborough on the afternoon Neil Warnock's side made their entrance to the Football League – and the behaviour of some of the visiting fans inside and outside the sun-kissed Athletic Stadium was lamentable.

One intoxicated supporter sustained serious injuries when crashing 30ft through the terracing roof on which he was standing; others became involved in violent skirmishes with their counterparts from the home club and Leeds United or indulged in mindless acts of vandalism. More than 40 arrests were made and Molineux officials, having had to explain similar riots at Torquay, Southend and Exeter the previous season, were hauled back before the FA.

Bull duly followed up his effort at Scarborough, where his right-foot finish beat a goalkeeper by the name of Kevin Blackwell – better known in recent times as the manager of Leeds and Sheffield United – by also scoring against Notts County at Molineux in the League Cup. But there was little cheering to accompany the next seven goals he scored on his travels. The FA banned Wolves fans from six successive away League matches from September 1 and the club added their own sanction by refusing to sell tickets for visits to Notts County and Hereford in the meantime. Those who cheekily found a way round the move sometimes had to sit on their hands when their team scored but were rewarded for their initiative by seeing him notch at Edgar Street, Cardiff, Peterborough and Carlisle as the team continued their encouraging start.

Daz Hale, now a respected reporter and presenter on BBC Radio WM, was a regular traveller, even when he should have stayed at home. "I was just in the habit of going to the games and didn't want to miss them," he said. "The same faces turned up at all the matches we were meant to be banned from. The vast majority of supporters weren't trouble-makers in any way and still wanted

## Scoring Sensation

to travel everywhere, so we found ways of getting our hands on some tickets.

"I got in at Hereford the day he hit that stunner into the top of the net from 30 yards and me and my mate walked up quietly and paid to get in at Stockport soon after. A lot of fans were still attending and it was an exhilarating time to follow the club. I had also been there the night Bully scored his first Wolves goal at Cardiff in 1986 but I'd be lying if I said I could recall it. I can't even remember if it was down at our end or not. At that stage, we weren't sure he wasn't going to be another Tommy Langley or Derek Ryan but it soon dawned that we might have a special player on our hands. The goals flew in and the more we worried he couldn't keep it up, the more he proved us wrong."

Thank goodness the pre-ban mob mayhem at the seaside had no part of 1940s and 1950s life when Wolves were playing regularly in front of 50,000 and 60,000. So crammed in were crowds in earlier decades that it wasn't unheard of for spectators to stick a hand in their pocket for a sweet at kick-off and not be able to extricate it and remove the wrapping until half-time. On the morning after Billy Wright and Co trooped triumphantly off Molineux after beating Honved in 1954, a female fan had to return to the ground to search for a shoe that had come off and disappeared down the South Bank. Another spectator turned up to retrieve a crutch.

It was an era without all-ticket matches, a time when fans merely started queuing at the turnstiles four or five hours before kick-off for big games and those who turned up in the last hour risked not making it in. If ever that period of massive crowds had been accompanied by the sort of outbreaks of unruliness that blighted Bully's early Wolves career, there would have been carnage.

At least the exploits of the no 9 saw to it that Graham Turner's hungry side started to write as many back-page headlines again as front-page ones, even if followers of their games remained low on creature comforts and even on intimacy with the players they were watching. Compared with the compact, throbbing theatre Billy was used to during his pomp, 1980s Molineux was still a bleak old place. In the middle of the decade, only the hardy few had been left standing on the giant South Bank, complete with its depressing segregation barrier, or sat in the relatively new John Ireland Stand.

The expanse of green had grown in the late 1970s with the demolition of the Molineux Street side of the ground and its replacement by a towering new structure, renamed by Derek Dougan and his board in 1982 in honour of the club's well-liked long-serving former chairman. With the stadium's other two sides shut as a safety measure after the fatalities at Bradford, Birmingham and in the' Heysel Stadium, the pitch was moved eastwards 20 yards or so. To those of us in the seats, it still felt like we were in a different postcode to the players.

If Wolves' famous old ground remained a sad sight, at least the mood was starting to pick up. And Steve Bull, who would amply prove he was the last to worry about architectural niceties, was at the heartbeat. All he was interested in was the whites of the keeper's eyes and, in particular, the white of that frame behind him. Having scored in six of the first seven League matches and hit a brace in the Littlewoods League Cup at County, he already looked good for a tally well in excess of 20. The season was barely five weeks old by the time he moved into double figures with one of the two that won a Littlewoods first-leg clash at Manchester City and he had a round dozen by September's end.

He was a fearsome sight for opponents; marauding, physical and often bearing one heck of a three o'clock shadow. Already, he looked a perfect fit for the club, even if he hadn't previously held any sort of a candle to them. Before and for some time after the first of his occasional shaves, he had looked to Liverpool, in particular Ian Rush, for inspiration, rather than to Molineux or The Hawthorns.

His game didn't show too much of the deftness with which Rush lit up Anfield but he was looking a class apart as Wolves started to claw back some of the ground lost during their deeply troubled years. As long as he stayed fit, he was going to score by the sack-load and, with each goal that hurtled in, the club took a small step back towards respectability and public recognition.

Waterloo Road had slipped off the radar of Central TV and BBC Midlands for several years apart from when a camera crew or reporter might have been scrambled to bring the latest on Wolves' brushes with extinction. Gradually, though, the likes of Billy Wright, in his office in Birmingham's Broad Street, were warming to the fact that the club were a good-news story again.

Billy despatched a Central crew led by Bob Hall to Wolverhampton's Goldthorn Hotel for the launch of Ted Farmer's 1987 book *'The Heartbreak Game'*. Not that a get-together of old pals with drinks close to hand was Billy's scene then. Having hardly touched a drop when playing, he was waging and winning a battle against alcoholism that included a successful spell in a clinic, while Bully was intoxicating us all with his rampages.

Bully was also known to like a drink. He and his colleagues were run extra hard in training on a Tuesday when there was no midweek game as Turner was

## Scoring Sensation

aware the players would often reconvene for a round or two in Birmingham, Wolverhampton or even the The Goal Post pub, no more than a cleanly struck goal-kick from Molineux's North Bank.

When informed by the management early in his Wolves stay that players were not allowed in licensed premises after a Wednesday night, Bully let it be known he had had a beer at home every Friday night for as long as he could remember. As he was by then starting to bang a few goals in, he was told to carry on if that was his routine. "The rules were more aimed at not being seen drinking in public after a Wednesday," coach Barry Powell said.

As Wolves' results occupied more broadcast time and column inches, so speculation surrounding Bully started with a vengeance. A host of scouts and managers from clubs higher up the ladder dropped in and he was linked, to varying degrees, with Derby, Oxford, Villa, Sunderland and even Liverpool and Manchester United as he and Mutch blitzed Fourth Division defences.

More than once, Turner was irritated enough to say he would refuse to comment in future on such interest, much of which he dismissed as speculation. Happily, he had boardroom backing, even from rugby-favouring owner Tony Gallagher, although chairman Dick Homden qualified the situation by saying: "I won't sell unless it's for silly money, approaching seven figures. I'd have to think hard if someone offered us a million, otherwise he's going nowhere."

The Shropshire businessman's comments were less a sign of weakening resolve and more a reflection of the saner fees that prevailed 20 odd years ago. He and Jack Harris were football-minded enough alongside the guiding hand of popular secretary Keith Pearson to know that, with Bully on board, Wolves were embarking on an exciting journey.

Not that there weren't setbacks. A week after scoring the only goal of the game at Carlisle on the day Billy's pal Jimmy Mullen died suddenly, the striker suffered the first sending-off of his senior career when booked twice by referee Roger Wiseman in a win over Tranmere. Scoring a net-full of goals wasn't the only thing Steve Bull managed that Billy didn't!

Four weeks and six goals later, he was again having exclusive use of the showers, banished by a referee bearing the famous Molineux name of Mike Bailey for alleged head-butting in a victory at Colchester. Turner was reluctant to criticise his star man out of fear of curbing his abundant aggression but, as if to underline Wolves' increasing profile, a Radio 2 reporter weighed in with the comment that Bully was the type who liked to get his retaliation in first. A one-match ban for his Tranmere indiscretions had cost the striker an unbroken run of 56 games. Now he had to contemplate a two-game suspension. The blow was softened in the meantime when he hit his second Wolves hat-trick – one that crushed any hope Cheltenham had of heaping more FA Cup embarrassment on Molineux a year on from the Chorley nightmare.

With 20 goals against his name, Bully was leading the Fourth Division charts by five from Crewe's David Platt, who had been watched by Wolves before and after scoring two goals at Molineux in the September. And he was without equals country-wide. The respective top marksmen in the other divisions were Liverpool's John Aldridge (13), Swindon's Jimmy Quinn (17) and Chester's Warwick Rimmer (16).

Less than 13 months into a Molineux stay that would stretch to nearly 13 glorious years, Bull was running riot. He had overtaken Mel Eves' 1982-83 tally of 19 and was Wolves' highest scorer in a season since John Richards hit 25 in 1975-76. And the campaign was hardly a third of the way through.

Central defender Robertson, having also seen the player at close quarters at Albion, was relieved to be captaining him rather than marking him. "Most strikers would be happy with 25 goals a season but I don't think Steve would be happy even if he reached 35," he said. "His finishing has become far more clinical and Albion's loss is certainly our gain."

Even Billy had not witnessed scoring deeds like these. Wolves were punching well below their weight at the League basement; they were prize middleweights in the same ring as lightweights and there wasn't a defence in the division who could live with their no 9. Actually there was, just the one. Bully's second Molineux year started just like the first with an emphatic home defeat against Wrexham and not a punch landed on the opposition by way of consolation. It was a quirky thing, amid the mayhem of his 71 goals in his first season and two-thirds with the club, that Bully faced the Welshmen four times and failed to score in any of the games.

Fortunately, he could run amok against anybody else – and did. He scored two against Bristol City in the Sherpa Van Trophy and, when he delivered another winning brace in the League against leaders Orient to put his side back on top, we started to wonder whether Dennis Westcott's 1938-39 all-time Wolves record haul of 43 goals in a season was going to fall. We didn't wonder for much longer. We just counted off the days. With Turner's team flying, the striker's total clicked on to 28 as he netted both against Hereford on New Year's

**Scoring Sensation**

Day and followed up with three of the four that felled Third Division Brentford in the Sherpa Van; three hat-tricks in nine months and in different competitions.

Not for three months had Bully done anything as trivial as scoring just once in a game but, after he had to settle for such meagre pickings against Cardiff, he returned to a more familiar output level within the next week by producing a double against Peterborough and a treble against Exeter – the latter his first hat-trick away from Molineux.

Mutch's tally at this stage was a more than respectable 17 but Turner resists the temptation now to take the credit for spotting how the two might dovetail and for signing one specifically as a foil for the other. "Bully wasn't bought to partner Andy Mutch," he said. "They both had strengths and weaknesses and we devised a system around them. But the fact they formed such a tremendous partnership was a terrific bonus."

By the end of February, thanks to a brace against Bolton, Bully had passed the best seasonal haul of Tom Phillipson, having already left behind those of Derek Dougan, Ray Crawford, Jimmy Murray and John Richards. Westcott's 1938-39 tally was a mere four away, with up to 17 matches still to play.

Shock horror, Bully didn't score in the first four League games in March, although he bagged a Sherpa Van winner against Torquay in the meantime. Then the floodgates burst open again with a hat-trick against Darlington, one of the three goals with which his side won at Burnley and both in a home win over Colchester at Easter. The Westcott family marked the eclipsing of their figurehead's record by presenting the 1980s man with an inscribed tankard.

There were two stock goals at this stage. One was the low right-foot shot across the keeper – on the run and usually delivered early – after Mutch had flicked on an accurate half-volleyed drop-kick from Mark Kendall. The other would see Bully gain possession near the left-hand corner of the penalty area and then manoeuvre himself, with no particular dribbling skills or element of surprise, across and in front of his markers until he had the time, space and angle to let fly a right-foot shot. Defenders and keepers knew what was coming but seemed powerless to stop it.

I'm indebted to Andy Mutch for an observation he made about his partner as late as the year 2008. Summarising on an official dvd of Wolves' Sherpa Van Trophy final win, he argued the significance of the fact that Bully was left-handed yet right-footed. The remark drew a snigger from the man at his side, Robbie Dennison, but maybe it takes a striker to fully appreciate the usefulness of being able to hold off a defender with your stronger left arm – as Mutch pointed out – and have the ball furthest from your marker as you strike it with your right. "He was just like Ian Rush in that respect," Mutch told me off-mike.

Bully drew a blank at Cambridge on the day his cousin Gary was in the home side and also missed out when Wolves finished 1-1 in a shortened game with Everton in the Mercantile Credit Classic tournament at Wembley before losing on penalties. But the club were on the brink of a much more significant return to the twin towers as they continued to sweep aside all before them in the Sherpa Van Trophy.

Only John Barnwell's Notts County stood between them and the final and, although the striker's superb goal at Meadow Lane was quickly equalised, he put the second leg to bed with an early double in front of Molineux's biggest crowd of the season. So joyous were the scenes afterwards that Turner allowed TV cameras into the dressing room, just in time to capture a memorable clip of a red-faced fan clenching his fist and yelling through the open window: 'Come on Me Babbies.'

"I don't remember any jealousy from the lads towards Bully," said Keith Downing, Wolves' other scorer against his old club. "He brushed Paul Hart aside in the games against County and took a lot of the spotlight but his goals swept us along. I recall the tremendous following we had at Meadow Lane and the celebrations back here. On top of that, of course, he was earning us more win bonus through all his goals!"

Curiously, as they were excitedly contemplating a Wembley date with Burnley, Wolves had a trio of consecutive matches against Welsh opposition that would more than likely see them over the line in the promotion race. Bully didn't disappoint, helping see off Swansea at Molineux and then collecting a first-half brace at the expense of ex-Wolves keeper Paul Bradshaw on the night his side won at Newport to ensure they were going up. The former fork-lift truck driver had 50 goals to his name in 1987-88 and added two more on May Day afternoon as Hartlepool were despatched and the title was lifted.

Compared with the Football League Championship Billy Wright had got his hands on 30 years earlier, it was trifling stuff. Wolves, the first club ever to win all four divisions, had been to death's door in the meantime, though, so the significance of this first step on the way back was not lost on the fans who had remained loyal to them during the darkest days.

A final-day win at Orient meant they finished with a club record 90 points,

## Scoring Sensation

five more than runners-up Cardiff, and set them up nicely for the training trip to Majorca that was scheduled into the three-week gap before the Sherpa Van final. There was also time for Bully to go back to Albion to play in Alistair Robertson's testimonial game.

Another link with Wolves' glorious past materialised when Bill Slater and Jimmy McIlroy were chosen as guests of honour at Wembley. Slater shares with Billy Wright the honour of being a former Footballer of the Year and with both Billy and Bully the pride of having letters after his name. In his case, it's double honours as he is an OBE and a CBE.

The level at which Wolves were now playing might have been alien to Slater but the crowd for the final was of a magnitude that would have made even him and Billy blink. The figure of 80,841 was more than 10,000 higher than for the England v Scotland game a week earlier and estimates had the gold and black representation at anything between 45,000 and 50,000.

Bully had scored in every round up to the final, including home and away against County, and owns up to the fact he was in a bit of a sulk after firing blanks at Wembley. "I was happy we won it but I wasn't in myself," he said. "As a goalscorer, I'd got a strop on me because I hadn't scored. Then I had a couple of pints and was back to normal." Needing a hat-trick in the final to overtake Peterborough forward Terry Bly's all-time record of 54 goals in a Division Four campaign, he had few chances, having to settle for once for an assist as Mutch opened the scoring with a header and a spectator role as Dennison completed it with a stunning free-kick.

The 2-0 win meant Wolves carried on the Wembley winning habit started when Billy was captain in 1949. In four successive subsequent visits, they have been victorious there, be it in FA Cup, League Cup or Sherpa Van finals, the club's flair for delivering on the big occasion also being underlined by their play-off final success at Cardiff's Millennium Stadium in 2003. Bully, with 52 goals in his first full Wolves season, was clearly destined for greater things and Turner excited supporters by telling them he realised they wouldn't be happy for long in Division Three. He targeted another promotion, believing, thanks to his strike-force, he had a nucleus of players capable of going up again.

Chapter Eleven

# Miracle Man

There were absent faces when Steve Bull looked round the dressing room as Wolves prepared for their next assault – on the Third Division. Micky Holmes's last involvement as a Wolves player before being freed was to be carried on the lap of honour on the shoulders of team-mate Jackie Gallagher at Wembley. Steve Stoutt was discarded as well while others, like Chris Brindley, didn't make the grade.

"I signed for Wolves just before Bully and became friendly with him," said Brindley, a former central defender. "He lived in Norton Canes, not far from the street in Hednesford I've lived in for 40 years, and we used to have a beer or two together. He quickly became the biggest figure in the team, although the big money didn't come for him until later. He was very much part of the backbone of that side and played week in week out. He never missed a match."

As in the previous season, Wolves and Bully started on an up-and-down note in 1988-89. They won two and lost two of their first four games, one of which brought him two goals in the Littlewoods Cup against Birmingham, but it was his only appearance on the score-sheet in the opening six fixtures. The Molineux management were concerned he was labouring amid the after-effects of a virus, so he was packed off to both the doctor's and a human performance unit at Lilleshall for a once-over. There was relief, not to mention a few raised eyebrows, when his stamina problems were put down to a change of boots that had caused an unspotted alteration in his running style.

Bully jabbed in the only goal against Aldershot in his 100th competitive game for Wolves and underlined his return to full health and fitness with braces against Swansea and Port Vale in the next two games. He and his side then got a win-less three-match spell out of the way before setting off in mid-October on a sequence of seven straight victories, to which he contributed six more goals and so moved into the teens for the season.

"Bully was always one of the lads despite setting the place alight," said young defender Nicky Clarke. "There were no airs or graces about him. In his early days at the club, I remember him having a dodgy old car that he had to park on a slope, facing forwards, so on cold nights when we returned from away games, he could bump-start it if necessary to get himself going."

The striker's season was no longer in need of such measures and he left a profound impression on one of England's finest as he continued to move through the gears. Who knows whether he had even heard of Nat Lofthouse but the Bolton legend loved what he saw of him in Wolves' autumn win at Burnden Park. "He didn't seem to touch the ball more than five times," the 'Lion of Vienna' wrote in his 1989 autobiography of the same name. "But they included a header just off target, two shots the keeper had to save, another shot that hit the post and a superb goal. Bully only knows one way to go…… towards goal. Show him the whites of the posts and he will have a shot."

Lofthouse was a long-time England team-mate of Billy Wright, who would soon be groomed for an emotional Molineux return. And he clearly saw a bit of himself in the man Billy would most often be lifted off his seat by. "We still have to see whether he can score goals at the highest level," he added, "but I think he will. He can be right up there. If you want to know how good a striker is, just look at his record. Count the goals and the number of games and you will soon see who the top men are. That's why I'll be watching the progress of the young Steve Bull very closely. He looks the genuine article to me."

The other side of an FA Cup exit at Grimsby, Lofthouse's judgement looked sounder still. At home to Preston, their hapless centre-half Sam Allardyce and all, Bully came up with his sixth Wolves hat-trick – one with a difference as it was the first time he had scored four times in a game for the club. And he repeated the feat in the next home game by hitting four more against Port Vale, then settled for just three against Mansfield four days later.

Molineux was in a state of delirium and the chants of 'Bully for England' that rang out in the slaughter of Ian Greaves's Mansfield were hardly fanciful. His conversion rate of chances had increased spectacularly and he was looking a special player. Fourteen goals in six matches spread across 36 days. Wow! The time of year when cricket and football seasons overlap had long since gone but here was a player hitting two fours and a three in no time.

Bully had been sharing top billing in the Third Division goal charts in late November with Sheffield United's Brian Deane, their tally of 13 lagging behind the totals of the sharpest shooters in the other three divisions. By Christmas, the Wolves man had 25 and was head and shoulders above anyone else in England. The well-known Bramall Lane goal firm of Deane and Agana had 17 and 16 respectively, Alan McInally was on 17 for Aston Villa and Tommy Tynan of Second Division Plymouth boasted 19, as did Ian Muir of Fourth Division Tranmere.

Amazingly, Bully wasn't even half-way to the figure he would finish the campaign with. He ripped past his pre-season target of a round quarter century of goals before the dawn of 1989, his late point-saver at Brentford on New Year's Eve bringing up his hundred with Albion and Wolves and taking his tally for the 1988 calendar year to a staggering 54.

"We had had this revolving door of players in and out after the departure of my early heroes like John Richards, Kenny Hibbitt and Andy Gray," said Daz Hale. "Then this figure appears and scores a ridiculous amount of goals in a short space of time. It was fantasy football. If Roy of the Rovers had been set in the Midlands, we all know who the main character would have been. Although we went to support Wolves, there always seemed to be an extra 5-10 per cent of gusto in the celebrations if the goal was scored by him. You always felt he was celebrating with you, whether it was with a somersault or the aeroplane impression."

Just as fans have their favourite players, so players have their favourite opponents. Billy Wright loved facing Arsenal and Manchester United, and Steve Bull, it would appear, never lost any sleep when Bristol City were in town. The striker made an utterly mundane start to 1989 with only two goals in four games, all of them won and the third of them (at Reading) attended by then Tottenham manager Terry Venables. Then the red, red Robins came bob, bob, bobbing along.

Looking for a different slant on this one-man trail of havoc, I invited former Albion captain John Wile – not long out of a management spell at Peterborough – to sit with me in the John Ireland Stand at the Sherpa Van Trophy tie at Molineux in late January. Wile probably didn't want to criticise Bully in a Wolverhampton-based newspaper any more than I wanted him to, which is why we both winced with every ball that cannoned clumsily out of his control and with every pass or cross he failed to read or reach. He didn't impress. "I don't feel I played very well," he admitted. "I was second to every ball and wasn't getting things together at all." But by the way, he scored three times.

## Miracle Man

His first was mis-hit with his left foot and barely trickled over the line, his second was down to a poor back pass by Steve McClaren – didn't he pop up somewhere else a decade and a half later? – and his third was a straightforward side-foot from 12 yards. Wolves had five wins out of five and Bully had passed the 100-goal mark for them. It was also his first hat-trick for five weeks........ phew, another worrying dearth ended!

No team suffered more at the player's feet than Bristol City, against whom he scored 13 times during his career. Fulham's defenders had their own tale of grief less than three weeks later, though, when he helped himself to three of the five goals by which they were beaten. It was his fifth hat-trick in eight home games, two of which had brought him hauls of four.

The international summons duly came and Graham Turner had a twinkle in his eye when he broke the good news of Bobby Robson's phone call to a group of children he was addressing at a local school. "Whatever you do," he said, "don't tell the newspapers. It's a secret between us for now." It was in jest only. Why wouldn't Wolves shout from the rooftops at the earliest opportunity about their star player's inclusion?

Bully was in Dave Sexton's squad for the under-21 trip to Albania and the fact the top-flight programme was cancelled in the build-up meant many Fleet Street writers were at the home game against Bolton on March 4 to catch their first sight of this prodigious Black Country upstart. He gave them plenty to write about by ripping in the winner with a stunning long-range left-foot shot.

"We had a go at him one day for being much weaker on that side and we worked him hard in training at the racecourse," said coach Barry Powell. "Not that it made him any better. He was still bobbling shots or ballooning them. Then, come the next match, he mis-controlled a ball off his right foot on to his left and then crashed a terrific shot into the net by the stanchion.

"It was the time when I would be in the dug-out and the gaffer was up in what we called the crow's nest in the stand. We used to communicate by walkie-talkie and as soon as the ball flashed in, my ear-piece was crackling and Graham was on, shouting: 'I don't \*\*&@in believe it!' Bully was almost uncoachable. If you put on sessions where he had no-one around him, he was hopeless. The more space he had, the worse he became. When he really came alive was when he had markers he could tussle with and get the better of. In a lot of ways, he was like John Richards, who I played with in my first Wolves spell. They both liked to run on to the ball rather than come deep and play."

# Billy & Bully

Bully goals had been coming at about one a game for well over a year and a half and, although he didn't score despite impressing in a win in Albania, he was taking rapid strides towards a haul of 50 for the second season running. He moved on to 40 in 40 club games when his sixth hat-trick in 16 weeks demolished Bury and gave Wolves the last in a run of 16 straight home wins.

In terms of scoring, Bully had tried relative normality in 1986-87 and decided it wasn't for him. He was a goal monster, insatiable and ravenous, and the sky was the limit. No wonder a rival manager shook Turner's hand after one game and said: "As long as you have Bull, Graham, you'll have a job."

Midfielder Keith Downing was from similar Black Country stock and said of his team-mate: "He had great pace and strength and what stood out was his shooting capacity. When the ball went into him in the penalty box, it rarely came out again without him getting his shot away. He had a selfishness around the area that all great strikers have."

You wonder how many more Bully might have scored had goalkeepers not been able to pick up back passes. The law was changed much later to eradicate an often negative, time-wasting tactic. Just imagine what extra mayhem there might have been with him bearing down on nervous keepers if they had to kick instead of handle the ball on bobbly or squelchy pitches.

Bull's international introduction was different from Billy Wright's. Whereas Billy had been blooded with his country by going straight into England's senior side, albeit initially in four Victory Internationals in the days when there was no under-21 or under-23 team, the golden boy of Molineux four and a bit decades on continued in the age-group side. After Wolves had emerged from an Easter wobble, he was chosen for the under-21s' return against Albania at Ipswich – a game in which he delivered his first international goal.

The three lions were fitting snugly on his chest and a whole new world, one about which Billy could tell him so much, was opening up. "With his shaven head and gum shield, his image really scares defenders," said Bury centre-half Kenny Clements. "He is a Mark Hughes sort of player, powerful and aggressive but actually taller and faster than Hughes and more awesome looking."

Clements was quoted in a Weekly News article in which he still considered Bully worth only £400,000, given that the striker was unproven in the higher divisions. Interestingly, Oldham manager Joe Royle said much the same and placed his value at slightly less while Garry Birtles, then a Notts County player, estimated he would be worth a punt at around £650,000.

## Miracle Man

Another transfer deadline had come and gone, so Wolves fans didn't have to fret for a few weeks while their star asset ran amok. Not that his glorious season passed without disappointment. Crushing disappointment, in fact. In the area final of Wolves' Sherpa Van Trophy defence, Bully seemed to have got his team off the hook when he struck twice in the last five minutes of the first leg at Torquay to turn a deficit into a 2-1 victory. But the return, three days after the Hillsborough disaster, was a nightmare. Wolves conceded twice in the first half and for once couldn't bring their enormous goal power to bear.

Plans for a return trip to Wembley were scuppered by Dean Edwards, a Wolves fan and player Turner had discarded at both Shrewsbury and Molineux. Bully had added seven more goals in the competition to the 12 he hit the season before and wouldn't play in it again. He would soon have bigger fish to fry.

## Chapter Twelve

# England Calling

There was no hugging, no pitch invasion and no lap of honour. Second Division football became a mathematical certainty for Wolves when their players had their feet up and a glass to their lips. The 2-0 May Day afternoon win against hapless Bristol City (Bull 2) became a promotion-securing one only when Port Vale lost at home to Northampton several hours later.

Anti-climax tinged the final accomplishment of the club's season-long target, even after the striker had contributed a goal to a follow-up victory over Northampton to make it 50 for Wolves and England under-21s for the season.

Molineux still had a big night to look forward to, with Wolves needing one point from their last three fixtures to clinch the championship and Sheffield United, with their own Bull-Mutch impersonators in Brian Deane and Tony Agana, arriving in the Midlands for Turner's men's last home game requiring a draw to be sure of finishing runners-up. In other words, a point apiece would leave everyone happy. And that's just what we got.

Bull, beaten by Liverpool's Steve Nicol after becoming the first Third Division player ever listed in the PFA Footballer of the Year voting, opened the scoring with his 50th Wolves goal of 1988-89, his header making him the first man to hit a half century of club goals in each of two successive seasons – a feat not close to being repeated since. Even so, the striker was delighted to see Robbie Dennison's curling free-kick equaliser after his side had trailed early in the second half. The two-sided Molineux, packed with 24,321, echoed to the celebrations of both sets of fans when the final whistle blew.

"I was pleased when they played for a point with 34 seconds to go," Turner said wistfully following a compelling 2-2 draw that had shades of when Wolves had won the 1977 Division Two title with a home draw with Chelsea that also saw the Londoners up. Of Bully's heroics, Turner added: "It's incredible. Who could have envisaged anyone scoring 52 goals one season and 50 the next?"

## England Calling

And to think Wolves had gone out of the two major cups at the first hurdle. Had they not lost on the away goals rule to Birmingham in the Littlewoods or fallen totally against the run of play in the FA Cup at Grimsby, there would have been more games for Bully to push his total up towards 60.

With Wolves lifting the Third Division title 12 months on from hoisting the Division Four crown and 30 years after Billy raised the League Championship trophy for the third and final time, Turner dropped his normal conservative guise to clamber on to a balcony above Molineux's main entrance and tell the fans massed in Waterloo Road that it was a case of two down, one to go.

The manager knew Wolves had to spend in order to challenge next time round but made it clear he wouldn't be cashing in the family silver to do so. To questions about whether he would sell Bull, he said in the Mail on Sunday: "That would be crazy. There would be a riot." Little could fans have imagined this was to be the last success their club would have in the 20th century. Many years of Division Two stagnation lay ahead but there was still some significant football to be played in 1988-89 before such challenges were confronted.

By now, Bull and Mutch knew they were going to miss the final game, at Wigan's tumbledown old Springfield Park, having been named together on England's B tour of Switzerland, Norway and Iceland. In the meantime, they had a trip to Preston, where Bully needed a seventh hat-trick of the season to eclipse his monumental club tally of 1987-88. You wouldn't have backed against it and Wolves duly scored three times on the Deepdale plastic but one of them was by Gary Bellamy and the other two by Mutch, whose Molineux future was in some doubt. He was out of contract in the summer and his 23 goals had attracted Albion's interest among others. "Obviously, I want him to stay," Turner said. "He has a proven partnership with Steve and I think they would make a considerable impression on the Second Division."

The two strikers weren't particularly close socially but had an excellent reading and appreciation of each other's game. As strike partnerships go, it was pretty special. "Although Bully might be looked at as the star, we all felt we were on the same level," Mutch said. "We worked really hard for each other and, if defenders were giving us a tough time, we stood up for each other rather than leave it to the other to sort out. I'm proud to have played up front with him and he reciprocates and says we were a fantastic partnership.

"I take a lot of pride from the fact he says I was the best striker he played with. We enjoyed playing together and his movement was superb. He was always on the move, hungry and looking for spaces. He had power, strength and pace. I could run with him in training and match him over 40 yards. But, over five, he would be half a yard ahead of me because of his power. When we got to Norway (on the B trip), we got a penalty and he had never taken one in his life but he grabbed the ball, took it and scored. That was his determination to score for England."

Bull, who went on as substitute in Stavanger for Paul Stewart, and Mutch missed Wolves' open-top bus tour of the town as well as the final League game. Their team-mates had some fun by thrusting hands through a cluster of bodies in supposed acknowledgement each time they heard the names of their absent friends were chanted. And Bully had lapped it up 12 months earlier, standing at the front with Andy Thompson once the official route had been completed and beaming hugely as they ducked under overhanging branches as the vehicle accelerated towards the Mount Hotel in Tettenhall Wood.

It wasn't long after the duo had been waved off from Molineux on their international travels that a story broke in the national Press about Bully supposedly considering his future. Media personnel recognised it as the sort of 'exclusive' reporters sometimes spin to justify the high outlay of foreign assignments and Turner was not particularly concerned.

"I'd be amazed if these words were accurate," he said. "I can just imagine what's going on out there among players and reporters." Nowhere does money talk louder than in England dressing rooms, and Wolves, after all, were still in the lower divisions, so their manager wouldn't have slept as easily as when Stan Cullis did when he used to send Billy Wright away on international duty, knowing there was no freedom of contract and the skipper's head wasn't going to be turned anyway. There were no bigger clubs than Wolves in the 1950s.

Bully, still with a couple of seasons on his contract, was keen to discuss a two-year extension and did himself no harm as a prelude to negotiations by also scoring in Reykjavik against Iceland B, Bobby Robson already having said he was considering giving him a senior debut on his return.

The manager flatteringly drew comparisons between Bull, who had been named Midlands Footballer of the Year in his absence, and Gary Lineker for the way both preferred the ball in front of them. They were intent on causing maximum damage rather than through the more modern way of holding it up with their backs to goal and bringing others into play.

Wolves, for all the players they have contributed to England teams down the decades, have not found it easy to supply centre-forwards for the side. Jack Brodie, a founder member of the club, filled the role for both in the 19th century, to be followed a few years later by Billy Beats and Dick Topham. But luminaries such as Dennis Westcott, Roy Swinbourne and Jimmy Murray missed out while Jesse Pye won a single cap, then John Richards's only outing in Alf Ramsey's team saw him used in an alien position wide on the left.

Here was Bull, though, bridging the gap between Third Division and international stage. With his under-21 and B achievements already added to his CV, he was selected for the seniors for the first time when a cluster of withdrawals, some of them caused by the Liverpool v Arsenal title decider, prompted Robson to ring Molineux again two days before the Rous Cup trip to Scotland.

There being no Internet in those days, many Wolves fans considering going to Glasgow rang the Molineux switchboard on the Friday for news of whether their hero was likely to set foot on Hampden. As it turned out to their disappointment, he was on the bench after John Fashanu had recovered from an ankle injury suffered against Chile in midweek.

Not that Bully's arrival was delayed for much longer. He went on as a 31st minute substitute for the still incapacitated Fashanu, who shouted 'All the best, babe' as they passed each other on the touchline, and stepped in among the Robsons, Gascoignes and Barneses to immediately make himself at home.

"Nobody had ever called me 'babe' before, particularly not another bloke, and I felt a bit overawed by it all at first," he said in his book, *'My Memories Of Wolves'*, a decade and a half later. "You just have to get the blinkers on, switch off to everything and get on with your game. Once my nerves had settled, I suddenly realised I wasn't out of place in such distinguished company. That surprised me a bit as I was still a Third Division player. No doubt a lot of the Scottish supporters hadn't even heard of me but they were already a bit subdued after Chris Waddle had put us ahead in the first half and I enjoyed every minute of it. I just wish I could go back and do it all again."

Bull had already gone close with one effort when, ten minutes from time, he challenged with Dave McPherson for Gary Stevens's high right-wing cross and seized brilliantly on a lucky bounce off his own shoulder to fizz a low shot from 15 yards just inside Jim Leighton's right-hand post. Billy Wright no doubt looked on with much Wulfrunian and English pride.

Remember those sterling performances by Billy and his men at Hampden?

## Billy & Bully

Well, here was one from Bully and the 1989 vintage. For three years, the striker had been used to being part of winning teams at Rochdale, Exeter, Chesterfield, Gillingham and the like. This was a cut above, though. Scotland 0 England 2 (Waddle, Bull). The lad who used to glue and screw together the ends of beds in the Black Country had played and scored for his country.

It was Bully's 106th goal in two extraordinary seasons and the 54th of his latest all-conquering campaign, his four for various England sides supplementing the round half century he had managed for Wolves. At Hampden, he slid on his knees in celebration towards the pocket of away fans and said later: "I could have cried." He was in a different stratosphere.

"The England team weren't as high profile as they are now but I still admired Bully for the way he came into the squad," said West Ham United's own late 1980s goal machine Tony Cottee. "It couldn't have been easy for him as a lower-division player because there were lads like Peter Beardsley and Gary Lineker standing in his way.

"The match at Hampden was the only one I started for England and I didn't play that well. I was alongside John Fashanu but I was back in the dug-out by the time Bully lashed that one in the bottom corner. It was a typical Steve Bull goal. I'm envious of him actually because I didn't score for my country at that level and it's such a thing for a player from outside the top division to get a goal in the national team. David Nugent was probably the next man to do it.

"We knew about the number of goals Bully had scored but little else because there wasn't the same coverage of lower-division games there is now. I suppose the question marks were whether he'd be able to carry on scoring in the Second Division but I had no doubt after seeing him in training. He was a good finisher. He may have been quiet with the lads but he was highly competitive and proof that if you're a goalscorer, you're always a goalscorer."

The attendance for Bully's big day was 63,000, around 67,000 smaller than Billy had encountered there three and a half decades earlier but it was probably no less raucous. By scoring his big goal, the country's newest recruit had done what no Scotsman had done in the fixture north of the border since Mark McGhee breached the English defence in 1984. At Parma Airport, where Turner and his players were waiting to board their flight home after a celebration holiday in Majorca, a glass or two of San Miguel was raised to him.

The events left an impression on BBC summariser Trevor Brooking. "He really is the old bull in a china shop, isn't he?" he said. And Wolves fans had no grumbles that one of the most memorable goals of Bully's career had come in a white no 16 shirt rather than a gold and black one bearing the famous no 9. So consumed were they all with pride. He was the first player to win a senior England cap from Division Three since Peter Taylor in 1976 and Molineux's first international for the home country since Emlyn Hughes had won the last of his caps in 1980. Furthermore, his startling continuing emergence was making quite an impact on a Wolves forward of the previous decade.

Bobby Gould, who had scored 39 goals in 93 senior games across two spells with the club, was more a brave, bustling predator than the explosive sort of finisher Bully had become. But he saw in him the same single-mindedness that had given himself a fine career with the likes of Coventry, Arsenal, Albion and West Ham, as well as Wolves, before his switch to management.

"I still have my diaries and can see that I rang Graham Turner on May 30, 1989, to ask about Steve," said Gould, then still manager of Wimbledon a year on from steering them to improbable FA Cup final glory against Liverpool. "The straight answer I was given was that he wanted to stay at Wolves but Andy Mutch would be available that summer under freedom of contract and I could talk to him if I wanted.

"I'm sure there were many others looking at them as well. Bully, in particular, was building a terrific reputation in the lower divisions and in the England teams and plenty of clubs would like to have had him. I was disappointed to be told no and to have to turn to other names on my list, like Clive Allen, Niall Quinn, Alan McInally, Marco Gabbiadini and Paul Stewart."

Despite the return of Lineker and Beardsley, Bull, who had attracted a bid from Leeds in the season, was retained in the squad for the home game against Poland, although he and Mutch lined up together as over-age players in an under-21 victory against the same country at Plymouth in the meantime.

Turner had never remotely considered using Bully from the bench but now found himself advocating him for that role. "He has shown he can give a team a real surge when he goes on," he said. "He would be very refreshing for the last 20 minutes or so. He has learned so much at Molineux and it's a general practice that we do a lot of shooting and finishing in training. I wouldn't say he's a natural footballer. Sometimes, he even treads on the ball but he often turns these things to his advantage because defenders find it hard to read him. He loves the club and his attitude after playing for England is a big boost for us because you often wonder whether contact at this level will change people.

He's a tremendous lad and I get the idea the whole nation likes him. If he had come from Manchester, Liverpool or Arsenal, people wouldn't have noticed him too much but this really is a fairytale story."

There were some concerns over burn-out when, after not seeing action against the senior Poles, he was retained in the squad for a trip to Copenhagen. He had already played 61 games (without being taken off in any of them) and scored 54 goals. And we were now well into June. In the event, a 20-minute run-out was the extent of his work against Denmark, then it was home for a five-week rest cure prescribed by his employers.

## Chapter Thirteen

# Sky's The Limit

The Second Division seemed to have much to commend it when Wolves graduated in the summer of 1989. Albion were there, so too were Newcastle, Sunderland, Middlesbrough, Sheffield United, Leeds and West Ham – clubs with considerable top-flight pedigree. It was only after many years of treading water that Molineux regulars started to call English football's second grade the division from hell.

Wolves had lurched close enough to death's door during their five years away from the elite to ensure that they appreciated their new surroundings, which were still alien to Billy Wright and his contemporaries but not Steve Bull. He had played at this level and, it is often forgotten, at the one above during his brief Albion career, so it wasn't totally a step into the unknown.

For the best part of the 1980s, though, Wolves fans had been starved of genuine heroes; men who could brighten mundane lives by tempting floating supporters away from their factories, offices and firesides. There had been precious little in the way of idolatry since Dougan and Richards and the rest of the League Cup winning heroes, not surprising really considering the top scorer in 1981-82 (Mel Eves) managed seven goals, the leading marksman in 1983-84 (Wayne Clarke) mustered nine and the most prolific men in 1984-85 and 1985-86 were Alan Ainscow and Andy King with six and ten respectively.

That Bully was cut from the same salt-of-the-earth stock as the fans made him manna from heaven when the goals came. Why, he had even turned his back on the Baggies to wreak his havoc with Wolves! Very quickly, he had become a god, his working-class Tipton roots, skinhead haircut and phenomenal success seeing to it that he was regularly immortalised in song.

He was often celebrated as a 'tatter' (the local dialect for a rag and bone man) and through renditions of the 1960s hit by Sam The Sham and The Pharaohs, *'Woolly Bully'* – so much so that a new version was recorded in 1991 by Midlands comedian and former drummer Ollie Spencer. At other times, he was celebrated by adaptation of the words of the 1968 record by The Scaffold, *'Lily The Pink'*, or even the Christmas song *'Mary's Boy Child,'* the lyrics of which fans adapted as 'A New King Born Today'.

It's doubtful Billy ever heard a crowd chant his name. Fans hardly sang in his day, unless it was *'The Happy Wanderer'* or other organised pre-match joviality. There wasn't the same hero worship then. Global figure that he was, England's captain was a star among stars, surrounded even at his club by internationals. Bully's popularity was all the greater because of the years of dross that had preceded him at Molineux. Not only did he hear the South Bank faithful endlessly honouring him in verse, he had an enduring fanzine and even a burger sold at a match-day food stand named after him. And it wasn't unusual to see fans wearing replica shirts with a no 9 and 'God' above it.

His following was colossal. He had the masses flocking to his feet with a public appearance after the publication of the first biography about him, *'Bully'*, by Black Country journalist Rob Bishop. Then he signed around 2,500 autographs when he was booked in for a promotion organised by his boot suppliers Qasar at the Sportsco branch in Cleveland Street, Wolverhampton.

"We thought the Qasar deal we did for Bully was great and then we did another one two years later with Adidas which was unbelievable," recalls Barry Powell, who, along with physio Paul Darby, started to handle the player's commercial interests. "He didn't know, of course, what he now knows about what money could be made off the field, nor did we. But I'm sure he trusted us to do the best for him. As far as I know, he never had an agent other than his father-in-law but it was tremendous to play a small part in the emergence of a local lad and I remember from the turn-out we used to get events, like the launch of his book, that the fans were ready to take a hero to their hearts."

Bully was a natural when meeting his public, particularly if there were young children at the front of the queue, and the extra money was nice. Yet all he really wanted to do was play for Wolves – and hopefully England – and score lots of goals.

On the night Billy Wright introduced several of his contemporaries on to the Molineux pitch, Bully netted two absolute beauties in a 3-2 midweek friendly win over Moscow Dynamo that rekindled memories of the club's pioneering floodlit matches of the 1950s. He was up and running. Predictably, goals didn't come at the same sort of rush in Division Two, though, and Wolves had what later became known as a wake-up call as they found themselves bottom after five League games. Bully made a better start than most by scoring in two of them as well as in a Littlewoods Cup two-leg win over Lincoln.

Ironically, it was in the striker's absence that the side turned the corner. For the first time in nearly three years as a Wolves player, he missed a game for fitness reasons when a virus ruled him out of the victory at Ipswich but the team's lift-off, at a time when he was also knocked out when scoring in a Littlewoods clash with Aston Villa, was the springboard he needed to net a brace in a draw at Barnsley and two more goals in a 5-0 follow-up crushing of Portsmouth.

"One of my challenges as physio was to encourage lads to train and play through problems but Bully always had to have reins on him," Paul Darby said. "The worry with him was that he might tell you he couldn't feel something when he could. That's how keen he was to keep going. He was a great trainer and could easily have overdone it because he had so much energy and was as strong as an ox.

"He had everything you wanted really in a player. He didn't shrug anything. He would put his head and foot in and didn't fret about injuries. He was very strong mentally. I hardly had to go on the pitch to treat him unless it was a clash of heads. You knew if he stayed down, it was a problem and he was more willing than most to try to run off a problem rather than come off."

The striker had a further taste of the international circuit when he played in the early weeks of the new season for England under-21s in Sweden. It seemed to underline the more demanding company he was now keeping, though, that he was on the losing side in this game for the first time with his country.

He bounced back, though, with a brace in England's under-21 international victory over Poland, then another first came along in mid-October when he faced his former club Albion amid the ending of the Black Country rivals' five seasons apart. It was a poignant day. Ever since Tipton Town's youth manager Sid Day had spotted Bully playing in a boys' match while he walked his dog, there was a greater likelihood of the player ending up at The Hawthorns than Molineux, if he was good enough to attract the League scouts. Sid and the more senior Tipton management were well connected at Albion and the lad who quickly started to bang in the goals for his team had cut his football teeth in 'Baggie' territory with West Bromwich-based Bustleholme Boys and then the prominent Sunday League side Newey Goodman, based just outside Tipton.

# Billy & Bully

The script could hardly have been written better for Bully on the day he went back to The Hawthorns in Wolves' colours. He drove in the late winner in front of the ecstatic gold and black following when set up by Andy Mutch and so gave Albion's board another sickening reminder of the monumental clanger Ron Saunders had dropped.

Bull and Mutch both scored in the win over Port Vale two days later – Turner's 100th as Wolves manager – and had ten and six goals to their names after two months of the season. But Wolves then lost at Leeds and drew with Oldham to remain in the middle third of the table. After two virtually unbroken years as pacesetters of their division, they were noticing the step up in quality.

Chief scout Ron Jukes, the man whose homework had done much to facilitate Bull's signing, neither had nor craved a public profile through his work. Reluctant as he was to be quoted in the media, he spoke to me off the record following one of Wolves' autumn games in 1989-90 to talk about the club's pursuit of a third successive promotion. "We can't really expect to go up again so soon," he said. "But, if the chance were there, we'd have to take it." It was a typically sound assessment by a man on whose judgement Turner heavily relied. Not that either man could really have foreseen the fireworks that were in store after they had splashed out their biggest fee so far in their time at Molineux by paying Norwich £250,000 for Paul Cook.

A game at Leicester gave the midfielder his first chance to impress on a Wednesday evening on which Bully had an extra agenda. England manager Bobby Robson was going to be at Filbert Street to watch him with a view to naming his side for the Wembley game against Italy later that month.

The game was going satisfactorily enough for player and team until just before half-time when Bull reacted angrily to provocation by home centre-half Steve Walsh and pushed him in the face. Bishop's Stortford referee Graham Pooley took the ultimate sanction and condemned him to the third dismissal of his career. Bully sat in the visitors' dressing room for the rest of the 0-0 draw, needing no-one to highlight the repercussions of his indiscretion. Even so, Robson made it clear next day he had been intent on recalling him to his squad. "I know I've blown it," Bull said at Molineux when handing me a few hand-written thoughts for the Express & Star column he penned at the time.

"I once made a promise to myself that I'd never get sent off again but there's only so much provocation I can take before something has to give. I'm sick and bitterly disappointed about my dismissal. It was purely frustration that led me to push him away. But I promise you all one thing: It won't happen again."

As Bully came to terms with the fact he would be facing Italy's B string at Brighton the night before he should have been lining up against the cream of Serie A, consolation lay just round the corner. When feeling a little down in the dumps, just bang in another goal for Wolves – that seemed to be the motto imprinted across his heart and it served him well only three days later.

By hitting the winner at home to West Ham, he lifted some of his personal depression and bridged what would have been a two-month absence from the score-sheet, his three-match ban spanning three painful weekends. There was no danger of Bully's name disappearing from the back pages, though, and Wolves owner Tony Gallagher used the suspension to spell out his value.

"We have already turned down approaches of more than £2m for him and he's worth at least twice as much to the club's future," he revealed. "Besides, I think I would have an entire town after me if I sold him."

Wolves' season had been meandering along with a series of low-scoring games containing as many defeats as victories. They remained in their shell and in mid-table without their talisman, although a 2-0 win over Middlesbrough on the final day of his ban was a fillip at the end of a run in which they had netted only seven times in nine matches.

Bully, resuming the no 9 jersey from South African-born John Paskin, didn't immediately cut loose again. His comeback game was at Brighton, the scene of his farewell with England B three and a half weeks earlier, and he failed to score there or at Oxford, both games being drawn. When he did return to the score-sheet, it was in a Boxing Day home defeat against Hull.

In the meantime, he had won a third England cap, impressing but failing to net in a 2-1 success over Yugoslavia that gave the country their 100th victory at Wembley. Italia 90 was six months or so away and he was clearly in Bobby Robson's thoughts – a point underlined when he was the only player from outside the top flight in a 30-man New Year get-together at Lilleshall.

Back on the club front, there was just time for Bully to partake in a revitalising Molineux victory over Bournemouth before he gave Wolves fans the most astonishing 45 minutes it was ever their privilege to see from him. And he did it despite the after-effects of a late-night drink beforehand behind the back of his trusty manager.

What made Steve Bull's four goals at Newcastle on the first day of the 1990s all the more remarkable was that they were so perfectly timed. Not only did they completely transform a tight game in which Mark Kendall's penalty save from Micky Quinn had kept Wolves level up to half-time but they came in a match in which the club's supporters created headlines of their own by flying to the north east in a squadron of eight planes.

Wolves' players travelled by coach as usual and Bully has since confessed to not having the clearest of heads for match-day after seeing the New Year in with a quiet tipple in his room along with a couple of team-mates. Unlike Billy Wright, who was teetotal throughout his playing career, Bully enjoyed a good drink when the time was right – and an occasional sneaky one when the coast was clear.

"The gaffer told us we could have a couple of halves, ring the missus at midnight and then go to bed," he said. "Thommo, Cooky, Mutchy and me were playing cards in the room where we'd had dinner and we had a couple of halves, then another couple and another couple. My glass was under the table and I regretted it – I'm sure we all did – the next morning. It had never happened before and it never happened again. I scored four goals, though, and we win, so perhaps I should have repeated it!"

By way of preparation, his indiscretion clearly did him no harm. Within two or three hours of Wolves' 882 airborne fans planting their feet back on terra firma, he had their heads in the clouds once more with his first four-goal haul away from Molineux. Three of them came in the space of nine minutes early in the second half, the result of quite brilliant finishing that did for Newcastle's former Wolves keeper John Burridge.

"People said I had dried up but this might make them think again," said the player, who had netted only once in his previous seven games for club and country. "It was an unbelievable way to start the year. I always think of the fans and it's great to give them something to cheer after they turned out in such numbers so far away from home."

The last two of the four goals that gave Wolves their first win at St James' Park for more than 30 years were made by Robbie Dennison, the Northern Ireland midfielder who said on a 2008 dvd: "Bully really came alive round the penalty box. He wasn't ever going to stand round watching. He was on the move all the time. His strength created a lot of chances and he was very difficult for defenders to handle. He was totally focused on what he did and, nine times out of ten, would hit the target."

Tyneside apart, Bully's progress was like the team's; quietly pleasing rather than a runaway success. He was still pure gold and Wolves acted accordingly by insuring him for £2m, well beyond a standard cover that, in the event of career-ending injury, would have brought them only £50,000. "It's just sensible business practice," said Tony Gallagher. "Premiums are substantial but, were we ever to lose Steve through injury, heaven forbid, our loss would be virtually incalculable." Gallagher, once so green in the game that he couldn't remember Bully's name, now truly recognised his value.

It was while Bully's life was racing through the gears with club and country that Billy became a bit misty-eyed about his, Michael Aspel surprising him with a certain red book and welcoming him on stage. Billy had tears in his eyes and a lump in his throat. "My life has been a fairytale," he said to the show's script writer Norman Giller. "Who would have believed all this could have happened to a lad from Ironbridge?"

Among the guests for Billy's second *'This Is Your Life'* appearance – his first was with Eamonn Andrews 35 years earlier – were three of his mates from Madeley Modern School whom he hadn't seen for more than 50 years, Arthur Russell, John Norry and the coincidentally named Lawrence Cullis, then all still resident in the Madeley or Dawley areas of Telford.

Billy, also greeted by a host of football friends, no longer wanted to be swanning around for too long in front of the TV cameras. Increasingly, he was being drawn back towards the club where he made his name and was delighted to be reunited there with a distinguished former international colleague on the February day Bully hit his 20th goal of the season – a header against Watford.

Bobby Robson was paying his first visit to Molineux as England boss and must have found it a different world from Highbury, Old Trafford and Anfield. The stadium was a lop-sided mess but thank goodness the man in the country's top football job had delayed his visit until then. When Wolves were on their knees a few years earlier, you wonder how he might have been greeted into the guest room. Maybe with the comment: "Only one bourbon today, if you don't mind, Mr Robson. We've got Halifax here on Tuesday."

Not that the finances were too clever even now, with the Gallagher Family running a tight ship prior to their sale to Sir Jack Hayward. The main stand, as Robson would have known it from his playing and Ipswich years, remained sealed off, so he watched from an executive box in the John Ireland Stand with Billy (by now mooted as a director in waiting) and chairman Jack Harris.

Robson was then good enough to cross the dark corridor following a reviving post-match cuppa and share with the Press his view that Bull had worked hard and taken his goal well. The manager proceeded to cause some raised eyebrows among the media representatives with the follow-up comment that he had been impressed by Wolves' no 7. Well, it wasn't every day Tim Steele, once of Shrewsbury, attracted glowing praise from an international boss.

What with Robson and Sir Jack, Wolves were attracting the right people. And the process moved on apace when Hayward showed some of his hand during the late-March weekend of a visit to Port Vale. "If I buy the club, I will ask Billy Wright to join the board," he said. "He's a great fellow, the greatest player Wolves have ever had. He's the type of character any club would be proud to be associated with and would be a welcome addition in the boardroom as far as I'm concerned."

They were words guaranteed to send an excited shiver down the spine of long-serving fans. Thirty one years after his departure from Molineux, Billy, having taken a step back into the fold with the formation of the Wolves Former Players Association and having known Jack Harris for decades through their friendship with full-back Roy Pritchard, became a regular at games.

Harris had not been in the best of health for 12 months and appreciated the extra company of Billy and Sir Jack's son Jonathan. Other than Harris, the club's directors at the time were Gallagher, his brother David and solicitor Peter Glaister – and only David of the three watched many matches. Billy, who had become Midland Cable Communications director since retiring from Central in 1989, had also been at the win at Plymouth in February when a meeting also involving Harris in Sir Jack's car outside Home Park had gone a long way to confirming that a change of ownership was on the way. But the ex-Wolves and England captain would be returning to a different club from the one he knew.

Neither Steve Bull nor any of Graham Turner's other players stood out in a 3-0 defeat at Vale that was preceded by a lunch meeting of would-be directors. Billy never faced Vale as a Wolves player and the club hadn't lost to them since 1926, so plenty of work obviously still lay ahead to wrestle free from the latter-day shackles despite the promising, spirited challenge for a place in the play-offs.

By then, Bully had netted against Portsmouth and Barnsley in successive matches and further exasperated Albion's top brass by scoring a late winner against the Baggies for the second time in the season. He wasn't going to get anywhere near the half century mark again but the total in the upper 20s for which he was destined was still excellent for mere mortals, especially in a first full campaign at this level.

Hat-tricks were also proving understandably more elusive but he registered his first treble at Molineux for more than a year when he and his side took full revenge on Leicester, public enemy no 1 Steve Walsh and all, in the shape of a crushing 5-0 victory. The second of his three lifted him above Peter Broadbent as the club's fifth highest scorer of all time while his hat-trick goal was the 150th of his career with Albion and Wolves.

There was one big scoring hurrah left in him in before the club season ended and left the stage clear for the World Cup. Having netted what would prove his last Wolves goal of 1989-90 in a home win over Oxford, he had Turner and the manager's backroom colleagues Powell and Darby in tow when he was named for England's April friendly with Czechoslovakia at Wembley.

The trio's pride was all the greater as Colin Taylor, who briefly threatened to become another prolific crew-cut no 9, went on and impressed in a 1-1 youth-team draw between England and the Czechs before the main event. The side were managed by former Wolves inside-forward Dave Burnside, who could hardly be accused of getting it wrong with his choice of lone striker. He backed Andy Cole, the scorer of his side's goal.

Bull had Alan Smith and Tony Cottee as competition in the race for an Italia 90 place but stole a march on them in only the 18th minute of the seniors' game when he crashed a right-foot shot past Ludek Miklosko from Paul Gascoigne's pass. "With the London bias in the Press, we felt Bully had to score that night to be sure of going, so I jumped up and punched the air when he got that goal," Powell recalls. "I was sitting next to Graham Taylor and he tapped me on that shoulder and said: 'You can relax, he'll be on that plane.'

"I don't know how much more he knew with being set to take on the England job but we started to believe him when Steve thumped in a header in the second half. It was a match when all Wolves fans felt very proud." Are we imagining it as we look back through gold-tinted spectacles or did Bobby Robson once compare Bully to the West German great Gerd Muller?

Nationally, it went down as Gazza's night but, 40 years on from when Billy had led his country in the tournament in Brazil, Bully had taken huge steps to becoming the first Wolves player to go with England to a World Cup since Ron Flowers in 1966. Despite Taylor's reassuring words, though, there was a scare the following day.

# Billy & Bully

I stayed over after covering the game so as to attend Robson's press conference at the FA's Lancaster Gate headquarters the following lunchtime and was delighted to extract from him a line that made big headlines in the Express & Star. The play-offs were unheard of in Billy's time but, yes, Robson was concerned about Bully's availability for the tournament if Wolves achieved the top-six finish that would take their season into overtime. "It's a real threat to his chances of going to Italy," he said. "It's a very bad state of affairs for him and us. Getting to the First Division is obviously very important to Wolves and there's not really anything anyone can do."

In the event, the conflict of interests didn't materialise, Sunderland winning at Molineux on the following Saturday to add to the defeats Newcastle and Hull had inflicted on Wolves in mid-April. Bully failed to score in the club's final three games of the season and the side finished an unflattering tenth after a last-day hiding at West Ham marked by noisy chanting from their fans for his inclusion in Italy.

By now, a man who knew a thing or two about England teams was quite literally stepping on board at Molineux. Billy Wright, the holder of the small matter of 105 caps, was officially and proudly unveiled as a Wolverhampton Wanderers director when Hayward assumed control in May, 1990. "At one match, it was in London if I remember right, I had asked Billy if he would come along as a director if I bought the club," Sir Jack recalls. "He had tears in his eyes, said Wolves were the only club he had ever played for and added: 'Just wait until I get home and tell Joy.'"

Martin Swain, the Express & Star's long-time assistant sports editor, was born in Coventry to a Wolverhampton-born, Wolves-supporting mother and was sent a simple message by her in the event of him being able to speak to Billy on takeover day: "Just tell him I love him." "She absolutely adored Billy from the time she watched Wolves while growing up in the town in the 1950s," Swain said. "He was obviously this glamorous figure, the idol of the English game, who filled everybody in the area with such pride at a time when football dominated people's leisure time even more than it does now.

"I had heard so many wonderful things about him from her and couldn't wait to meet him. When I did, I found him every bit as warm and distinguished as I'd hoped. I remember writing a piece for the Express & Star which they headlined 'A Postcard Home' and which was presented in the style of me reassuring her that I'd found meeting him a memorable experience.

# Sky's The Limit

"He was such a lovely, lovely man who never disappointed you. I met him half a dozen times and he never ever let himself down by saying a bad word against anybody. I recall being at a Midland Soccer Writers lunch once with Billy as guest of honour. Our chairman, David Harrison, stood up and went through Billy's career…….the Cups, the caps, the titles. Then he paused for a moment and said: 'Now that's what I call a legend.' It brought the house down. Everyone was on their feet clapping this guy, yet Billy just sat there, totally humble and probably a little embarrassed. He was a top bloke, a real champion.

"My dad worked in the car industry in Coventry, so my parents settled there – and I've stayed there, too. But it's interesting that my youngest son, although surrounded by Sky Blues fans at school, has chosen to be a Wolves fan. I took him on a tour of the grounds round here as he was trying to decide which was his club. He took one look at Billy's statue at Molineux and that was that. Having had the privilege of meeting the guy, it sent quite a shiver down my spine. My boy's instincts were pretty good, if I say so myself."

Swain was on Bully-watch when he departed for reporting duty at Italia 90, carrying with him a sack of fans' good-luck letters the paper had offered to pass on. Before his back started to creak under the load, the player said he had never felt better, fitter or stronger and thanked Wolves supporters for their unstinting devotion. "No matter what happens over the next four weeks, you have made this an experience I shall treasure for the rest of my life," he said.

By now, it was clear Molineux's Boy's Own Hero was seen as back-up to the likes of Gary Lineker, Peter Beardsley and John Barnes, a feeling underlined by his introduction as a substitute in the pre-tournament games against Denmark and Uruguay.

He stepped from the bench again to stoop and head in Barnes's cross for a late equaliser after the squad had made a detour en route for Sardinia to fulfil a friendly in Tunisia. His stock was high. Seven games in the senior side had brought him four goals at the rate of better than one every 80 minutes on the field, not forgetting the five he had managed in England's lesser sides.

As Bully scored twice in a warm-up game against Cagliari and two more against a Sardinia Select XI, the clamour for his inclusion in Robson's starting side intensified, not least when Jimmy Greaves appeared on TV in a t-shirt bearing the message: 'Let the Bull loose.'

As the only player in the squad from outside the top flight, a goalscorer at that, he was big news. Wolves were having to work hard to prevent the story spiralling out of control, their newly-appointed vice-chairman Jonathan Hayward reacting to suggestions that Genoa were eyeing him by saying: "They are wasting their time. It doesn't matter how many millions we are offered. We don't need their money and consider him the best striker in the country."

Unfortunately, Robson didn't and used him for only the final seven minutes of the disappointing opening draw against the Republic of Ireland, who had a certain Mick McCarthy in their defence. "I think that was the only time I played against him," says Wolves' 2009 Championship-winning manager. "He may have come from the lower divisions but he was one of those players you always knew was going to be a threat. He was always putting you under pressure. He was a real grafter who would run the channels and never let up. I remember managing Millwall later when we played Wolves and he was still going strong. He always carried that goal-scoring threat and had a phenomenal record."

Bully had 32 minutes in place of Chris Waddle in the more encouraging stalemate with Holland and was finally given his head in the decisive group game against Egypt. Alas, it was an opportunity he couldn't take and his satisfaction in helping England to a victory secured by Mark Wright's header was not reinforced by any particular glow from his personal contribution.

With the team decamped to the mainland for the knock-out phase, Barnes's withdrawal against Belgium in Bologna gave Bully another run-out and I wasn't the only one guilty of temporary mistaken identity when England's winner flashed in a couple of minutes from the end of extra-time. Okay, the decisive volley was from the right foot of David Platt, not Bully, but we were in the last eight – and Wolves had a player helping them get there.

By now, Italy's various charms were wearing a bit thin with the striker. While his room-mate Platt was sufficiently falling in love with the country as to jump when Bari, Juventus and Sampdoria moved for him in the next three years, Bully was longing for a plate of fish and chips and a glimpse of Cannock. What kept him going was the thought that England were on a roll and in with a chance of emulating 1966 and all that.

Without calling on him, they hit back to oust Cameroon in the quarter-final and he had gone further in the tournament than Billy Wright ever managed. The end came, though, for the first and certainly not the last time, on penalties. West Germany did what they do by withstanding a terrific performance from Robson's men, holding on at 1-1 after extra-time and winning the shoot-out. Bully, used neither in that game in Turin nor the third-place play-off against the hosts in Bari, was nevertheless given a hero's reception, along with his colleagues, when their plane landed at Luton. Despite the frustrations of his limited involvement (around 135 minutes of playing time) and his occasional boredom, it had been an experience he would never forget.

"With Wolves not in the top flight, it made it even more difficult for him to break in," Robson said. "It would have been better for him to be in the top division and he suffered for that. But I looked at him and liked him. He was aggressive and he was a goalscorer. He wasn't a dribbler or hugely talented in terms of technique but a bit like Lineker. It's not by luck that he scored all those goals. In Sardinia, there were always a lot of fans watching our training sessions and we were doing heading practice. Each time he nodded one into the net, there was this big roar. He was a nice character, a little bit shy. That's how most of the players saw him. He didn't put himself around much but he looked around him and he loved being in it."

The furthest Billy went in the competition was to the quarter-finals in 1954 and, patriotic Englishman that he was, nothing would have thrilled him more than to see Bully play in a side who lifted the Jules Rimet Trophy in Rome's Olympic Stadium. He wasn't downhearted, though. How could he be with new horizons opening up ahead of him as he took his seat in the directors' box?

## Chapter Fourteen

# Second Coming

Despite having played all his matches for Wolverhampton Wanderers at the highest level, Billy Wright had no trouble firing his enthusiasm for the task of aiding the club's push for promotion from the second grade. He became a virtual ever-present at games Graham Turner's team played and was a frequent visitor to Central League fixtures, too, even ones that entailed long midweek trips from his London home to Yorkshire and Lancashire.

"Billy had worked all his life, in football and TV, and loved being involved with Wolves again," said fellow director John Harris, son of then chairman Jack Harris. "It was a new lease of life for him. He went on the overnight trips with the team but would invariably go back to London afterwards. He loved beans on toast and used to enjoy getting home for a late-night snack!"

He was, needless to say, a delightful addition to the travelling entourage. Opposing chairmen were always thrilled to greet him at their door and the likes of Harris Snr and secretary Keith Pearson were pleased to have him, Sir Jack and Jonathan Hayward in their midst after a year or two of turning up at some grounds with a full row of seats allocated for the visiting club – and not many bottoms to plonk on them.

"I recall people wanting to shake Billy's hand and strike up conversation the moment we got out of the car," Harris Jnr added. "He was a very ordinary man in terms of his attitude to others. He didn't make himself important. I suppose he received more attention at the bigger clubs where directors were perhaps more attracted to glamour. One night, as we left Nottingham Forest, Brian Clough spotted him, came over and gave him a big kiss which Billy wiped off as soon as he was out of Cloughie's sight!"

Just imagine the thrill of such VIP company for Turner, a boyhood Wolves fan who was brought up in Ellesmere Port at the opposite end of a terraced street to where the Cullis family lived. "I remember, when I was 14 or 15,

All smiles for Billy and the women in his world on the set of This Is Your Life after host Michael Aspel had surprised the Wolves and England legend with his famous red book in 1987. It was the second time he had been the 'victim' on the show.

Hey, shouldn't you be on the other side? Steve Bull holds his smile in place as he spots a photographer's blind-side 'run' during the annual photo call in the late 1980s. Wolves, at the time, had the promotion knack and the striker was a 50-goals-a-season performer.

Right: Bully getting stripped for action in the little-seen home dressing room at Molineux. The occasion in question was not a match day, though, but an adidas photo 'shoot.'

Below: Move over Shilts! Molineux's record-breaking striker shows he is not averse to stopping goals as well as scoring them as he demonstrates his agility between the posts.

Images of a great night at Wembley. Steve Bull may not have scored there for Wolves in the Sherpa Van Trophy final but he netted twice for England in April, 1990, against Czechoslovakia and so booked his trip to Italia 90. As a result, he once more found himself as a photographer's best friend, although there was still a scare the next day when Bobby Robson discussed his World Cup prospects.

Billy Wright is all eyes and ears as Sir Jack Hayward outlines his ambitious plans on the morning of his Wolverhampton Wanderers takeover in May, 1990. It was the day on which a proud and delighted Billy joined the board at his beloved club. In the background, waiting for his interview chance, is Phil Shaw, a Midlands-based reporter for The Independent.

Billy has full-back Brian Roberts for company as he leaves Molineux's old main stand behind and sets off on the walk for the John Ireland Stand at a Boxing Day game against Kenny Dalglish's Blackburn in the 1991-92 campaign.

Was there ever a more memorable day in the decades-old worship of Stephen George Bull by Wolverhampton Wanderers fans than this one? Supporters are in festive mood (above) as they wait on the tarmac at Birmingham to board the plane that would fly them to Newcastle on the first day of the 1990s. And, once in the north-east, they had the unforgettable sight of Bully (pictured breaking away below) scoring all his side's goals in a 4-1 victory at St James' Park.

Only Port Vale suffered more at the mercy of Steve Bull over the years than Bristol City did. The West Countrymen are the opponents here on a day early in 1990-91 when Bully didn't disappoint, hitting yet another hat-trick at a time when he was still in a World Cup glow.

All nice and friendly for the pre-match formalities at Molineux in August, 1992 - but it didn't stay that way for very long. Leicester skipper Steve Walsh was sent off for a tangle with his opposite number, who plundered the 200th goal of his Wolves career in a 3-0 victory.

Steve Bull leads Aston Villa duo Kevin Richardson and Steve Staunton a merry dance on the day he netted twice against them in a friendly to mark the 1992 opening of the Stan Cullis Stand. Billy was at the great manager's side (right) during the formalities as the ribbon was cut on the impressive new structure at what had always been known as Molineux's North Bank. On the right of the picture is Eddie Stuart, the man who in 1959 took over from Wright as Wolves captain.

Left: Steve Bull and Andy Mutch - partners in goals for seven years to magnificent effect and also colleagues in England's under-21 and B sides. Below: An evening for smiles and nostalgia as Billy finds himself reunited with Ferenc Puskas, the legend who tormented him in England's two notorious defeats against Hungary before revenge was taken in Wolves colours on a magical 1954 night. The two are together here in 1993 for the opening of the Molineux stand that bears the Wolves great's name.

Never a sadder day. Molineux is awash with grief (left) after news broke of the death of Billy Wright in 1994. From all over the world, the outpouring of sorrow was intense.

## Second Coming

writing to Billy asking for his autograph without sending a stamped addressed envelope or anything like that," he said. "By return of post, I got a programme, with his picture at the back signed by him. I still have it now, wrapped in foil, in pride of place in the house. He was, without a doubt, my big hero."

Not that Billy interfered with team affairs – or showed much inclination to join in the tactical debates. "He stepped on the coach once as we prepared to leave after an away game and stood in the well while Graham, myself and Garry Pendrey or Barry Powell were in discussion," said ex-Wolves physio Paul Darby. "Someone suddenly said: 'What do you think, Bill?' And he said: 'There's no substitute for ability.' And that put everything into context really."

Steve Bull had no yearning for airports and the babble of foreign languages after Italia 90 and settled for topping up his Southern Europe tan in Great Yarmouth with girlfriend Julie. Before loading up the car, he signed another new contract. "My dad always said Steve was the best player to do wage negotiations with," added John Harris. "He just used to say to him: 'Now, come on Bully, what do you want this year?' And that was usually that."

The player didn't hang around either when 1990-91 kicked off. His sights sharpened by six pre-season goals that included a hat-trick past former Wolves keeper Mark Kendall at Swansea, he looked the part as he opened the scoring against Oldham on day one after five minutes and added a second. The trouble was that Ian Marshall had the audacity to hit a hat-trick at the other end.

Thanks partly to another Molineux brace, this time against Plymouth, Bully had six goals on the board inside a month, with Andy Mutch scoring one and making one prior to a four-month absence caused by back surgery. Not that the Liverpudlian was unhappy in his supporting role. "People said I created a lot of Steve's goals," he said. "But my passes or headers wouldn't have looked anything like as good if Bully hadn't put them away, which he usually did."

With John Paskin and Paul McLoughlin tried at his side, Bull's contribution was unwavering, although he felt the boot on the other foot at international level when taken off and replaced by Chris Waddle at home to Hungary after being named in the starting line-up for Taylor's first match. The response with Wolves was hugely enjoyable. He netted twice and hit the woodwork at home to Charlton and put poor old Bristol City to the sword once more four days later, the 14th hat-trick of his Wolves career making them the first side against whom he had netted ten or more times. With 11 goals from 11 games, this was his best start to a season.

# Billy & Bully

"There were so many games where it would be tight and not much between the teams and suddenly Bully or sometimes Mutchy would pop up with a goal that turned a probable 1-1 draw into a 2-1 win or a 1-0 deficit into a draw," said midfielder Keith Downing. "Bully, in particular, had that wonderful knack of getting on to something and just making the difference.

"Obviously, having the two of them went a long way towards dictating how we'd play and Graham was sensible enough to adapt our style accordingly. It would have been unwise to develop a sophisticated passing game while the strength of those two was turning and running goalwards. We were inevitably going to be fairly direct and our approach was too much for many teams."

What was still working for Wolves was no longer quite the ticket with England. Bully had held off the rival claims of Ian Wright when selected against Hungary and was retained for the Euro qualifier at home to Poland – the first time he had started successive internationals. The Arsenal legend was now breathing down his neck, though, so was Peter Beardsley.

Billy Wright had had to tolerate occasional questioning of his claims to an England shirt but he was the centre-half and captain of a Wolves side at or very near the summit of the domestic game. Bully was forever striving to justify himself as a gatecrasher from outside the top flight and Taylor knew it. He gave him 53 minutes against the Poles, then Beardsley went on for him and added a beauty to the goal with which Lineker had drawn first blood.

We didn't know it, although Turner suspected it and even said so, but the on-field part of Bull's England career was over. "I felt he was discarded too early," the manager said. "A lot of players' careers were coming to an end and I thought he was ready to really go on and establish himself."

Whether you thought Bully was unlucky probably depended on your pull towards Molineux. Wolves fans thought he could do no wrong and saw him as the new fresh face and legs to replace the ageing Lineker. Others considered him too rough and ready for such rarefied company and Sir Alf Ramsey put in his twopenneth by saying he should be dropped.

Whereas Billy had enjoyed 13 years with England and played 70 successive matches, Steve Bull was given but 13 games and only four times had the luxury of playing more than 70 minutes. He didn't, of course, even sniff the captaincy – a role Billy carried out 90 times. But the latter-day star had a more than satisfactory record. His four goals in the senior team came at the rate of about one every 154 minutes, a higher scoring frequency than Bobby Charlton and

# Second Coming

very similar to the time Alan Shearer had to wait between goals, so that's something to tell the grandkids. Not forgetting he also scored twice for the B team and three times in the under-21s.

With Wolves at least, Bully remained totally sure of his place and standing. He scored in wins over Hull and Middlesbrough in consecutive matches and burst out of a five-game League famine with a couple against Ipswich. To his great regret, he had left the 50-goals-a-season plundering in the lower divisions but this was still what you might term heavy accumulation.

He was again the country's top scorer and had the boost of another England call-up, albeit for a draw in Dublin where he wasn't used. To mere mortals, it would have been dizzy stuff. As Bully winters go, though, this was sedate; a smattering of goals largely in ones, an England B outing in Swansea and a promotion bid that promised up to March and then imploded horribly.

On the day Paul Birch made a scoring Molineux debut, Bully hit the winner against leaders West Ham – the third time in 15 months he had netted a decisive goal against them – and, in lifting Wolves to a first win in seven, had taken his tally for the club to 168, ahead of Billy's great pal Johnny Hancocks and into third spot in the club's all-time scorers' list. "I'm flattered when I'm described as one of the greats, even if I'm being compared with players I have hardly heard of," said Bully, who then made his manager's 250th game in charge a memorable one by scoring twice in a home win over Port Vale.

The brace took him level with Billy Hartill on 170 Wolves goals, with only John Richards ahead…about a year ahead at his Division Two strike-rate. Amid the continuing rampage, though, Billy was about to discover that the club no longer found winning anywhere near as easy as they had in his hey-day.

From standing fifth, well in the running for the play-offs, they fell away horribly to finish 12th, a dozen points short of sixth place. They won only two of their final 15 matches and such was the scale of the blow-out that even when Bull came up with his 15th hat-trick for the club, Oxford hit three second-half goals of their own to snatch a draw and turn the Molineux mood ugly.

"Billy didn't get too upset about a defeat," added his fellow director John Harris. "He was disappointed but his attitude was that you can't win every game and there was always another one coming up to put things right. The most critical he became was to tap his chest around his heart if he thought someone wasn't putting everything into it on the pitch."

Turner, already the subject of suggestions he lacked what it took to complete the journey to the top flight, acknowledged that the direct style on which he had built success around the potency of the Bull-Mutch axis had to be replaced by a more cultured style. But how would the duo cope with the tinkering? Amid Wolves' nosedive, Bully failed to score after late March, his barren six-game trot compounded by fitness problems. The miracle man had to admit defeat to a pulled hamstring at home to Hull and missed the last three matches – the first time in five years he had been sidelined by injury.

   He had still added 27 goals to his 27 the previous season but the fact an England squad were named in the meantime without him underlined one fact; that, unless your name is William Ambrose Wright and you can stay at the top, time eventually catches up with you. Steve Bull was not finding life as easy, although he was destined to remain a force for some years yet.

## Chapter Fifteen

# Record Breaker

When did consolidation give way to stagnation in the life of Wolverhampton Wanderers as a Second Division club? Certainly, we can look back to the autumn of 1991 as the time when the exhilaration of two successive promotions was largely forgotten amid the gloom of competing much nearer the bottom of the table than the top.

Two and a half years on from waving goodbye to the Third Division, Wolves had lost their momentum and were seeking a fresh foothold on their climb back towards the elite. At least the team as a whole were. Steve Bull, having wed in the summer and signed a two-year contract extension that made paying the bills in the marital home a little easier, was still very much in the goal-scoring groove.

He made his lean end to 1990-91 a distant memory by netting in the first three games of the new season and, after unusually missing out against Port Vale, hit the target in the next five as well. Nine goals in nine matches added up to his best start as a Wolves player – a strike rate sufficient enough to prompt a spying visit from Graham Taylor, only for the England manager to still omit him from his next England squad.

Glenn Hoddle, then player-boss of Swindon, added his voice to the theory that Bully needed more to his game than sheer volume of goals to win his place back on the international stage. It wasn't what the player wanted to hear and he said on video many years later: "I think they gave Ian Wright around 18 caps in a row and he scored three goals. If I had played 18, I think I'd have scored ten."

Bully had to do without Andy Mutch for eight games in the autumn, both strikers being sidelined on the gloomy November afternoon their side lost at bottom-of-the-table Plymouth to go 16th. While the side languished and looked in need of surgery, though, it was a time of great change elsewhere in the club.

## Billy & Bully

Sir Jack Hayward launched his massive Molineux makeover by overseeing the flattening of the North Bank shortly before a Bonfire Night home defeat against Bristol Rovers in which Bully scored twice. Exciting redevelopment plans were in place but there was considerable doubt over whether Graham Turner would be around to see the first bricks laid in the replacement structure, the manager's position increasingly becoming a subject of debate.

Steve Bull would have run through a wall, new or old, for his gaffer, and Billy Wright was another firm ally of the manager's in his hour of need. It was perhaps surprising, though, that the trickle of goals that turned the corner for the 44-year-old came not from the striker but from midfielder Paul Birch. Bully, totally out of character, managed only one appearance on the score-sheet between November 5 and January 15.

Once under way again, though, the striker hit another purple patch. He netted in four matches on the run, including the winner at home to Leicester on the day of Turner's 300th match in charge, before Wolves' sequence of five straight League wins tailed off again into indifference. Then another entry into the history books loomed, his venomous 'strike' against Bristol City taking him on to the 193-goal mark, one behind John Richards.

With a better sense of occasion, Bully would have used a vibrant Molineux as the setting for catching and overtaking the 1970s 'king.' Instead, by way of a reminder that he was happier than anyone to get his hands and knees dirty in the humblest of workplaces, he was at Bristol Rovers' rented tumbledown home at Twerton Park on the night he became the club's joint heaviest scorer of all time.

Remember Keith Downing's quote about tight games suddenly being turned round in Wolves' favour or impending defeats being offset as satisfactory draws? Wolves were trailing 1-0 with 13 minutes to go on a miserable might at the non-League venue until Bull popped up on the end of a right-wing cross by Kevin Ashley to head an equaliser that had barely looked like coming.

Three games later, the record was his outright as, within a minute of Birch equalising at Derby, he hooked in the decider in a 2-1 Wolves win on March 21, 1992. Downing was first on hand to congratulate him but, while no doubt aware of the record-breaking significance, would have been happy to leave the finer detail of the moment to the anoraks.

John Richards's last goal as a Football League player had also come at the Baseball Ground (when he was on loan with the Rams), as had his first in the

## Record Breaker

FA Cup. What's more, Bully, whose haul was now a round 20 in a disappointing 1991-92 campaign for the club, had also netted his third and final Albion first-team goal at the venue.

It was only the second time in around 60 years that the mantle of Wolves' all-time leading goalscorer had changed hands, Richards having left Billy Hartill (170) behind late in 1979-80. The comparison in games played makes interesting reading. JR's 194 Wolves goals spanned 486 matches while Bully had reached 195 in only 283, not much above half the number. It has to be pointed out that the latter-day star didn't make any of those appearances in the top flight, where the vast majority of Richards's outings came, but the gulf is still eye-opening.

"There were no strong feelings for me when the record went to Bully," Richards says. "I was sad to lose the accolade but it had been fairly obvious that it was only a matter of time until he overtook me. Given the way he was scoring goals, it didn't come as a shock and I was happy to hold up my hands and say 'well done' because he had been absolutely brilliant for the club."

Thank God for Bully. Without his latest slice of Molineux history, which came a week before his 27th birthday, the campaign would have died even earlier than it did for Wolves. It was the first season in which he had failed to score a hat-trick but Andy Mutch stepped in to fill that particular void by netting three times in a spectacular 6-2 home victory over Newcastle at a time when Kevin Keegan's new charges were flirting with the threat of relegation to the Third Division - a fate that eventually befell Albion.

There was just time for one more highlight in that 1991-92 campaign – the 200th goal of Bully's Baggies and Wolves career as his side came from behind to win at promotion-bound Blackburn – before Turner's men finished a very distant 11th. It says much for the striker's worth that this had been the leanest of his five and a half Molineux years to date, yet he had still helped himself to 23 goals. For the fifth successive season, he had netted more than twice as many as his nearest challenger at the club but would he be content to remain a part of a team he had clearly outgrown?

## Chapter Sixteen

# Deeply Devoted

Just how devoted Billy Wright still was to the Wolves cause became apparent when he accompanied Graham Turner and his players on their pre-season tour of Scotland in the summer of 1992.

For a man who had dipped his toes in the Atlantic along Rio's Copacabana Beach, met Juan and Eva Peron in Argentina and performed in Paris, Rome, Milan and Madrid, friendlies against Dumbarton, Partick Thistle and Dundee could easily have been viewed as an endurance. But you wouldn't have guessed it from his constant good humour and boyish enthusiasm.

"Billy was a legend," says former Wolves centre-half Derek Mountfield. "He was always on the team bus and glad to talk with you about the game. I remember in Scotland in the early 1990s when we were given a day off to play golf and he and Jonathan Hayward were the last group out and the heavens really opened. I'd never seen rain like it. Billy obviously had no waterproofs or brolly because he was like a drowned rat when he came in wearing nothing more substantial as protection than a Pringle jumper. He was totally fed up but soon perked up over a cuppa and was his chatty, cheerful self again in no time."

Although Billy once partnered Gary Player in a tournament and got down to a handicap of four, he wasn't always the most enthusiastic of participants in later years. "He turned up once at Patshull Park with no clubs and no shoes," said John Harris. "He was prepared just to be there in attendance rather than necessarily play but, being Billy Wright, he soon had people running around making sure he had all the right equipment, so he could join in."

In golf terms, Wolves would become seen as a fancied player who was always in contention before writing a couple of ugly scores on the card near the end and ruining the whole round. Either that or, it has to be said, they tended to blow up at the play-off stage. At least, though, they still had something in the bag that was the envy of everyone else in the field.

## Deeply Devoted

By now, they were well used to seeing and hearing Steve Bull's name mentioned alongside those of various big clubs but one link was stronger and longer-lasting than all others. Aston Villa had been on his case since Graham Taylor's time there before the 1990 World Cup, a tournament at which their chairman Doug Ellis had invited him on to a private yacht for 'a chat.' Now the whispers connecting him to the Second City were becoming a din.

For the first time, Bully's head was turned early in the summer of 1992. It may not be going too far to say he was unsettled because he was certainly considering his options. Although Ron Atkinson tells me Villa did not bid for him, they were strongly linked with a move and the player wondered, with Wolves marooned in mid-table after three years in the Second Division, whether he needed a change. The doubts soon wore off.

Having requested a meeting with Graham Turner in late May, he made it clear the following day through his father-in-law and agent Gene Dace that he was going nowhere. "Steve has given the matter an awful lot of thought and he's quite happy to stay," Dace said. "He's still very popular here, not only with the fans but also the rest of the staff, and the club have always made it clear they don't want him to go."

It can be argued that Bully went closer to leaving when Coventry had a bid accepted in 1995 but I believe this interest of three summers earlier is the one that most makes him wonder all these years on. He doesn't regret not joining the Sky Blues, nor Leeds, Celtic, Genoa, Wimbledon or any of the other clubs keen on him. But Villa, a thriving club on the doorstep who were playing exciting football under Big Ron, mmmm……..maybe.

Judging by what he subsequently did at Molineux, he still had five good years in him and at least three or four of them may have been spent in the Premiership. That said, what price could be placed on the seven years' further adulation he received as a player at Wolves and then the continued post-career connections that that service helped to bring about? Perhaps it was a no-lose situation for him.

Villa were reminded of the explosive finishing power they might have tapped into when they made the short trip across the Midlands for Stan Cullis's testimonial game. On an August Sunday lunchtime on which Billy Wright was once more very much to the fore, Bully did his stuff yet again by scoring twice in an entertaining draw to which Tony Daley also contributed a couple of goals.

Billy was busy assembling his former team-mates for the ribbon-cutting ceremony in front of the structure that had replaced the North Bank, joining in with gusto in the singing of *'The Happy Wanderer'* as he was flanked by the likes of Cullis, Dicky Dorsett, Harry Middleton and Johnny Walker.

Bully had become a dad at the age of 27 for the first time that summer and had invested in a box in the John Ireland Stand for his growing family. If his head was meant to have been turned by the earlier uncertainty over his future or thrown into a spin when his nights were interrupted by young Jack, it didn't show when the 1992-93 campaign kicked off.

He now had another string to his bow – that of the captaincy in place of the injured Mark Venus – and took that step-up like he had taken every other; in his stride. For the fourth time and the third successive year, he was on target on kick-off day as Wolves put away newly-promoted Brentford at Griffin Park, then he struck twice in a follow-up victory at home to Leicester to take himself to the 200-goal landmark for the club.

That the striker's old adversary Steve Walsh was sent off in the latter fixture made it an even more special night for the home fans, who were now spread around three sides of Molineux, rather than two. "The atmosphere is brilliant now," Bully said in a TV interview after the game. "They are starting work on the other stand as well and, when that's completed, it will be an even greater pleasure to play here." About reaching his double century for the club in well under six years, the player added: "It had been mentioned in the newspapers over the last few days but I don't take any notice of that. My job is to get on with it and score goals. I set my targets every season for 25 and I have (always) reached it so far. I just hope I can do the same this time."

Following three goals in two games, six points out of six for the team and a successful start for the improving stadium, he was bubbling. Why, he even found it in himself to call Walsh 'an absolute gentleman' after the Leicester skipper and hard-man had gone into Wolves' dressing room following the game to apologise for the tangle that earned him his sending-off.

A visit by Glenn Hoddle's Swindon started a run of three matches without a Bully goal before another flurry of landmarks came in September. What was already Graham Turner's best start to a Wolves season was underlined by his 150th win as their manager when Peterborough were beaten 4-3, Andy Mutch's first goal of the afternoon taking his combined tally with Bull to 300 while his second made him only the 15th player to hit a century of goals for the club.

Bully also netted against Posh but not in the follow-up televised draw at

## Deeply Devoted

Leicester, where he played his 300th competitive Wolves game. Two headed goals against Watford took him back above Mutch in the Molineux charts, then he had to settle for a sincere thank-you from Darren Roberts after the rookie striker had hit a sensational 31-minute first-half hat-trick in the derby dismantling of Birmingham at St Andrew's.

As early as seven years before Bully's retirement, a man well versed in similar deeds believed the no 9 already had a goal tally that no other Wolves player would ever threaten. "There's no way his record will be broken," says John Richards now. "For that matter, I don't think anyone else will ever pass my figure either. Not unless the club spend many years in the bottom division and unearth a real talent who lacks the ambition to move on.

"It was such a freakish set of circumstances with Bully and Wolves. He was a magnificent scorer who got all those goals in the lower divisions early in his career and was then happy to stay for so long in the Second Division because he knew there was always a chance of another promotion. So the club didn't hinder his progress.

"For somebody to break his record, they would have to score more than 30 goals a season for ten years and that isn't going to happen. If a player was to achieve that sort of figure for a couple of years, the chances are that Wolves would be playing outside the top flight and then be unable to hang on to him. Bully was a one-off in being happy to stay."

As their centre-forward went off the boil in 1992-93, so Wolves lost their edge, although a run of draws ensured they remained the last unbeaten side in any of the four divisions. They lost for the first time when confronted by Millwall on a waterlogged date with the TV cameras in the docklands, the satisfaction of a club record equalling 12 League games unbeaten at the start of a campaign eroded by the fact they were no longer playing well.

Bully was misfiring, too, a heel injury ruling him out of a game for the Football League side against a representative team from Italy's Serie B and contributing to a run of seven matches without a goal that made this the driest spell of his career. He bounced back with a brace against bottom club Bristol Rovers that took him past Billy Hartill as Wolves' highest all-time scorer in League games but he was part of a side who now looked distinctly ordinary.

Turner's position was again under some scrutiny and calls for his departure intensified during the winter, Wolves by now having Jonathan Hayward as one of the League's youngest chairmen after Jack Harris had retreated into a regular seat on the board alongside Billy Wright. How the club could have done with their former skipper sprinkling some of that 1950s magic dust over Molineux.

Bully's goal tally was comfortably into double figures by Christmas but more than once he gave a passable impression of a one-man team, Mutch missing more than two months of football though injury before he and his strike-partner both scored in a big FA Cup win at Watford that proved to be another false dawn. Amazing though it seems, there were actually a few boos as Bully missed several chances in the Cup defeat against Bolton at Molineux and he revealed in one of the club's publications that the reaction hurt him, even if it was understandable. The message was accompanied with the inevitable rider, though, that he was still putting his heart and soul into the cause.

"Bully was always a leader by example on the field," said midfielder Keith Downing. "Even if things weren't going his way, you could rely on him to be harrying and unsettling defenders. They never had an easy time against him. He gave it everything in every game and I'm sure it was that attitude, as well as all his goals, that the supporters warmed to."

The player promised that one goal, no matter how scruffy, would set him off and running again and was true to his word. Much though the team remained in the doldrums, he hit the heights again between two suspensions he incurred in quick succession for amassing too many bookings and, from late February, scored in five consecutive matches, including twice against Notts County at Molineux.

In the meantime, a tentative approach from Newcastle had been rebuffed by the Bully camp, who soon found themselves sitting down to negotiate yet another new contract for him. Jonathan Hayward, in hinting at a major spending spree the following summer and making it clear Turner would be the man with his hands on the credit card, said he hoped Bull would stay at Wolves until 1999. The chairman made mistakes while in office but this at least was an accurate prophecy.

Despite the upturn in the player's fortunes, 1992-93 proved to be different to him from other Molineux seasons. For the first time in a full campaign, he failed to reach 20 goals, being marooned on 19 when he limped off with the recurrence of an Achilles problem shortly after scoring the equaliser in a midweek draw at Luton. It was an early sign of the injury ravages that would blight much of the rest of his career.

## Deeply Devoted

Bully missed the last six games and, despite a home win over Newcastle and then two goals against Mick McCarthy's Millwall by Shaun Bradbury on the day the giant South Bank was used as a terraced area for the final time, the inconsistencies that were underlined by the side's unsatisfactory 12th-place finish bore out the need for reinforcements to Turner's stagnating squad.

There was personal consolation for the striker in the form of yet another record. With his 16 First Division (second grade) goals, he had emerged as the club's top scorer in League matches for a seventh time, Richards and Hartill having previously shared the mantle by each leading the Wolves charts six times, 40 years or so apart.

That apart, supporters had found the season's main saving grace to be the on-going work on the magnificent Billy Wright Stand. With the demolition of the old Waterloo Road Stand soon after Molineux became a bizarre target for firebomb-planting arsonists during the final weekend of 1991-92, the players had to change in Portakabins for several months but the gradual materialisation of the new structure was a captivating sight.

Billy was entitled to puff his chest out with pride every time he stepped inside the stadium anyway but this development was an extra reason for his heartbeat to quicken. Understandably, he loved to keep an eye on the work, so much so that he was once present to bump into Hugh Curran in midweek while the former Wolves striker was back at the stadium to do an anniversary feature for Swedish TV. "I remember walking round the pitch and being very flattered when Billy recognised me," Curran said in 2008. "We hadn't met before and it was quite a thrill to be back after all those years and to meet the most famous player the club have ever had. He was very nice to me, as you might expect, and it was a big shock to hear the news about him the following year."

## Chapter Seventeen

# The Last Stand

Wolverhampton Wanderers gave every impression of being a club in a hurry as the final few bricks were laid in the new Billy Wright Stand. Molineux had undergone a spectacular metamorphosis and now boasted a new executive club and presidents' club which soon sold out, state-of-the-art changing rooms, floodlights on the roofs of the stands, under-soil heating, a fitness centre and hairdresser among other swish amenities.

To anyone who had seen games at the ground as recently as early 1991-92, it was a breathtaking transformation and Sir Jack Hayward was delighted to be able to attach the names of Stan Cullis and Billy to the two structures he had rebuilt at a personal cost of around £10m. Not that he would have any truck with suggestions that he should be similarly recognised. "Billy and Stan are the two greatest players who ever played for this club and I don't want to be compared with them," Hayward said. "I don't want any part of it named after me." And he warned younger generations: "Don't ever change the name of Molineux. It's so famous. If you do, I'll come back and haunt you."

There was a feverish expectancy about everything Wolves did at the time. Sir Jack, never slow to speak of wanting to live his football dreams before being tapped on the shoulder by the Grim Reaper or invited into the care of men dressed in white coats, had turned 70 and his reign had produced finishes of 12th, 11th and 12th – disappointing results a few years on from the club's successive promotions.

Then there was all the talk about the need to overhaul Molineux first and the team second. So now the stadium was changing massively for the better, what could possibly get in the way this time? Even Steve Bull, who had refused to speak to the media for long spells after evening newspaper coverage of his wedding to second wife Julie in 1991, broke his ban to talk up Wolves' chances.

"I have not looked forward to a season so much since I first signed for the club," he said. "The fans didn't see the real Steve Bull last season. For the last 18 months, this Achilles problem has been nagging away at me and, although I don't want to make excuses, I can really feel the difference now I have had it cleaned up."

Bully had recovered from a close-season operation on the injury and was going to be part of a very different side. Times were changing with such haste that some of the old guard were bound to suffer because, by Second Division and 1993 standards, the recruitment of Geoff Thomas, David Kelly, Kevin Keen, Cyrille Regis and Peter Shirtliff in one summer added up to an orgy of spending.

Bully was still the idol of the masses but no longer stood head and shoulders above everyone else in the dressing room in terms of profile. Thomas, whose arrival laid down a marker when it emerged he had turned down Manchester City in favour of Molineux, was a big character, not long out of the England side. So was Kelly and Bully, by contrast, was shy. But he said: "The new signings and the ground have given everybody a lift. The past couple of seasons have been a little bit flat but now there's such a buzz about the place, I can't wait to get cracking. I will set my usual target of 25 goals and, if I get that and David Kelly matches it, we'll be on our way to the Premier League."

While Bully even revealed at the annual photo call that he still harboured hopes of playing for England, citing Gary Lineker as an example of what could be achieved by thirtysomethings who looked after themselves, three stalwart members of Wolves' double title-winning line-up of the late 1980s were less enamoured with the changing landscape. Andy Mutch, Andy Thompson and Robbie Dennison were all left behind from the tour of Sweden and also unkindly positioned off-camera when the squad picture was taken at Molineux. Such was the apparent strength of the squad that Thompson, signed on the same day as Bully seven years earlier, found himself with the reserves from the first day of training while Mutch was so marginalised that the highlight of his pre-season was a run-out at Shifnal, where he scored twice.

In the wake of Kelly's signing, Bully had cautioned against writing off the man with whom he had wreaked such havoc in Wolves' colours but the parting of the ways was indeed imminent. Mutch left in the August to join top-flight newcomers Swindon for £250,000, his own Molineux job handsomely done in the shape of 105 senior goals from 338 appearances.

Dennison and Thompson, whose contribution to the cause was summed up by their combined 550-plus tally of matches to that point, were also available for offer, the impish utility man going close to a move to Huddersfield. Much more was to be seen and heard of them, though, even if it did take a few weeks for bridges to be rebuilt after their somewhat clumsy handling.

The long-serving trio weren't in Scandinavia with Wolves in the July but Billy Wright was. Three miles from the Baltic Sea in the south of a country in which he had led England at the World Cup 35 years earlier, he was again something of a star turn, with officials at the host clubs flattered by the presence of one of world football's biggest all-time figures. "Everywhere you go, everyone knows Billy," Graham Turner wrote in his programme notes shortly after returning home. "I must confess that when it was first announced he was to join the board, I had my misgivings. At times, it isn't the best for a manager to have a former manager on the board of directors. But I have to say Billy has been nothing but a great help and a source of great encouragement."

Wright's attendance sheet was covered in ticks, determined as he was to take as full a part in Wolves' activities as he possibly could. "He rarely misses even a reserve match or midweek youth game and, given that he lives in Barnet, that demonstrates his commitment to the present set-up," Turner added. "I can't think of a more worthy name for the new stand."

The Swedish teams Wolves encountered would have been surprised, though, at how Billy whiled away the time while the players trained. The man who was introduced on the pitch before the fourth of the five tour games happily acted as ball-boy during the various drills and practice matches. "Hopefully, all the shots and headers will be on target in the matches," he smiled. "But I'm here to clear up anything wild for now."

Bully, at least, adjusted his sights sufficiently to make an impact. Having previously been to Sweden with both England under-21s and Wolves, he scored three times as this trip began with friendlies on successive nights and would net once more before returning home. His pay at this stage reflected the fact he was essentially a Premier League player operating in the First Division. The wolf, if you'll pardon the pun, was not at his door and he stuck his neck out to say how he thought he could boost his earnings further. "I'm so confident we'll go up that I would bet half of my year's wages on it," he said.

Wolves had been installed as third favourites for the title behind Nottingham Forest and Derby but had a setback when their warm-up programme again took them out of England. Just how much more Steve Bull relied on a bit of brawn than Billy Wright ever had was underlined in a game at Wrexham, where the striker was involved in a clash that left home defender Mel Pejic nursing a gash under his eye. No card was shown but video evidence brought him an FA charge of misconduct and a ban for three matches.

How Billy and Bully would have fared against each other is anyone's guess. They would both have known they had been in a game, that's for sure, and you could argue that the one who played in the 1940s and 1950s had attributes that are more readily associated with the modern-day game while, in the marauding centre-forward who pulled them up by their bootlaces two decades ago, Wolves had a player whose style was a throwback to a more distant era.

Billy was more reliant on his skills than his muscle. He had guile, balance, anticipation and spring. He was pure class, even when switched to centre-half in an era when no 5s, or pivots as they were known, were meant to be big and bad. He would surely have been a legend in any team any time but you can well imagine how Glenn Hoddle, in particular, would have loved him in both his England and Wolves sides for the way, among other things, he could distribute the ball. By the same token, just as Billy warmed to Bully's barnstorming deeds from his seat in the Molineux directors' box in the early 1990s, so Cullis would surely have welcomed to his side a centre-forward who had brawn, bravery, singular vision and an overwhelming desire – qualities which meant he occasionally overstepped the line.

As the pre-season programme continued victoriously, Billy renewed fond acquaintances before a game at Bloomfield Road with his England team-mate Jimmy Armfield, who was Blackpool's vice-president as well as a respected media pundit. But he had a good reason for missing the game at Crewe. He was at Wembley on the same day to present the Charity Shield to Manchester United captain Steve Bruce after their win on penalties against Arsenal.

Despite the glut of captures, Steve Bull was intent on retaining his familiar centre-stage billing. He needed only nine minutes of the first League game to make his mark, sliding towards the magnificent new Billy Wright Stand in celebration of netting a beauty against Bristol City, the only pity being that there were just a few workmen in McAlpine jackets behind the goal to see it.

There was a second goal from the player in the same victory but the club's next home game was even more memorable with Billy officially opening the showpiece £5m structure named after him. Whatever sadness he may have had in watching the bulldozers move in on the Molineux he best remembered, there was no denying that a gleaming new stadium was springing up in its place. It wasn't only Wolves colleagues like Peter Broadbent, Eddie Clamp, Billy Crook, Stan Cullis, Norman Deeley, Malcolm Finlayson, Johnny Hancocks, Bill Shorthouse, Bill Slater, Roy Swinbourne and Bert Williams who turned out on his big night of August 25, 1993. Among the stars from the wider football world who also showed were Bobby Charlton, Bryan Douglas, Ronnie Clayton and Don Howe.

Needless to say, the evening didn't pass without Billy joining The Beverleys in the singing of *'The Happy Wanderer'*, the main man cutting the ribbon and waving happily to a crowd reduced in capacity while the South Bank was still being redeveloped as the Jack Harris Stand. One other big name was present that night – Mick McCarthy. His Millwall side were on to a loser after being reduced to ten men early on and were despatched by Bull's 150th Molineux goal and Kelly's first. Well, it wouldn't have been like the big playing hero of the day to let such an occasion pass unheralded, would it?

Kelly, signed at high cost following his 28-goal contribution to Newcastle's enthralling promotion journey under Kevin Keegan the previous season, was delighted with his strike partner. "The 'Pit Bull' is a tremendous fella to play alongside and we hit it off as mates when we roomed together on the tour of Sweden," he said. "I've played with a few good goalscorers like Mick Quinn at Newcastle and I've never known anyone who works harder. He puts his effort in outside the area as well as in it and there's no-one, Sir Jack included, who wants Premier League football more than he does. This is his club and his town and, with an attitude like his, we must have every chance."

Wolves' high-octane start to the season wasn't long in burning itself out. The opening burst of seven points from three games was followed by a sobering sequence of six matches without a win, during which Bully marked his first appearance as a substitute for the club by lashing in a late Anglo Italian Cup goal against Stoke and netting in his latest return to The Hawthorns. The game against Albion ended in an exciting defeat, though, and there was another down-side with the striker pulling up clutching his hamstring and facing another absence. How much the side still relied on him became clearer as the pressure mounted on Turner despite assurances from Jonathan Hayward that he was not under pressure – 'and never will be while I am chairman.'

There's nothing to suggest Billy Wright was anything other than supportive to the manager in his hour of need. Wolves' board was not a radical one given to knee-jerk reactions, and it's easy to assume the young Hayward adopted Turner as something of a hero, given that he latched on to the club while the goal-filled rise from Division Four, via Wembley, was being masterminded.

Bully was open in his support of the man who had signed him and unleashed him on to an unsuspecting world but, partly through the three-game ban handed to him for his indiscretions at Wrexham in pre-season, he played only one of the next ten matches. Just two of them were won, one a second-leg Coca-Cola Cup success over Swindon which was rendered inadequate because Andy Mutch had helped give the Wiltshire club a two-goal first-leg lead.

Wolves, for all their big spending and gung-ho vocabulary, were 18th in the table after visiting Southend at the end of October. A 1-1 draw there was no great shakes either as they came to terms with the loss of Geoff Thomas to a serious knee injury but at least Bully was fit – and he exploded back to life just when Turner's need was greatest. He scored once in a crisis-easing midweek win over Notts County for which the crowd dipped below 16,000 and then three times to destroy high-riding Derby at the Baseball Ground. It was a stunning performance, from player and team, and a glimpse of what Wolves' talented squad should have been producing on a more regular basis.

The treble took Bull level with Billy Hartill as scorer of the most hat-tricks (16) in Wolves' history and he promised afterwards that the match-ball he was clutching was for his son Jack. "I should have had five goals but three will do," he said of a Sunday TV matinee that inevitably led to renewed calls for his recall by England. It soon became clear that that would no longer be an issue for Graham Taylor, who resigned after a 6-1 away win over San Marino had proved too late to salvage a World Cup finals place from a torturous qualifying campaign. There was already talk of Taylor being eyed as a Wolves manager, although Turner's star rose again in a 12-game unbeaten run that would stretch almost to Christmas and include a terrific Bully brace in a draw at Leicester.

With 11 goals already to his credit in 1993-94, the striker was very much in the groove once more and didn't miss out either in an easy win against Barnstaple in a North Devon bonding break that included a training match between Billy Wright's Invitation XI and Keith Pearson's All Stars on Saunton Sands. But there were fewer smiles when he appeared for the last time in front of a deserted South Bank.

The massive stadium redevelopment was now virtually complete and Wolves had arranged to mark the occasion in some style once they had fulfilled an early, bruising return with Derby. The date with the Rams saw horns locked aggressively and Bull, in his 300th Football League appearance, followed up a first-half equaliser by being caught on the knee by a poor Martin Kuhl challenge that caused him to be led off by physio Paul Darby in a finger-waving fury. Turner, not normally one for brash comments, said he thought his prize asset had been 'assaulted throughout the game.' Another injury worry…..

No-one more deserved to run out in front of a packed and fully open Molineux than the striker but he was soon ruled out of the historic date with prestige opponents. It being almost 39 years to the day since the club, led by Billy Wright, had beaten Honved in arguably the most exciting game ever staged at the ground, the Hungarians were invited for a third visit, having also played a friendly in 1962. They were a big draw, too – or rather the occasion was, tickets selling at twice the rate they had for the televised visit of Derby. Ferenc Puskas, Billy's tormentor-in-chief on the international stage, was asked along, although he must have been left wondering whether this was the same ground as the one he and his team-mates had departed, exhausted, in 1954.

Where smoke had once circled tall floodlight pylons high above cramped stands and terracing that dropped within a few feet of a muddy pitch, he now saw four pristine structures, with the light coming from state-of-the-art lamps on the roof of the Billy Wright and John Ireland Stands. We even had the planned switch-on of the new £200,000 video-wall, complete with 240 TV monitors.

Everything had changed but, if Puskas had looked hard enough, he would at least have seen the famous Molineux clock. Nearing the end of its sixth decade, the timepiece was by now perched on the Stan Cullis Stand rather than the long-demolished zig-zag Molineux Street Stand, the bulldozers having dropped it into the rubble in the late 1970s before its salvation and subsequent overhaul by a firm of Whitchurch specialists.

Puskas was working as an official for the Hungarian FA and flew in separately from the Honved squad who had already been beaten by Manchester United in that season's Champions League. And, despite looking forward to throwing his arms round Billy once more, it's unlikely he would have been able to add much to the meagre knowledge the visitors had of their 1990s hosts.

"All I know about Wolves is that they are very famous and they have Steve Bull," said their Finnish coach Martti Kuusela, understandably unaware of their stirring 3-2 win over Honved before 54,998 enthralled spectators almost four

## The Last Stand

decades earlier. "But the new stadium looks fantastic and we shall enjoy playing there."

This, in many ways, was Jack Harris's night. Long chosen by Sir Jack as the man worthy of having his name on the new stand at the South Bank end of Molineux, he took it upon himself to meet the reigning Hungarian champions at Heathrow and act as guide while they were transported to the West Midlands on Wolves' team coach. Then he lapped up all the nostalgia as 'his' stand was used for the first time. Emotion hung thick in the air as Billy and Puskas, the latter much more portly in these twilight years, embraced at a civic reception the night before the game. Two footballing greats from the 1950s were now both in their late 60s and in the spotlight once again in the 1990s. Flash bulbs went off at 20 to the dozen.

"He was the greatest inside-forward I ever played against," Billy said. "He was a powerful finisher and always seemed to hit the target with his efforts on goal. We have seen each other in the last two or three years at a TV function in Madrid but it's great to see him back at Molineux."

The entire Wolves line-up from the victory were present again, including Leslie Smith, the man who was having a lengthy run on the left wing in 1954 in place of Jimmy Mullen. And, whereas Cullis's men put the Hungarian flame out in those pioneering floodlight days, there was a black-out of more serious proportions 39 years on. An hour before kick-off, Molineux was plunged into semi-darkness by an electrical fault that pushed proceedings back 15 minutes. The PA system and crowd control computer were among the essential devices knocked out of action and food provisions were badly affected. It was not the most auspicious start for the Jack Harris Stand, a safety certificate for which had been obtained only two days earlier.

The video-wall was not switched on after all but, thanks to the willingness of the teams and local referee Terry Holbrook, the game started, albeit in partial light until full power was restored at 8.25pm. Billy and his contemporaries must have seen the irony in how their big night against Honved had gone much more smoothly in front of 54,998 than this version before a 28,041 audience, Wolves' biggest crowd for 13 years.

We were assured there was no truth in the rumour that Sir Jack, amid his £15m rebuild, had simply forgotten to pay the leccy bill! By the time he and Harris did a lap of the perimeter track in an open-topped vehicle to wave to fans at the end of the game, he was just relieved that the big night had not been wiped out. The result was satisfactory, too, as Andy Thompson's equaliser brought a 1-1 draw.

A transformer fault was blamed for the problems but normal power was established for the League game against Watford three days later – and normal service was resumed on the field as a fit-again Bully helped seal a comfortable victory by fittingly becoming the first player to score in front of the now populated Jack Harris Stand. He salvaged another point when bludgeoning the equaliser at Tranmere just after Christmas and went into the New Year on 14 goals – a promising return that kept him propelled towards new targets. "I've got 230 for Wolves but want to make it well over 300 before I'm finished," he said. "I've got a few years in me yet and I want to fill them full of goals."

The following few weeks were bizarre in that Wolves set off on a revitalising run of post-Christmas victories at a time when their main man's own scoring contribution dried up. The goals were shared among others, including the by now restored Thompson and Robbie Dennison, as the side won five games in a row without conceding a single goal.

Draws at Nottingham Forest and Stoke were a reasonable follow-up but Bully was at the start of his longest injury absence to date when Billy Wright celebrated his 70th birthday on February 6, 1994, the day after Wolves had left the Victoria Ground with a point. He had been caught by an awful challenge from behind in the previous weekend's FA Cup victory at Port Vale and was found to have ruptured ligaments and a torn cartilage in his left knee. He was still sidelined when Wolves, having drawn at home to Premiership side Ipswich in the FA Cup, went to Portman Road for the fifth-round replay and won thanks to two first-half goals. Billy, present as usual, was caught on camera leaping out of his seat in celebration but didn't cut such an excited figure when live TV was again there for his club's exit at Chelsea in the quarter-final.

Both Billy and Bully were saddened by the events that followed. Only two nights later, in a cruel run of six away games out of seven for a side having to catch up on their fixtures, Wolves surrendered meekly at Portsmouth in a 3-0 defeat that prompted Jonathan Hayward to stand up and lambast the players as their coach approached Molineux on its return journey.

Graham Turner, unwilling to see his authority undermined in such a way, resigned the following morning. His reign had encompassed all of the games and goals in Bully's Wolves career so far and spanned seven and a half years – long service that was more in keeping with the Wright and Cullis era than

## The Last Stand

the increasingly impatient 1990s, complete as they became with their angry phone-ins.

Bully spoke to Turner urging him to reconsider his decision but found him steadfast. "He called for me in the treatment room to tell me and, as soon as I found out, I shot into the office," the player told me this year. "I more or less pleaded with him not to go and told him not to be hasty. But he said he couldn't stay when he had been humiliated like that. It was the last straw."

Of all the men Wolves could have appointed as Turner's successor, they chose Graham Taylor. He was seen as the man who had ended Bully's England career and he carried a foyer-full of baggage following his unhappy experiences with the national team. He did, however, have a brilliant track record from Lincoln, Watford and Aston Villa of delivering promotion teams and no less a man than Billy Wright quietly said to the Express & Star's representative at a game shortly after the unveiling: "I think we've got it right." It shouldn't be forgotten that Taylor had tried to take Bully from the late 1980s lower divisions to Villa and the manager said early on: "I'm looking forward to working with him and can't wait to have him fit again. Wolves rightly said no to Villa and it's exciting to have the chance to work with him at club level now."

Bully had been out nearly three months by the time he returned in an April 16 win at Notts County in Taylor's sixth game, three of the previous five having been won. He stayed in the line-up for the five that remained but Wolves did what they so often did by threatening to reach the play-offs, then falling short.

Although the striker scored at home to Sunderland, it was a sad end to a season that had started with high spending and high hopes. With 15 goals, he had finished as the club's top marksman for the eighth time in eight years but Wolves had blown a massive chance. And a few months later, it became clear that Billy Wright would never be able to sit in his stand and watch them playing in the Premiership.

## Chapter Eighteen

# Saddest Passing

We didn't know it at the time but June 24, 1994, the day The Queen dropped by to officially open the redeveloped Molineux, was the last time Billy Wright set foot in the ground he illuminated more than any other player. It was in the same month that he and his wife Joy had what she called their last date – a trip to the Chelsea Flower Show. The phrase 'end of an era' was invented for momentous times such as this.

Wolves' best and most famous all-time player must have had some regrets at the complete change in identity of the stadium he knew and loved in his majestic pomp but thank goodness he lived long enough to see how the club had changed with the difficult times and come out of their crisis much, much stronger. Thank goodness, too, that he had been around to be reminded that, while Wolves fans knew how to celebrate the deeds of present-day heroes, they never turned their backs on giants of the past. The showpiece stand which was adorned by Billy's name was almost a year old when the patriotic Sir Jack Hayward decided the job of officially opening the rebuilt ground could only be entrusted only to regal hands.

Not for almost 20 years had The Queen been to the town but, as part of a West Midlands tour that also took her to Dudley and Bully's birthplace Tipton, she agreed to fit in a visit to Wolves and the nearby Dunstall Park racecourse; with conditions, that is. Namely, that a full-length mirror and coat stand be provided for her use in the flat that the Haywards had built for themselves in the Billy Wright Stand.

Beatties fulfilled that need but there was no sign of another Wolverhampton institution on the big day. Steve Bull was away on holiday. As a result, the club – excited that they had become the first ever to have a ground opened by the reigning monarch – lined up Paul Birch, Tony Daley, Graham Taylor, groundsman Bill Pilbeam, long-serving manager's secretary Dot Wooldridge

## Saddest Passing

and former players Ron Flowers, Roy Swinbourne and John Richards as a welcoming committee.

Sir Jack, of course, was her main escort, demonstrating his ability to shine through the formalities by thanking her for wearing a gold hat – even if many observers thought it was tangerine. He also told her to make sure she was at Wembley when Wolves were there for the following season's FA Cup final! There to shake her hand as well, as he had been when receiving the Cup from the then Princess Elizabeth after the 1949 final against Leicester, was Billy. No wonder she said to him: "I know your face, don't I?"

"It has been a tremendous day," Wright said later. "Not only for me and the club but for the town. The Queen's visit has been the icing on the cake for the club." And, with that comment and a lunch hosted for all the dignitaries by Wolverhampton Council in the Hayward Suite, Wolverhampton Wanderers' most famous player retreated from public view for the final time.

His illness had already taken hold but wasn't a matter of public knowledge for another couple of months, during which supporters were counting down excitedly to Taylor's first season in charge. Billy, still well connected in FA circles, looked beyond his own problems to nurture considerable hope for the club at a time when the Molineux spotlight was partly on Taylor's relationship with Bull, the ending of whose international career he had effectively brought about by not playing him again after the autumn of 1990. And some of the new boss's early close-season moves would have found favour with the striker as he went into the transfer market to sign two wingers.

It will take a sea change of Tsunami proportions for Bully's Wolves goals record ever to come under threat but you wonder how many he might have scored had he been born 40 years earlier and played in a more cavalier era in the same team as Billy. True, he would have had some serious competition to dislodge in the likes of Swinbourne, Jimmy Murray and Dennis Wilshaw and he would have been playing only in the top flight but he would surely have been Stan Cullis's type of target-man.

The Iron Manager didn't like fancy-dan footballers and shuddered at the thought of his centre-forward pirouetting off his marker to link up the play. He wanted him stampeding towards goal to make full capital out of Wolves' reliance on fast, direct attacking. And how Bully would have loved to have wingers like Hancocks and Mullen supplying his bullets!

In his 13 years at Molineux, Bull never had the luxury of two quality wingers providing ammunition. Taylor pinned his strategy on just such a policy by gambling on the suspect fitness of the Aston Villa pair of Tony Daley and Steve Froggatt – and losing. Daley suffered a serious knee injury on tour in Sweden before kicking a ball for the club and Froggatt was hurt at Reading in the December and played only a further six matches for the manager.

Under Taylor, though, Wolves had the feel of a big club just waiting to take off. A home friendly with Manchester United, arranged as part of Darren Ferguson's signing the previous winter, attracted 28,145, pulled in record receipts of £228,000 and contained a lovely ninth minute finish from Bully – a lob over the giant Peter Schmeichel. The Premiership champions for the previous two years hit back to equalise through Paul Ince and win 2-1 but Sir Alex Ferguson sensed things were stirring at Molineux. "I like Steve Froggatt and, if Wolves can get Tony Daley fit to create chances for Steve Bull, they should do well," he said. "Looking at the clubs who have come down, I don't think any are better than Wolves but it's a tough division to get out of."

Bull was himself now picking up injuries. He limped off in the follow-up friendly against Coventry with a pulled hamstring on the day he chipped in a beauty for his tenth goal of the pre-season programme. At home to Mark McGhee's Reading the following Saturday, he failed to score on the opening day of a campaign for the first time in five years and, to make matters worse, his troublesome hamstring again forced him off in the first half. This time it was clear he faced a substantial lay-off and he was still on the sidelines when Wolves became a club awash with grief.

It hadn't been widely reported that Billy Wright was seriously ill, although many at the club had a clear idea. And, in a brief emotional visit to see me in the press room after the second home League game of the season, Sir Jack Hayward made it clear the happiest and most famous Wanderer of them all wasn't coming back. "We're losing Billy," he said, choking back tears. "If the paper are planning any special tributes, now is the time."

Wolves, recently back from a successful Anglo Italian journey to the heel of the famous boot, followed up with their first win over Albion in five attempts and then a defeat at Taylor's former club Watford. The manager and his squad were then holed up in their overnight hotel before their game at Sunderland when news came through of Billy's passing at the age of 70.

'Billy Wright Dies At Home' read the main heading on the Express & Star's front page on September 3, 1994. Sir Jack broke down when he spoke of 'a great player, friend and gentleman.' "He was just a wonderful person, England's finest player and gentleman," he said. Billy had been diagnosed with cancer of the stomach a month before The Queen's visit to Molineux.

Joy Beverley quickly set minds at ease by saying the funeral would be in the town where he was most revered. "Billy loved Wolverhampton and its people," she said. "I don't think it would be right to deny them the chance to say goodbye." She said he had died 'peacefully and without any fuss or complaints' at 4.20am at their home in Barnet, North London. Thankfully, he had survived for the arrival in the April of the couple's first grandchild, a daughter Kelly to their own eldest daughter Victoria.

Billy's illness was similar to the one that had taken his brother Lawrence three years earlier, the family last having been together at the funeral of their aunt and uncle, who were tragically overcome by coal fumes at their home in Broseley, near Ironbridge.

Flags at Molineux flew at half mast and Wolves' players wore black armbands as they formed an arc round half of the centre circle for a minute's silence before kick-off at Roker Park. The result seemed secondary at a ground where Billy had featured in some stirring encounters, not least against the Sunderland of Len Shackleton fame in front of 62,000 in 1951. Another clash of the clubs, also in the FA Cup four years later, attracted 55,000, with snow having to be shovelled off the pitch. In 1994, Mark Venus's equaliser earned Taylor's team a lower-key 1-1 draw.

It was the saddest of days and Taylor spoke eloquently in a post-match TV interview on the pitch of a man known to him during his England days as well as over five months at Molineux. Some heart-rending goodbyes lay ahead. The news was felt well beyond the Wolves community, England coach Terry Venables saying of his status as national skipper: "He was a tremendous role model for younger players." Billy's England team-mate Don Howe, later an assistant to Bobby Robson, described himself as 'terribly upset' and The Times' David Miller wrote: "Never in his life did he do a mean thing."

Tributes from those who inhabited the Molineux dressing room in the 1940s and 1950s were predictably fulsome. Ron Flowers, recalling how Billy had put him at ease soon after his own arrival by telling him to call him by his Christian name rather than Mr Wright, said: "He was an unassuming player who enjoyed his privacy. He didn't rant and rave as captain but went in hard and fair and was a very, very good player."

## Billy & Bully

Bert Williams said: "It's a terrible shock. I have known the situation for months and had hoped against hope that this wouldn't happen." And Bill Slater spoke of Billy's global impact by saying: "He was a remarkable player who had many friends in other countries and was respected across the world of football. It's a very serious loss." There had never been an outpouring of emotion at Molineux like it. Almost immediately, scores of scarves, bouquets, messages, photos and shirts were laid outside the stadium's main entrance and fans queued for more than an hour to sign a book of remembrance, alongside which stood a pair of the player's old boots.

Just before the following Saturday's home game against Tranmere, Bill Shorthouse, Eddie Stuart, Billy Crook and Sammy Smyth carried into the centre circle a huge floral tribute in the shape of a gold and black no 5 shirt. Bill Slater, Peter Broadbent, Bert Williams and Ron Flowers did likewise with a design in the form of an England jersey while four Wolves directors carried an arrangement depicting the famous wolf head.

A lone bugler played the last post in the warm sunshine and it was to the refrain of *'The Happy Wanderer'* that Billy's long-time team-mates left the arena, their sad duty done. Visiting Tranmere fans behaved impeccably during solemn formalities that put lumps in 27,000 throats.

Funeral day was the following Monday. The heavens weren't as kind and hundreds stood in silent tribute in the rain as the seven-car funeral cortege pulled quietly away from Molineux at 1.45pm after the vehicle containing the hearse did a slow lap of the pitch. Nearer the town, thousands lined the streets to pay their respects. St Peter's Collegiate Church was full to the rafters as friends from TV and football were joined by MPs, councillors, police leaders and other town officials.

Around 40 members of the Wolves Former Players Association that Billy had helped to set up following Jimmy Mullen's death in 1987 formed a guard of honour, a tape of the Beverleys singing *'Love Me Tender'* providing a moving backdrop during proceedings. Among the chosen hymns was the mournful FA Cup final anthem Abide With Me. The tributes were led by Sir Bobby Charlton, who had also been present at Molineux two days earlier. He described Billy as a leader and a gentleman and someone whose face was always lit up by a smile. "In the 1950s," he said, "he was the heart-throb and glamour boy of football, always immaculately dressed. In today's market, he would have been worth many millions. He was strong in the air and brave and

# Saddest Passing

fair in the tackle. Without question, he had great leadership qualities for both club and country."

Singer Gerry Marsden recited a passage from 'If' – the Rudyard Kipling poem that had also hung on the wall of Graham Turner's office during his Wolves reign – while club secretary Keith Pearson read the lesson.

An all-star gathering hung on their every word and those of the Reverend John Hall-Matthews. As well as Wolves' playing staff, the packed building seated the six pall bearers – Pearson, Sir Jack, Jonathan Hayward, Jack and Jonathan Harris, and club solicitor and director Nic Stones – plus Sir Stanley Matthews, Tom Finney, Nat Lofthouse, Jack Charlton, George Graham, Bill Nicholson, Don Howe, Jimmy Greaves and Frank Clark.

From the TV world came Nick Owen, Gary Newbon, Trevor East and ITV head of sport John Bromley, and they heard renditions by the orchestra and choir of Billy's old school in Ironbridge, by now Telford's Abraham Darby establishment. His was such a rich life and many of the people touched by it were represented in some way on the day he took his last journey. The hearse, with the words 'I Love You' spelled out in flowers along the side, was taken for private cremation afterwards at Bushbury Crematorium, then his ashes were spread on the pitch. Billy Wright was never meant to be far from Molineux. "It's appropriate that this is his final resting place," said his widow.

In the programme for Wolves' next home game, she wrote: "I would like to extend to the people of Wolverhampton all my heartfelt thanks for their caring and kindness. My family and I will forever be in your debt. I would like to tell you how much my darling Billy loved you all. I always said he had two hearts: one at home with me and our children, and one in Wolverhampton."

The couple's daughters said in a message in the same publication: "To all the wonderful people of Wolverhampton, thank you from the bottom of our hearts for all the flowers, teddy bears, shirts, scarves and loving tributes for the best Dad in the world." Why, William Wright even shared the same initials as Wolverhampton Wanderers – it was a match that was meant to be.

Within days, it was reported that a statue of Billy was being considered, as was a posthumous award of the Freedom of the Borough that he and Sir Jack missed out on because of political squabbling in 1993. "The statue is an absolutely wonderful idea," said Joy, adding that she felt overwhelmed by the prospect. Majestic and proud, he would retain a presence at Molineux.

## Chapter Nineteen

# Goals And Nearly Gone

With one Molineux hero laid to rest, another re-emerged with a flourish. Steve Bull, whose last competitive goal had been against Sunderland the previous May, returned for the home game against Southend the day after Billy Wright's funeral and rounded off the scoring in a 5-0 victory that took Wolves top; a position in the table with which Billy had had more than a fleeting acquaintance. Then the striker kept his side there by heading the only goal at Burnley.

During Bully's injury absence, Graham Taylor had signed Mark Walters and Paul Stewart on loan from Liverpool. At the other end of the age scale came the disclosure that young right-back Jamie Smith was being rewarded for his first-team emergence by not only being handed a new contract but also by being watched by England under-21 coach Dave Sexton – news that would have earned Billy's seal of approval.

By now it had emerged that the five-year deal Bully was sitting on had been reduced to three, with his wages increased so as to make up much of the difference. He was said to be in agreement with the change, which did not threaten the testimonial he would be due by completing ten years' service in the 1996-97 campaign. His close pal Andy Thompson was also on renewed terms which made him another beneficiary.

Bully drew enthusiastic praise from Taylor's coach, Steve Harrison, in the confined corridors of Saltergate after his two late goals had salvaged a 3-1 League Cup first-leg victory from the clutches of potential embarrassment against a Chesterfield side in the basement division. The brace meant he had scored 48 goals in 56 cup games for the club. Not that he appeared to be guaranteed a part in the Taylor blueprint. Despite scoring twice against Millwall and then rescuing a point at Stoke while the club were still top, cracks were evident in many areas of the side. And he was taken off for the first time for tactical reasons when the manager sent Neil Emblen on his place at half-time in the home defeat against Luton in early November.

Taylor felt compelled to insist there had been no dressing-room bust-up but appeared to be leaning towards a Kelly-Stewart partnership in attack. A heel injury, different from the one that had necessitated surgery 18 months earlier, took another chunk out of Bully's season, his month-long absence coming as Wolves lost the leadership of the division to Middlesbrough, then regained it and promptly handed it back.

The deficiencies obviously weren't escaping Taylor's attention. In a manic few weeks which appeared to be at odds with the relative transfer-market quiet of the summer, five new players arrived, financed in part by the sale of three surplus-to-requirements midfielders, Paul Cook, Kevin Keen and Chris Marsden, for total fees exceeding £1m. John de Wolf and Don Goodman signed on one early December day, then Brian Law, Gordon Cowans and Jermaine Wright followed. The recruitment frenzy underlined Taylor's view that his side lacked the mental toughness to handle the enormous expectations they were carrying. "Having got to the top of the table, some of the players have found it difficult to cope with the pressure," he said.

The joint £1.7m investment in De Wolf and Goodman made this the heaviest day of spending in Wolves' history, the striker becoming only the fourth seven-figure buy made by the club after Andy Gray, Steve Froggatt and Tony Daley (all from Aston Villa) when valued at £1.1m. Clearly, the former Sunderland man would become another threat to Bully's place if the two of them didn't gel.

Almost immediately, a story broke in the national Press about Wolves supposedly trying to sign Leeds central defender Chris Fairclough by using a certain Molineux striker as bait. Worried fans swamped the club's switchboard and Taylor was sufficiently irritated as to tell reception staff to inform them the report wasn't true. "Steve Bull is going nowhere except into my first team," he said. "The story is pure and absolute fabrication and I know nothing about it. I am very reluctant to feed speculation but the sooner all this ends, the better. It seems to go on and on. First we had the rubbish about there being bust-ups here and now this. I don't think it's as much about speculation as lies."

Taylor was unequivocal in his insistence that Bully was staying and went on to make it clear he had the striker's long-term health in his thoughts as well. "I want Steve fully fit and scoring plenty of goals for Wolves, as he has in the past," he said in the Evening Mail. "And I will continue to stand my ground on another thing: I'm not going to play an unfit or half-fit Bull. I think he is suffering from playing previously when he has not been totally fit and that's partly his fault. He is of an age where he needs to be protected and to play him when he is not ready would be doing no favours to him or to the club."

Chairman Jonathan Hayward said his family were happy to splash out but added: "If Bull and Goodman don't hit it off together, that's when I might call it a day." It was a tongue-in-cheek remark but indicative of how a £1.7m splurge was seen as much more of a gamble a decade and a half ago.

De Wolf, the holder of full international caps, scored from a penalty in a shoot-out against Willem II with his last kick before leaving Feyenoord and delayed his transfer in order to walk on the pitch at their home game the following Sunday to say a tearful farewell to a 32,000 crowd who showered him with flowers. He was described as the biggest character in Dutch football – big enough certainly for the TV station RTL5 to make immediate plans to cover all of Wolves' home and away games and so put some money back in the depleted coffers. Foreign players were still a novelty in 1994 and his arrival at Molineux was a huge story.

The curtain call he took before his adoring supporters meant he missed Wolves' televised Sunday defeat at Millwall in the meantime but underlined that Bully now saw a few big egos as well as big characters when he looked round the dressing room. At The New Den, the side lined up against a team who included Alex Rae and Mark Kennedy and had David Kelly's dismissal as a further headache as they reeled from four defeats in five matches.

De Wolf turned 32 the day he made his Wolves debut at home to bottom club Notts County and, having been described by Taylor as 'a leader of men,' was handed the armband in the absence of the injured Geoff Thomas. Bully was overlooked for the job but continued carrying off the one he had done for eight years. He scooped in the only goal of another fraught afternoon.

The striker then struck in the TV date at Reading the week after but Simon Osborn levelled and Michael Gilkes scored twice to secure a home win a few days after Mark McGhee's Elm Park walk-out. As if to emphasise the changing times, De Wolf made history in the alarming Boxing Day defeat at Oldham by becoming the first Wolves player ordered off to remove his ear-rings.

The side's performances may have been deeply flawed but there were mitigating circumstances. Six players had already undergone surgery during the season and Bully was pencilled in as the seventh when his heel injury worsened and forced him on to the sidelines for an estimated six weeks after he had scored in a comfortable revitalising victory over Charlton.

It had been hoped he would be able to play on into the New Year first but he limped off against Alan Curbishley's team and into his fifth substantial absence in little over 18 months. Much though his game was about aggression and power, it's worth reflecting again on how lucky Billy Wright was by comparison to escape relatively unscathed from an era of heavier pitches, heavier balls, much greater tolerance from referees and no substitutes.

Billy, once established in Wolves' post-war team, never suffered anything like the ten-game absence Bully was now condemned to. By the time the striker returned, he would have missed 56 competitive first-team games in little more than two years, the vast majority of them through injury. It was a far cry from his proud record of not missing a single match on fitness grounds in almost three years at the start of his Molineux service.

Initially, goals came bountifully enough without him – ten in four games – but the next six yielded only five and Taylor brought him back for a visit to Port Vale, anxious as he was to lift the gloom that had descended with a home defeat against Middlesbrough in midweek. Bully's hopes of match practice had been washed out by the postponement of a reserve game just before but he was needed so he played…….a familiar story. And Wolves' fans duly had a hat-trick to celebrate in the sodden Potteries but not from Bull. Never in the Billy Wright era and never, in fact, since Ted 'Cock' Pheasant against Newcastle in 1902 had a central defender scored three times in a game for the club but De Wolf, replaced as captain that day by a fit-again Peter Shirtliff, did just that and even put Bully through to lob a comeback goal as well.

The striker then scored the only goal against Portsmouth and was on the team sheet for both games in the FA Cup quarter-final clashes with Crystal Palace – the most advanced stage of the competition he had ever figured in. Alas, all he could do was admire Palace's explosive finishing power in a 4-1 replay victory in what was his 200th game at Molineux.

That, amazingly, was his fifth comeback of the season as he had missed another game and a bit with a hamstring problem picked up at Albion in March but he kept the promotion candle flickering by taking his tally for 1994-95 into the teens by netting against Burnley a few days before his 30th birthday and followed up with the decider at Southend – his 200th Football League goal.

## Billy & Bully

So many goals, so many stats.........but the issue that most interested Wolves and their fans was whether this was going to be the year the Holy Grail was finally reached. Although only one automatic promotion place was on offer that year because of a restructuring of the divisions, they still had the leaders in their sights as the campaign entered its final month. Unfortunately, Wolves, as if to underline Taylor's early-season remarks about another leak springing as soon as one was plugged, suddenly started shipping goals a few weeks on from the knee injury that had ended De Wolf's contribution in early March. As freely as they scored by hitting three at Luton, Derby and Sheffield United, they let them in at the other end, all three games being drawn.

In between, Bull's two headers at Charlton meant he had topped 200 League goals for the club but a defence reinforced by the capture of Dean Richards crumbled again and a 3-2 defeat left Wolves contemplating the play-off route to the Premiership. Bully (who else?) tucked in the equaliser at Tranmere that got them into overtime – a fitting way to mark his entry into a fifth century of League and cup games for the club.

After six years of trying and failing to graduate from this level, Wolves at least had a foot in the door that led to the big time. The years were creeping up on Bully and there was a hint of impatience as he said before the first leg of the play-off semi-final against Bolton at Molineux: "I still fancy our chances and think we'll be okay. I certainly hope so because I'm fed up of this division."

Taylor's team looked the part as they blitzed the visitors' rearguard and deserved much more than the breakthroughs achieved by headers from Bully and Mark Venus either side of half-time. But Jason McAteer looped in a goal in between for a side for whom Bull's England World Cup colleague Peter Shilton made his one and only appearance, the quality of the keeper's performance restricting Wolves to a 2-1 win. The frailty of the lead was exposed by Bruce Rioch's team in the second leg but there was bitterness when their decisive second goal came from John McGinlay after he had stayed on the field despite blatantly flooring David Kelly with a left hook.

Bully, as he had been twice before, was marooned on 19 goals for the season and, for the first time in nine years, didn't finish as Wolves' leading scorer. Kelly emerged on top of the pile with 22, including a November hat-trick at Bristol City. By coming up with over 40 goals between them, though, the duo appeared to have done their job, even if we looked back at little moments and wondered……

## Goals And Nearly Gone

At Burnden Park, for example, Bully could possibly have made the difference had he not skewed wide an early chance at 0-0. He was heartbroken and that pained pose he struck on the pitch at the end – seated and head bowed – might well have proved to be the last one of him in the colours with which he was synonymous, given the summer bombshell that was to hit Molineux.

The man who had scored 251 goals for the club was controversially up for grabs because, when Coventry bid for him, Taylor agreed a £1.5m deal with his Highfield Road counterpart Ron Atkinson. Despite having tried to take Bull to Villa, Taylor could now clearly visualise a Wolves side without him. Much though he and Stan Cullis may be seen as similar in insisting their sides did not over-elaborate, the younger man appeared to want a striker better able than Bull to play with his back to goal. He had seen Ian Olney perform the role superbly in Villa's sustained title challenge under him in 1989-90 and considered Wolves' style to revolve too much around the no 9.

There is a school of thought that, if Taylor no longer wanted Bull spearheading an attack he had led so spectacularly for almost nine years, he could have eased him out by using him more sparingly in the shadow of his successor. Maybe, though, he worked out that no striker would have the freedom to shine before a Wolves crowd who, if things weren't going to plan, would be chanting Bully's name while he warmed up on the touchline or even sat, suited and booted, in the stand. No tongs had yet been invented for handling potatoes as hot as this because no player in decades – possibly even in Wolves' history given that the Billys, the Mullens, the Slaters, the Dougans and the Richardses had performed in much more successful Molineux times – had garnered such popularity among supporters as Steve Bull.

As a storm began to erupt around him, Taylor said he was merely being honourable by letting Bully speak to the Sky Blues. "I always said that if we didn't go up and a Premiership club came for him, I would tell him," the manager said in the Evening Mail on July 10. "That's happened and I have kept him informed. I'm not pushing him out. I have kept my word and told him what's going on. Now it's his decision."

In the eyes of fans, it didn't help Taylor that he had tried Bully in his England side and deemed him not up to it. The backlash was immediate when the story that Coventry had lodged an official bid broke on July 9, 1995, Atkinson having decided that a man he had also admired from Villa Park would be a good foil for the height of Dion Dublin and the raw pace of Peter Ndlovu.

# Billy & Bully

A hundred times, Wolves fans had seen Bull's name linked with other clubs. This was different, though, because this time there was a willingness for him to be sold. On the very day Wolves' players reported for pre-season training, striker and manager went into talks as a fans' campaign to prevent a parting of the ways was launched. "The first thing that has to be said," Taylor told the Express & Star, "is that no-one at the club wants him to go. Coventry have put in an official bid and it has been discussed by the board here. I was honour-bound to put this to Steve. I am sure no supporter would begrudge him the opportunity I have given him. If people want to criticise me for that, that's up to them. He has spoken to Coventry and it will all hopefully be sorted out in the next day or two. If he wants Premiership football almost on his doorstep, it's there for him. If he wants to stay at Wolves, we will be quite happy to get on with things here."

By accepting a bid of £1.5m, of which a third would go to Albion, Wolves certainly didn't seem to be fighting tooth and nail to keep the player. And why would a promise have been made in the first place to keep him informed of enquiries from the Premier League if he was still as highly valued as he should have been by those in power at Molineux?

Wolves supporters would not have begrudged Bully joining an Everton, a Manchester City or a Tottenham, saddened though they would have been. But they saw Coventry, who already had coach Garry Pendrey and midfielder Paul Cook on their books, as a considerably smaller club than their own – and subsequent events have proved their judgment correct.

There were early signs that the pull of Molineux would prove too great for Bully in the end but three days of anxiety and no little anger lay ahead. It was widely assumed Coventry would not be able to match the estimated £6,000 a week he was on at Wolves and that their three-year offer to him was a way of paying him more over the piece than he would receive from the two years left on his Wanderers contract. Cue another strand to a story that gripped that densely populated corridor between Wolverhampton and Coventry……

Jonathan Hayward took his turn to meet Bully on the Tuesday – a day on which Taylor, who was absent from the talks, set about deflecting flak. "I am heartily sick of rumours that Steve and I don't get on," he said. "One way or another, by the time the season kicks off, this matter should be sorted out once and for all. I have to think of the dressing room and the stories that are continually going on. I have had to bite my tongue but I live in the present, not the past. The England thing is history, it happened nearly five years ago. It's his decision whether or not he goes. If Steve decides he wants to stay, I will be pleased as anyone and we will have laid this thing to rest. Fine."

In a straw poll on the news pages of the Express & Star, fans came down heavily in favour of Wolves keeping their star asset, not least because they thought he was being undervalued at £1.5m. Gordon Davies, from Bilston, said: "There's no way he should go. He is too good for Coventry and worth at least £3m. He has got plenty left in him."

Martin McGrellis, from Seisdon, near Wombourne, said: "I am absolutely gutted. Last season, scoring goals was not a problem. All the trouble was at the other end." Elaine Dodd from Wednesfield said she couldn't imagine Wolves without Bull while her daughter Louise was quoted as saying she would go as far as considering a boycott of games if he left.

It was just after 2pm on Wednesday, July 12 when the super-hero Steve Bull told Graham Taylor he was going nowhere, the press statement Wolves subsequently issued being preceded by minutes by the disclosure from Atkinson to the Coventry Evening Telegraph that the deal was off. What then emerged was that, amid the negotiations, Bully had tried and failed to have a year added to his Molineux contract. His reaction to that development created yet more column inches.

While insisting that he had been unable, when push came to shove, to turn his back on the Wolves masses who idolised him, he opened a new can of worms by revealing: "All I wanted was an extra year on my contract and they wouldn't give it to me. I have had loads of letters and they (the fans) have supported me for nine years. I'm staying because of them.

"I have another two years left and, if the board kick me in the teeth then, I will know where I stand. I have no grudges about the people I play with. It's just the people who run the club. I would like them to have given me a bit more loyalty like I have given them. But I will keep my head down and just give it my best. My heart ruled my head because of the people of the town. I will always give 100 per cent because the fans are people of my own heart. I love them. It was not about the money. It was about loyalty. I was very tempted to go to Coventry but I now hope to have one of the best seasons I have ever had and get Wolves into the Premiership."

Bull, having initially gone to Pendrey's home for talks with Big Ron, rang him to thank him for his interest and tell him 'no deal.' He later said it was the toughest decision he had ever had to make in his career. Atkinson was philosophical. "We always knew it would be an uphill battle," he said. "With the Wolves fans' reaction, it may well have become a pressure situation."

But the former manager has gone a step further with me in a conversation in recent weeks by revealing: "We had agreed a deal with Wolves and I don't quite know why it didn't come off. I understand from having spoken to people like Peter Shirtliff and Gordon Cowans that Bully said his cheerios there and he was about to come. I can only assume he had second thoughts about leaving there.

"Funnily enough, I might have taken him to Manchester United a decade or so before if I had listened to a friend of mine. My accountant Roger said there was a kid at Albion who I ought to sign. They were both from Tipton and that's all Roger was basing his judgement on when he said he must be good. I don't think he'd seen him play."

Leeds, Genoa and Villa had already been strongly linked with Bully and, within hours of the rejection to Coventry, Celtic came in as well. Taylor, who declared himself 'very pleased' that the striker was staying put, sidled over to him on the training ground to tell him, knowing full well what the answer would be.

## Chapter Twenty

# Born Again

Steve Bull got back to business in the way he knew best by scoring in Wolves' opening two pre-season friendlies and also netted on the opening day of the campaign in a second draw at Tranmere in the space of three months. It proved to be his only goal in the first five matches, though, as the side's form wavered and hit a downturn when they were beaten at Mark McGhee's Leicester.

A brace for the striker in a big home win over Grimsby promised better things but it was the end of October before his total clicked on to four. It was his slowest ever start to a Wolves season and Taylor, having signed experienced South African striker Mark Williams in the summer, was under fire. Wolves were 18th and the travelling fans unusually massed between the dug-outs and the directors' box for the follow-up defeat at Barnsley turned on Jonathan Hayward. There were loud calls for Taylor's removal and several hundred fans staged a post-match protest outside that was dispersed by police on horseback.

The manager's response, before a Coca-Cola Cup replay at Charlton, was to drop Bully for the first time in his 255-goal Wolves career. The striker had been named as a substitute against Stoke earlier in the season after completing a two-match ban following a sending-off versus Norwich but this was new territory. The mood was lightened both by the presentation to the Haywards of a bust of Billy Wright by sculptor John Lamont and by a 2-1 win at The Valley, where Taylor said of his team selection: "You have to take these decisions. We have been struggling to score goals and I thought we looked quite bright in this game. But Steve played his part when he went on for extra-time."

Predictably, Bully's name was regularly chanted in South London – just the sort of reaction his manager had expected. It was a reminder of how a Wolves XI with a fit Bully on the outside looking in might never work. And he didn't intend recalling him for the next game as a solution to the thorny dilemma.

## Billy & Bully

Following the tie, Hayward Jnr caught a small private plane to Newcastle en route for his home in the border country and composed a column for the programme that would three days later be read as an anguished release of his feelings. Wolves were playing Charlton again on the Sunday, this time in the League, and his words were of jaw-dropping significance.

"Last Saturday (at Barnsley), I felt as low as I have ever done in the five years I have been involved at Wolves," he wrote. "I spent the early hours of Sunday morning asking myself some fundamental questions. Why have I spent the last five years putting this club before my young family? Why have I put this club before my health? Have I got the guts to make hard decisions? Have I got the vision to make the right decisions?"

His words were bizarre in as much as they seemed to be an admission that he was considering sacking Taylor, Sir Jack having spoken in the week about the 'hell' the family were going through. The manager is said to have offered his resignation before that live TV date but had it declined, only for Wolves' miserable performance in a 0-0 draw against a team reduced to ten men before half-time to keep the subject of his future at the forefront of everyone's mind.

Another post-match demonstration by fans, this one noisier and bigger, turned up the pressure and the manager, who had vowed after the game to battle on, was summoned next day to a meeting with Hayward that dragged on for several hours. It was mainly a discussion about the terms of severance. Taylor appeared in the press room around 3.30pm to read a statement that confirmed his 594-day reign was over.

Jonathan Hayward said: "I had faith in him right up until the Barnsley game, then my confidence was shattered." The parting with others at Molineux wasn't easy because Taylor was well liked by those around him and had no trouble filling his office when he called a farewell get-together of administrative staff shortly afterwards and cracked open a couple of bottles of wine. So, despite being the man who almost sold Steve Bull, did he go too soon?

Bully has since gone on record to say he did and the bald facts are that the manager had taken Wolves to their highest finish in the League ladder (fourth in the second grade) since 1984, further in the Coca-Cola Cup (the last 16) since they had last won the competition in 1980 and further in the FA Cup (to a home quarter-final replay) than they had been for 14 years. The lamentable subsequent struggles to win promotion inevitably added weight to the theory that the club acted too hastily and that all would eventually have come right. I

# Born Again

applauded his appointment but, much as I liked him, I can't say my faith in him, as manager, was anything other than dented by the time he went.

For a man who likes to build clubs, his reign was very messy. The football wasn't attractive with or without Tony Daley and Steve Froggatt, the two wingers with suspect fitness records on whom he had based much of his strategy, and he always seemed to be papering over cracks. There was rarely consistency of performance or the feeling the side were in control. That said, he might have got Wolves promoted in one had serious injuries not deprived him of Mike Stowell, John de Wolf, Peter Shirtliff, Geoff Thomas, Daley, Don Goodman, Froggatt and Bully himself – all big players. And we should always recognise him as the driving force behind the new training ground.

He was a man with a vision for the whole club, the magnificent Compton training ground complex bearing Sir Jack Hayward's name having his fingerprints all over it – a fact recognised when he was invited back to its opening in 2005. He traced the decline of several clubs other than Wolves back to when they had lost their own training headquarters and saw a quality work environment for players as a must.

Taylor visualised himself working for Wolves for many years and planned to move from Sutton Coldfield with his wife into the area, maybe to Tettenhall, and one day take a role upstairs, with someone else in charge of the team. The chance didn't materialise, though, and Molineux had become an unpleasant place in the late autumn of 1995, with fans' patience undeniably reduced by the Bully-Coventry saga. By presiding over the proposed sale of the unimaginably loyal star player, Taylor had opened a can of worms and the stench was soon overpowering.

No sooner had Taylor gone than Bully was scoring again, at Huddersfield first – the 50th club ground on which he had netted for them in competitive games – and then at Luton while Bobby Downes and Robert Kelly were in caretaker control. But he left the goal-grabbing honours to Darren Ferguson and Mark Venus when Coventry, the club in whose colours he might by now have been playing, were beaten on a riveting Coca-Cola Cup night at Molineux.

Among the men touted as possible successors were Gordon Strachan, Ron Atkinson, Steve Bruce, Chris Waddle, Bryan Robson, Ray Wilkins, Joe Kinnear, Danny Wilson and even Mick McCarthy, then at Millwall. But one name was being mentioned ever more loudly. In joining Leicester the previous winter, Mark McGhee had gone back on his word and jumped ship after developing a rapidly rising Reading side. Now, in order to join Wolves, it seemed he was prepared to do the same. His work at Filbert Street had furthered his reputation despite relegation from the top division and there were even supportive words from Alex Ferguson, his former Aberdeen manager.

McGhee described Wolves as five years ahead of Leicester in terms of development and his employers-in-waiting certainly went the extra mile, eventually agreeing to the East Midlanders' compensation demands of around £500,000 – a sum that covered the recruitment of no 2 Colin Lee and assistant coach Mike Hickman as well. All three had had to resign, though, and a lot of bad blood was spilled along the M69 and M6 with the upheaval.

"I now hope Wolves get relegated and I speak for all the players," said Steve Walsh, the robust skipper with whom Steve Bull had famously tangled more than once. It was a remark the centre-half later qualified by saying he meant no particular ill to Wolves, only to the manager who was about to join them.

Much as Wolves fans were thirsting for a more attractive brand of football, Jonathan Hayward might have been better advised not to kid along the assembled media on unveiling day by saying: "And, now, I'm pleased to introduce the new manager of Wolverhampton Wanderers…….Dave Bassett. I mean Mark McGhee." Two and a half years later, Bassett was taking Nottingham Forest to automatic promotion while the McGhee reign was on its last legs in the middle of the Championship.

The Scot, who signed a contract for more than three years, would have plenty of those 'Doh, did he have to say that?' moments of his own. His opening gambits were music to the ears of Steve Bull lovers, though, especially those who might have been fearing that the striker's direct style would not mix with his new boss's possession football philosophy.

McGhee appeared on a Radio WM phone-in to predict big things for the two together, saying: "As far as I'm concerned, Steve Bull has 100 goals left in him for this club. It's entirely up to him. If he has the desire to continue playing for Wolves, he has a major part to play in the next three or four years. This business of his age is a joke. And to say I don't want him because he won't fit into my style is rubbish. He is a quality player who will respond to good football and will enjoy the style we play. I moved from Celtic to Newcastle at 32 and went on to score 26 or 27 goals in my first year. Steve is 30 and we feel we can get as much out of him as anyone. He's a better scorer than I ever was."

The manager made it clear he was retaining Bully as captain despite the return to fitness of John de Wolf, who had caused ructions during Wolves' spell under caretaker control by refusing to play in a Central League match. Around the same time came confirmation of further posthumous recognition of a man who had worn the no 5 shirt without a flicker of such controversy.

Just over a year on from his death, Billy Wright was being honoured with the building of a £50,000 bronze statue by Warwickshire artist James Butler. The Snow Hill area of Wolverhampton, as well as Molineux, was under consideration as a site but the Mayor, Councillor Margaret Benton, assured fans: "I feel the design selected would please everyone who remembers him. The pose of him leading his Wolves team out is so fitting."

McGhee's reign began bizarrely with three successive home matches followed by three consecutive away derbies – a run that would have stretched to four had a New Year's Day trip to Birmingham not been postponed. After an opening-day flop against Port Vale, the Scot collected his first point when Bully hit a beauty against McCarthy's Millwall. Given that the Londoners had lost their previous five matches, it was a disappointing result, although Bull's brilliant early volley on the turn was described as his best goal for years.

Bully was on target again in another draw, this time from 2-0 up against Portsmouth, to suggest all was well within his own world, even if the side he was captaining were taking time to adjust to new methods. The point was underlined when a tremendous looping header from near the edge of the area in the draw at Birmingham brought him his 50th goal in cup competitions and first FA Cup goal for three years.

McGhee gave an early indication of the abrasiveness he would occasionally extend towards opposing clubs when, before the tie at St Andrew's, he said of Birmingham: "Nobody should be kidded. They aren't a great side by any means." He qualified the remark by saying the same of his own team, which was just as well as Wolves trailed their third-in-the-table near-neighbours by 17 places. After the League Cup quarter-final defeat against Aston Villa, he used graphic language to sum up Wolves' placing in the bottom third by saying it was a 'disgrace' they were so low in the table. On this occasion, though, he was emphasising that they had much more in them, judging by the quality of their performance against Premiership opponents.

Bully played at Villa Park against the club he might well have joined several years earlier and, after a goalless draw at Albion in which Mike Stowell saved Andy Hunt's penalty, continued his bright start under new management by grabbing one of the goals by which Wolves overcame Blues in their Cup replay – and another when Tranmere were sent away from Molineux point-less.

By scoring seven times in less than two months since Taylor's departure, he had dwarfed the output of four goals he had managed while the former England manager was in charge for the first three months of the campaign. "There are elements of his game people have questioned," McGhee said. "But I think he now knows our belief in him is genuine. He is a good player and he's showing it again."

There was a whiff of a first competitive reunion between Bully and his first Molineux boss Graham Turner when Wolves were paired with Hereford or Tottenham as their reward for overcoming Barry Fry's Blues in the FA Cup. It nearly came to pass, too, as the underdogs did everything but win at Edgar Street, only to lose in a replay to opponents who also took care of Wolves at the second attempt during a snowy snap.

The next entries Bully made on the score-sheet, in mid-February, were the stuff of pure legend. If young Joe Bull ever asks "Dad, what did you do on the day I was born?", he had better pull up a chair because it's quite a story. For a player who dealt in hat-tricks in record-breaking numbers, this was one of a kind. The striker's weekend began normally enough as he stepped aboard Wolves' team coach on Friday afternoon for their game at Norwich. No sooner had the squad arrived at their hotel in East Anglia, though, than he received a call informing him he had better turn round pretty quickly if he wished to be present at the birth of his second child.

He set off westwards in a taxi at 6.45pm and arrived at Stafford District General Hospital three hours later – in good time to see wife Julie give birth to a brother for three-year-old Jack at 5.50am next day. The 6lb 4oz bundle of good news would have been enough to sustain mere mortals for a few days. But Steve Bull didn't quite think his work had been done.

After the luxury of a single hour's sleep, he had a breakfast-time bath and made the round of 'It's a boy' phone calls before zipping up his bags once more and being picked up just after 8.30am, this time by Wolves commercial manager Gary Leaver at the wheel of manager Mark McGhee's club Jaguar. Bully managed a nap on the 200-mile trip back to Norfolk and had a spring in his step as he walked back into the hotel, with the management determined to keep his exhausting movements a secret to their opponents.

Events at Carrow Road, given the build-up, were astounding. The striker

# Born Again

scored twice in the first half, first with a brilliant 25-yard chip that underlined the feeling he was adding more craft to his game. Gary Megson's Norwich, who pulled back to 2-2, had won only once in 17 games and that was confirmed as one in 18 by Don Goodman's second-half decider.

Even reporters who thought they had heard it all were flabbergasted by what McGhee told them in his press conference. "He's unbelievable," the manager said. "We would have accepted it if he had said he didn't want to travel back for the match after what he had been through. His commitment is invaluable." Bully, having bagged his sixth and seventh goals of the Scot's 13-game reign, wondered what all the fuss was about when asked for his reaction. "The baby's fine," he said. "It was all a bit of a rush but it has been a great day. I've scored two goals and become a father again – that's quite a hat-trick." How different his emotions were from when he was sent off against Norwich in the autumn.

He scored again when Leicester visited Molineux in the midweek but Iwan Roberts equalised and two goals by Emile Heskey bore out the theory that the game, based on Steve Walsh's words a few weeks earlier, probably meant more to the East Midlanders than it did to their mid-table hosts. Bully was by now sensing Wolves had too much to do to make even the play-offs and was again looking for crumbs of consolation. One came with his opportunist winner at Millwall, another when he stunned Birmingham at Molineux in the fourth meeting of the clubs in two and a half months with a late deciding goal he subsequently described as the best he had ever scored for the club.

"Simon Osborn played the ball through from midfield and I hit it on the run," he said in his 2003 book *'My Memories Of Wolves'*. "I was almost lying down when I struck the ball and, whenever I see the goal again, it makes the hairs stand up on the back of my neck. The Birmingham fans had given me a lot of stick, particularly when their team were in front, so that was the best possible way to answer them."

What he most craved, though, was evidence that the club could challenge strongly for promotion the following year, which made an eight-game run-in comprising four defeats and four draws hard to stomach. He scored only once in that stretch and the team managed a pathetic four goals as 1995-96 went downhill and Don Goodman, with 20, did what David Kelly had done 12 months earlier and beat him to the mantle as the club's leading marksman.

Chapter Twenty-One

# Last Chance Saloon

Wolves had gone through six seasons and tried three managers since last winning promotion and the 31-year-old Steve Bull probably sensed in the summer of 1996 that he had one final chance to make a telling impact for the club in the Premiership – one that hinged on Mark McGhee's ability to recruit expertly in the transfer market. If the Scot got it wrong, Bully's big dream would go up in smoke with a few more cheque stubs.

The club had limped feebly across the finishing line in 20th place, looking up in their despair at the likes of Tranmere, Southend, Oldham and Grimsby. The lowest final placing Billy Wright had known in 20 years as a player was 16th in 1951-52 and that, of course, was in the top flight, so it appeared either that new players were now needed or McGhee's coach Colin Lee had to work wonders with the existing ones. In, during their Molineux summer, came central defenders Keith Curle and Adrian Williams, full-back Serge Romano and a battering-ram strike partner for Bully, Iwan Roberts. With Simon Osborn and Steve Corica added the previous winter, there was considerable new blood, albeit some of it quickly spilled as Williams joined Tony Daley in being flown home with an injury picked up on the club's pre-season tour of Austria.

Curle subsequently went lame with a calf problem that restricted him to one appearance before Christmas and it all added up to a depressingly familiar tale of woe to which Bully came up with an equally habitual antidote in the form of a first-day hat-trick at Grimsby. It was the 17th time he had achieved the feat for the club and meant he was the outright holder of another Molineux record, Billy Hartill having had 16 Wolves trebles to his name.

There was a curious twist to the post-match exchanges at Blundell Park, with the hero of this and many another day tipping his club for relegation, so tired was he of backing them for promotion and seeing them fall short. He repeated the prediction after hitting the only goal against Bradford seven days later, then went into his shell and found no-one else able to step up to the plate.

Bully was in a mini famine of five games without a goal when the spotlight switched once more to Billy Wright on September 12. Amid some ordinary performances, Wolves had faded after their winning start by the time several hundred fans assembled in front of Molineux on a sunny Thursday lunchtime that McGhee succinctly said could have brought a tear to a glass eye.

Ron Flowers, Bert Williams and Stan Cullis, whose combined total of England caps came in exactly 20 short of a certain team-mate's individual tally at 85, formed a semi-circle as Joy Beverley took the wraps off a magnificent £50,000 statue to her husband. "It's fitting Billy should be honoured in this way," she said. "He was a great man. All over the world, he was admired and loved and he always played the game fairly." A rendition of *'The Happy Wanderer'* followed from The Beverleys, members of the crowd joining in as they blinked and marvelled at this wonderful addition to the Waterloo Road landscape, all nine foot of Wulfrunian pride as it was. How Wolves could now have done with him pulling on that shirt, taking the ball and leading them out.

"It's a fitting tribute," said Cullis, by then 79. "I'm very proud to be associated with someone I had a great deal of time for." From keeper Malcolm Finlayson came an interesting take. "Billy would probably have wondered what all the fuss was about," he said. "He was an unassuming, modest bloke really. He would be amazed at all this commotion but the statue looks superb."

As Sir Jack Hayward enthused at this 'wonderful likeness to Billy for all to see for all time,' Joy wandered among the spectators. At her side was her second grandchild, a 14-month-old lad given the name of William. And while the area started to clear, Steve Bull was upstairs in Molineux's corporate areas hosting winners of an Express & Star competition over lunch. Bully and his team-mates seemed inspired as they won 4-2 at Albion three days later, the captain's goal being overshadowed by three from Roberts in the club's first Black Country derby win in four attempts. But the follow-up was discouraging – three defeats out of four – and they were struggling desperately at home.

Sheffield United, Bolton and Reading all came and conquered and, when Wolves also allowed Port Vale to escape with three points in mid-October, they were the joint lowest home scorers in the entire Nationwide League. Their output going back to the previous spring stood at a pathetic six goals in ten games – and that total included two penalties and a Bully winner against Bradford with a striker, Carl Shutt, as acting keeper.

# Billy & Bully

Conversely, away results were excellent – and needed to be. After a Friday night success at Swindon, Bully scored once at Southend and twice at Portsmouth to harvest four more points and, on a personal note, set up the televised trip to Manchester City at the end of October as another special day. His first 477 Wolves games had brought him the small matter of 279 goals and there was still time before his tenth Molineux anniversary for him to write another piece of history. Starved of possession and support when used as a lone striker at Maine Road, he lit up an otherwise miserable 400th League game for Wolves by latching on to a chance 11 minutes from time and brilliantly rifling in the decider.

Quotes from Steve Coppell as City manager are few and far between as he lasted only 33 days in the post but he said: "If you stop Steve Bull, you have probably gone 75-80 per cent towards stopping Wolves. My centre-halves did very well but the ball skipped away from Kit Symons once and I knew where it was going to finish. Bully worked his socks off as the lone front man and that's the quality I have to bring here." Beyond earning Wolves three points, there was much significance about the goal. It was his 280th for the club and so took him past Albion legend Tony Brown as the highest scorer of all time for any of the West Midlands clubs. Brown had coached Bully as a member of the Hawthorns backroom staff just over a decade earlier and was generous in his praise when summoned to Molineux for a photo call the next day.

"I am sure Steve will go well ahead of my total now," he said. "He could go on to finish with around 350 if he stays at Wolves for another few years – and good luck to him. Records are there to be broken and I said a few months ago that this one was going to Steve. I'm very pleased for him and admire him greatly for what he has done. He's a genuine lad with great loyalty and he's a genuine goalscorer. I watched the match on TV and it was the only real chance he had. Typical of him, he put it in."

Brown expressed the hope that Bully would go on to play in the Premiership because 'he will regret it in the future if he doesn't.' As for the Wolves striker himself, he was as economical with his words as he was becoming in his chance-taking. "I get paid to do a job – that is to score goals," he said. "It was a case of one chance, one goal for me."

Bully reached double figures for the season by netting against Barnsley six days later and quickly added to his tally by scoring against Birmingham. But three successive home games post-City brought only two points and it was typical of Wolves' season that the grumblings of discontent were repelled only with a thrilling win away to a Crystal Palace side containing Kevin Muscat, Marc Edworthy, Dougie Freedman and George Ndah.

Billy Wright's name figured in the headlines again in the meantime and November 20, 1996 was not a day that sat easily with his legions of admirers. Exactly ten years on from the morning on which Steve Bull signed at Wolves, memorabilia belonging to the club's most famous player were sold at a Christie's auction held in buildings at 164/166 Bath Street, Glasgow.

Many would have preferred such heart-stirring souvenirs of a playing life dedicated to Wolverhampton Wanderers and England to have gone on view for the masses if the Wright family were correctly advised in deciding they were a potential target for burglars. After all, the reception area of the stand bearing Billy's name already had superb showcase cabinets while, one floor up, was Billy's Boot Room – a stylish facility paying homage to him and frequented for pre-dinner drinks by users of the adjacent Sir Jack's Restaurant. Joy Beverley let it be known, though, that her husband had agreed shortly before his death to the sale. And, in the city in which he remained unbeaten in six trips with England, sell they did, spectacularly and rapidly, in some cases for more than ten times their reserve price.

One buyer bought around £30,000 worth of Wolves and England history, including, for £14,500, a two-handled gilt trophy presented to Billy by guests at the 1959 banquet staged in commemoration of his 100 caps. The item had been expected to fetch around £7,000, so bidding was started at £3,200, only to rise very quickly. The same purchaser walked away with the first of the 68 lots, the skipper's 1949 FA Cup winners' medal (for £5,000), and his three League Championship winners' medals went for £3,400 (1954), £3,000 (1958) and £4,000 (1959).

A rose bowl, also handed over in recognition of Billy's England 'century,' realised £7,200 – more than ten times its expected price – and there was a similar mark-up on a cap awarded for his participation in the Home Internationals for the last time, the £8,000 purchase price coming in more than £7,000 higher than expected. At least the cap presented to him after the international against Ireland in 1948-49 went for £1,050 into Wolverhampton hands, the buyer saying: "I have been a supporter since 1945 and I'm just so pleased to have got one of Billy's caps. He was very special." Even caps from two of England's most notorious defeats, against the USA in the 1950 World

Cup and Hungary at Wembley three years later, raised four-figure amounts.

The couple's North London home might have become safer with the auction. A bank account or two also changed for the better. Some £101,530 – a record for a footballer's private collection – had been raised by bedecking mantelpieces in several mystery locations around the country with some of the English game's most valuable souvenirs. "It was upsetting to see the keepsakes sold," said Steve Gordos, the Express & Star sports editor who was despatched to report on the day's events. "I was horrified. As someone who had been there to see Billy win his 100th England cap and lift the Championship at Molineux in the same year, I found it very sad. What a pity they couldn't have gone on show at Molineux, elsewhere in the town or in Ironbridge, his birthplace."

The memorabilia trade grew quickly in the 1990s and remains strong, the 1951-52 England cap presented to Billy following the game against Wales raising £2,500 (almost double its recommended value) at a Bonhams auction at Chester in the summer of 2009. The headwear was among 38 items put up for a sale by a mystery fan, who also decided to part with a pair of gloves and a tie worn by Joy and Billy respectively on their wedding day.

The jaw-dropping 1996 sale of family silver was at least followed by a big win at Molineux against Manchester City. It was Wolves' first home victory in eight attempts since the unveiling of Billy's statue and, despite subsequent losses when Oldham and Portsmouth came visiting, a corner was finally turned, McGhee's side taking maximum points from four consecutive home matches, including Albion. Bully was relatively quiet in mid-season but stepped up a couple of gears by driving in a last-minute winner at Sheffield United and adding goals in wins over Swindon and Stoke that took Wolves second behind Bolton. When he netted in another victory at Huddersfield next time out to take his tally for the season to 17, promotion seemed very much on.

"The only thing he got real pleasure from was scoring goals," McGhee said in more recent years. "Take away his tally or reduce it by 50 per cent and in certain situations, Wolves would have been down and out. He would have got to his tally in the Premiership week in week out, no doubt about it."

The other side of a winter break in La Manga and a dismal homecoming against Crystal Palace, the flame burned more brightly still still when the striker was among the scorers in a fine win away to arch-rivals Barnsley. And two more victories were just around the corner against Birmingham and Tranmere, with Bully totalling three goals in them and taking his career total in club and international football to 300 with the first of his brace against the Merseysiders.

He had also gone past the 20 mark for the first time in five seasons and had the bit between his teeth, only for a moment's indiscipline in a game at Oldham on March 15 to prove costly. Having hit his tenth goal in ten games, he retaliated against central defender Craig Fleming with a push that was deemed a red-card offence. It was 1-1 when referee Roy Pearson made his fateful decision at the end of the first half and, although Wolves should still have had enough about them to emerge with something from the bottom club, a goal at the other end three minutes from time condemned them to defeat.

No-one can go through a career without a blemish, not even a bloke who scores 306 goals in 561 games, and this was not Steve Bull's proudest hour. It's impossible to know how the never-even-booked Billy Wright would have reacted to the provocation of a defender who had a brief loan spell at Molineux nearly a decade later but Wolves could well have done with their skipper and no 9 staying on the field that afternoon.

Even before the start of a three-match suspension doled out for the fifth sending-off of his career, the side lost at both Stoke and Bradford as well; a run of 12 wins in 18 League games had been followed by three defeats in three matches. The door was open for Danny Wilson's Barnsley to take second spot and Bully was powerless to prevent them striding through despite a goal on his comeback in a thumping win over Southend. He managed just that one goal in his last eight matches of the season and another promotion challenge faltered in the play-offs, this time against Crystal Palace. In 1995, it was that seated pose at Bolton that haunted Wolves fans. The expression photographers captured two years later was one of even greater desolation and dejection.

His 23 goals made him the club's top scorer for a tenth and last time but, in terms of aspiring to play at the top level, the game was virtually up. Even if Wolves won promotion the following year, he would be almost as close to his 34th birthday as his 33rd one by the time they reached their promised land and would he be in the right state to do himself justice there?

Steve Bull, directed to Molineux's departure lounge by Graham Taylor, only to then tear up his ticket at the gate, had nevertheless bounced back in a big way. Two subsequent seasons had brought him 40 goals and taken him close to a hundred ahead of John Richards, Wolves' second highest scorer of all time. But change was still in the air – and by no means all of it was for the better.

The summer of 1997 was the one in which Sir Jack Hayward rocked the club to their foundations with his 'golden tit' outburst, having exasperatedly reached the point at which, following seven years of pumping in money, he feared he was becoming a soft touch; a push-over both for his son Jonathan, in the chairman's office, and for McGhee a few doors down the corridor.

Hayward reined in considerably and ran the club along more business-like lines. In other words, the books would have to balance and the manager would need to generate his own spending money. So, with the funds accrued when Bully waved off another strike partner, the moderately successful Roberts, McGhee got down to work. Extensively travelled though Billy Wright was with club and country, he could always be sure of returning to Molineux and hearing English as the only language spoken. In the six years that followed his passing, though, Wolves went from being foreigner-free to signing John de Wolf, Mark Williams, Serge Romano, Hans Segers, Robbie Van Der Laan, Jens Dowe, Mixu Paatelainen, Dariusz Kubicki, Jesus Sanjuan, Isidro Diaz, Robert Niestroj, Fernando Gomez and Haavard Flo, as well as Australians aplenty.

For many years, Bully had known the Molineux dressing room to be overwhelmingly dominated by British players and had had trouble even with the Mutchs and Dennisons when it came to communication! Now, thanks to McGhee's recruiting, he was playing alongside most of these imports from Europe and beyond and even having his place threatened by one or two. It was all rather bewildering, too, for Wolves fans, who were haunted for a long while by another of the deals, namely the decision to send Mark Venus, one of Bully's long-time Wolves pals, plus £150,000 to Ipswich in return for Steve Sedgley. It proved to be a grossly ill-considered piece of business.

McGhee, with Sir Jack's outburst in mind, called it 'the mother of all summers of discontent' in his programme notes for the first home game of the season, although such disharmony clearly didn't diminish his confidence. He still felt he had the makings of a squad who could not only challenge for automatic promotion but also 'just about be good enough' to survive once they made it. When quizzed again on the subject a few weeks later, he said he would put his house on the club going up.

One other change was made and, true to form, there was no protest from Bully when McGhee announced his decision to take the captaincy off him and hand it to Keith Curle. The manager had said 18 months earlier that Bully would always be his skipper but, as from Wolves' pre-season tour of Scotland, he would no longer fulfil a role Billy Wright had until the very end.

## Last Chance Saloon

"Steve has enjoyed his time as captain and has risen to the job but he knows this is a huge year for us and he wants to concentrate his mind on scoring more goals than last season," McGhee said. "For that reason, he might need to be a bit more selfish and not have to think so much about his team-mates. He will be free of the extra responsibility he has had in the past. He will retain the club captaincy, though. That means he will still be a point of contact for me and no doubt be seen as an ambassador when he's out and about. Keith Curle plays in a position which better lends itself to organising a side. He is a natural organiser and motivator and is good at marshalling the players round him. Bully is more a leader by example and I'm sure he'll still be an inspiration to the other lads."

Wolves fans hardly needed to show again how much they appreciated a man who was about to embark on his 11th full season with the club. Nevertheless, they had another chance that summer as the predictably successful testimonial year marking his decade at Molineux culminated in a game against the legendary Brazilians Santos on the final Sunday before the campaign dawned. The turn-out of 20,871 was disappointing. It would have been fitting for Bully to walk out as he did, with his eldest son Jack holding his hand and his youngest Joe in his arms, and see every one of those gold and black seats occupied. His great pal Andy Thompson had been honoured by a 24,000 crowd at his game against Chelsea 12 months earlier, with the respective ticket prices seen as a factor behind the difference.

But the acclaim for a striker now within three dozen games of Billy's Wolves tally of 541 was unmistakeable on a day that featured a Samba band and a former players parade led by Graham Turner. "Later, I had my MBE and the stand named after me but that was one of my best days," the player told me this autumn. "It was superb and put a little tear in my eye if I'm honest. When I signed, having been told my knee wouldn't stand up to pro football, I never thought I'd be fit enough to spend ten years at one club for a start.

"There were times over the seasons that I thought my knee was locking up and I wondered whether my time was up. After a hard tackle, the floating bone would pop out and I'd push it back in. You can see me doing it if you look closely at some of the games on dvd and video. So you can imagine how I felt that day against Santos about how well things had gone for me for so long – and then to have my two lads with me as I walked out."

Bully, at 32, was not far off twice the age of the team-mate who lit up the early weeks of the 1997-98 season. Robbie Keane, just past his 17th birthday, scored twice in an opening-day win at Norwich and netted two, as did his senior partner, in a home victory over Bury three weeks later that fell several hours before Princess Diana's death. When Bull completed another brace, this time in the home win over Charlton, it meant he had left John Richards's 15-year Wolves record of 194 goals exactly 100 behind. There were worrying defeats, too, but Bully scored in four successive League home matches, the last of them against Huddersfield taking his goal tally for Wolves and Albion to exactly 300 and suggesting it was business as usual for him.

Troubled times lay around the corner, though. McGhee, his position under increased scrutiny after he appeared to mouth obscenities to supporters after a home draw, was waiting to eat into the money he had raised by selling Neil Emblen when he pulled off his best deal as Wolves manager, signing Dougie Freedman and Kevin Muscat from Crystal Palace in exchange for home-grown right-back Jamie Smith. Freedman immediately clicked – and needed to. Bully was sent off for the sixth and final time in his career during the new duo's debut at home to Swindon and, having added to a League tally standing at six with his first cup goals in 21 months, was then diagnosed with a bone spur in his left knee – a condition that required a substantial operation in the November.

Richards knew all about such problems, having had one cartilage operation and two lots of cleaning-out surgery, all on his right knee. "People talk about the mental torment of endless recuperation and the risk to your well-being in later life," he said. "But, at the time, I'm not sure you think that way. Very few footballers think long-term. It's all about the next game, then the one after that. You always want to play."

It was over three months before Bully played again and, in the meantime, Wolves did what they so often did in that division by bobbing around on the fringe of the promotion race without breaking in at the forefront of it. With goals coming reasonably freely in his absence, supporters were reluctantly having to consider a Wolves without him but a few curtain calls still lay ahead and, when he returned to first-team action in mid-February, he added another magical chapter to his story. Without the luxury even of a reserve game by way of a warm-up, he was sent on for the final 16 minutes of the home match against Bradford City and scored the 90th minute winner with a diving header in front of the awe-struck Stan Cullis Stand.

It was his 300th Wolves goal, no fewer than four months after his 299th, came in his 450th appearance in League football and left him thirsting for more.

## Last Chance Saloon

"Whether I'm playing a full game, half a game or 20 minutes, I will carry on trying to do what I've done all my career – score goals," he said from what can accurately be described as a post-match 'high.' I'm a born scorer and I'll make my next target 325 and then 350 but you don't know what's round the corner. It might all end tomorrow. This was just another goal to me but one day I'll look back and think '300, well done!' The most important thing was it won us all three points. I didn't know whether to head the ball or kick it and I'm not sure what it went in off. It took an unbelievable time to go in the net."

Bull celebrated by lifting his shirt to reveal a t-shirt from Wolves' main sponsors that bore the message: '300, What a Goodyear!' He had worn the same garment at Stoke in the final match before his lay-off, only to then forget about it until reminded by Adrian Williams to put it on for a game that lifted the club back into the First Division's top six.

Alas, any hopes that this was the start of a scoring run turned to dust. He didn't hit the target again in 1997-98 and, for the first time in his phenomenal Wolves career, couldn't make it into double figures for the season, showered as he became by the fall-out of a bewildering signing frenzy by his manager in the latter stages of the club's exciting FA Cup journey.

Despite being drawn away each time, Wolves knocked out Darlington and Charlton while Bully was out injured and despatched a then-Premier League Wimbledon in a fifth-round replay with him on the bench. Then their advance really came to life when they unexpectedly won away in the quarter-final against a Leeds side sitting seventh in the top flight. It was there that Bull made his first FA Cup start of the season but the goal-scoring glory went near the end to Don Goodman, a former Elland Road ball-boy, on a day Dougie Freedman and substitute Keane were also on duty. It was a handsome array of weaponry but any assumptions that McGhee had enough striking power at his disposal would soon go flying out of the window.

Wolves were on their way to using no fewer than 35 players in the campaign – enough for three full teams and a couple of subs – and Sir Jack Hayward saw fit to publicly remark as the club's promotion hopes began to fade in April for another year that he considered one of McGhee's strengths to be his ability to remember the names of all his squad members.

Even allowing for Bully's injury problems, it was no wonder he wasn't getting a regular game. There weren't enough shirts to go round. He went on for the last quarter of an hour of the win against Crewe as Hans Segers saved another penalty a week after denying Leeds' Jimmy Floyd Hasselbaink from the spot, then appeared a few minutes earlier than that in a draw at Swindon.

McGhee was sufficiently perturbed by the shortage of goals that he held a meeting of four senior members of his scouting team at the full-time whistle at the County Ground, his dissatisfaction then underlined when his team, with Bully in from the start for only the third time since November, crashed 3-0 at in-form Ipswich. Nine League matches had produced five goals.

The response was astonishing as the manager unveiled five new signings at the same pre-deadline media conference at the club's training headquarters, two more forwards, Steve Claridge and David Connolly, among them. Everything pointed to Wolves having seven senior strikers to choose from for the Cup semi-final against Arsenal – a game managing director John Richards called the club's biggest for 17 years. Already there were club record marksman Bull, the prodigiously talented Keane, leading scorer Freedman and quarter-final hero Goodman, plus Mixu Paatelainen, the outsider of the group despite scoring four goals in the run to the semis and five in all in the cups that season. That's without Jason Roberts, who was an unused substitute at Leeds and who never kicked a ball for the club's first team.

Bully was facing a battle to nail down a place and McGhee let him know it. "You can't be sentimental," he said. "I don't think Steve would expect that. If we feel he can help us beat Arsenal, he will play. But for no other reason." Of the spree, which also included Robbie Slater, the loan of Rangers full-back Stephen Wright and the buying-back of Neil Emblen, McGhee said: "We're not scoring enough goals and we could either have sat around and hoped the goals started to come again or do something about it."

Amid the chaos, Bully was demoted to substitute the day after his 33rd birthday for a Sunday win at home to Portsmouth, at which Wembley fever was in short supply. The crowd of 20,718 was Wolves' lowest of the season in the League and the team's average age was 29 – a far cry from the vision of 22 and 23-year-olds of which McGhee had spoken soon after his appointment. Bully was happier when re-promoted for the April 1 draw at QPR four days before the Villa Park date but still there were no goals, for he or anyone else in a gold shirt. Sir Jack Hayward may have been planning to climb off his Los Angeles sick bed to attend the big game despite having had quadruple heart bypass surgery but the team were still in dodgy health.

Players probably didn't know whether they were coming or going and, although the unavailability of Connolly slightly narrowed down McGhee's semi-final options, there was still much uncertainty. "The competition for striking places is so intense here now that none of us can be sure of our places," Bully said diplomatically. "We have all had to be patient and accept it if we have been left out. Whoever plays, this is a day when we all have to be together, united in the cause. It's going to be a great day, one of the best I will ever have known as a Wolves player. We have to go and enjoy it but remember Wembley would be even more memorable."

The game was the most lucrative in Wolves' history but far from the most special. Claridge was named as a lone striker, with Goodman on the right and Steve Froggatt deployed as a wing-back. There was no little consternation among fans that a centre-forward with 300 goals and close on 540 games for the club should find himself in the shadow of the journeyman Claridge for such a big tie. Keane was alongside Bully on the bench. True, Arsenal were on their way to winning the double with the first of Arsene Wenger's great teams but the Division One side's approach only rarely gave any indication of a belief they could win – or even a genuine desire to try to do so.

It was much easier to detect a damage-limitation policy. They played with three centre-halves and another player who had operated as one, Steve Sedgley, in midfield. They didn't lay a glove on their opponents in the first half, did better in the second but had few complaints that the tie finished, as many games did at that time, 1-0 to the Arsenal. Bully, rapturously acclaimed when going out for the warm-up, was introduced for Goodman for the final 22 minutes and Keane was added for the last seven. It said everything about the respective strengths of the clubs that Wolves barely threatened despite having strikers falling over each other while Arsenal were without leading scorers Ian Wright and Dennis Bergkamp and won in comfort with a Christopher Wreh goal.

In 1949, Billy Wright used his first taste of FA Cup semi-final day to produce, against Manchester United, what he regarded as the best performance of his Wolves career. Forty-eight years on, the same occasion had largely past Steve Bull by in terms of opportunity to impress. And, unlike Billy, in whose Cup-winning season Stan Cullis fielded 24 players, there would be no more chances for Bully to play at such rarefied heights.

## Chapter Twenty-Two

# The Final Curtain

Mark McGhee had taken 21 players to Villa Park and increased that number to 22 – the equivalent of two full sides in an era when only three substitutes were named – for the League trip to Charlton just over 48 hours later. Officials from the home club couldn't accommodate all those who weren't on the team sheet and many of the unused eight had to go and sit with Wolves fans behind the goal. It was a bizarre time.

The club had failed to score in 14 away games in 1997-98 and any realistic chance of promotion had gone. Quite what Billy Wright would have made of it all is anyone's guess. He was well used to competition for first-team jerseys and knew what big playing staffs were all about. In his day, though, the club had a proper structure and a seventh-choice striker would have been a lad playing in the Worcestershire Combination side or something similar, not a senior pro who had cost big money.

Robbie Keane escaped the bedlam for a few days by flying to Dublin to make his full debut for the Republic of Ireland, who had Mick McCarthy in charge. And the manager felt compelled to say after the 17-year-old's eye-catching performance against world champions Argentina: "He has been saying how proud he is to play alongside a few of these established internationals but they will now be saying they are proud to have been on the same pitch when Robbie Keane made his home debut. He has set himself a hell of a standard. I can't expect him to play like that every match but I hope I am wrong. I can't deny the man of the match award going to Ariel Ortega but, from an Irish point of view, Robbie would have been a very worthy recipient."

Bully, a mentor to the Irish teenager, was more in the team than out of it in the dying weeks of the campaign, Wolves failing to score on their travels for the 15th time when Dave Bassett's Nottingham Forest thrashed them on Easter Monday on their way to automatic promotion. Jonathan Hayward, who had poked gentle fun at Bassett the day he appointed McGhee, left the board at the end of the season after a well-publicised row with his father over finances.

Bully's leanest Wolves season to date had left his goal tally marooned on nine, two of them in the League Cup at Reading. He had played 39 games, of which about a quarter were from the substitutes' bench, and even had the indignity, in the last-day defeat at Tranmere, of being thrown the no 10 shirt while the one that had been soaked in his sweat for a dozen years went to Mixu Paatelainen. He had netted only once in 17 games since his absence of more than three months with knee trouble and nobody enjoyed admitting what was blindingly obvious: he was a hero on the wane.

Bully could never claim to have emulated Billy's status as a great player in a great team. He was a colossal scorer, a fearsome opponent and a man driven to extract every last drop of energy from his body for the cause. But how he must wish he could have surrounded himself with better players at Molineux in the endless days in the Second Division. Just as Graham Taylor would later speak of having encountered a money culture at the club, so Bully believes there was a loss of team spirit in the second half of the 1990s while McGhee was at the helm. "He simply got it wrong…….we're not all naturals when it comes to man-management," the player wrote in the *'My Memories Of Wolves'* book he brought out well after his retirement.

For manager and player, there was to be one final hurrah, Wolves starting 1998-99 with four successive victories following their ninth-place finish the previous spring – one rung beneath Stockport County. And Bull, having used a tour game against Carl Zeiss Jena to end a goal-less run stretching back to February, was so sharp in the opening weeks of 1998-99 that we dared to believe he had one more big season in him.

He was particularly sharp in the televised Friday night success at Watford that formed the last leg of that quartet. That Taylor was now back in charge at Vicarage Road meant there was an excellent sense of timing as well. Bully scored against the Hornets but the side's early promise soon evaporated, so did the no 9's after his reminder of glories past. He was already top of the pile for Wolves hat-tricks when he netted three times in a Coca-Cola victory at Molineux. It was only against Barnet, the club closest to Joy and Billy's home in North London, but it felt as good to supporters as it did to him. Five goals to his name by the end of August…..this seemed like the old days.

Bully had been paired with a host of strike partners since getting on so famously with Andy Mutch, among them David Kelly and Don Goodman. Now he was with the one who would go on to have the most illustrious career of the lot, Robbie Keane. For a few weeks, the union of old master and young prince was highly promising, not least as they shared the five goals that retrieved a first-leg deficit against Barnet. "He was a great inspiration to a young professional like myself," the Irishman says.

Soon afterwards, Bully scored the only goal at home to Bury but, while his precocious partner went from strength to strength, it became a depressingly familiar tale for the man the Irish teenager so looked up to in his formative months. As Wolves' team coach pulled up for the game at Crewe in early October, talk was rife among supporters that another lengthy absence loomed. He had played the first ten League games of the season, missing only the two legs of the Coca-Cola Cup second-round defeat against Bournemouth, and also put himself around in his usual way at Gresty Road in a game in which Wolves deserved better than the 0-0 draw with which they emerged.

Maybe the danger signals were evident in the way McGhee had departed for a scouting mission with his managing director John Richards to Germany the previous night. Albanian international striker Igli Tare was quickly revealed as their target – more food for thought that the manager's previously declared statement that Bully's knee worries had eased were a shade on the hopeful side.

Sure enough, three days after the Crewe game, McGhee revealed that the striker was to undergo yet another operation on his knee; exploratory surgery that would probably result in the removal of some foreign bodies or floating bone but with the ominous rider that there appeared to be 'some sort of arthritic condition and rubbing together of bones.' Whereas Billy was able to play through a glorious climax to a carefully chosen end point to his career, with Wolves at the pinnacle of English football, the club's record scorer was limping desperately towards the finishing line, his hopes of spearheading their attack on the top-flight stage now in tatters on the physio's floor.

McGhee, his position under intense pressure as Wolves' strong start quickly subsided, had hoped for an absence of around three weeks. He quickly amended that, post-op, to 'a minimum of a month – and even that's optimistic.' "It was a cleaning-out operation and has been dealt with," he said. "There's a lot that might have been dealt with long-term but that wouldn't have helped him play football. He's had as little as could be done."

Richards, similarly plagued with knee trouble during the second half of his

## The Final Curtain

career, was a shoulder to lean on if Bully needed it. "I had three operations, the first in 1976, and they eat away at you," he says. "It becomes very tiring managing an injury and playing with it. You're not training fully because you're protecting yourself, so, when you play, you under-perform. You wake up each morning hoping for a miracle and that you will be pain-free. But, with a permanent injury, you are never going to get back to full effectiveness. You slip behind the other players as your fitness drops and it's just a matter of how far down the slope you're prepared to let yourself go before you call a halt."

The McGhee reign ended in a whimper at Ipswich in early November with a fourth defeat in six games and 11th place in the table. The Scot was intelligent, engaging company who had firm friends in the club but few fans look back on his time at Molineux with affection. Finding a case for him to have been given longer, as some argued with Graham Taylor, was a challenging proposition. With no little irony, the goals flew in for his successor and long-time coach Colin Lee. David Connolly ended a 14-game personal duck by rattling in four during a 6-1 crushing of Bristol City at Ashton Gate and Wolves followed up by hitting back from behind – something they hadn't been able to do for ages – to beat Sheffield United and Birmingham.

It wasn't always so invigorating under the caretaker control of a man who had long since grown apart from McGhee in his thinking but, from his position on the sidelines, Bully would have detected some managerial method compared with the madness of the previous year or two. With John Ward in as assistant boss, Wolves became a hard side to beat and dangled the carrot of a stronger promotion challenge in front of the rehabilitating striker.

Five wins and a draw in six games from the start of March had him counting the days off to his return but the efforts of both the player and his team-mates were to end, as they often did in the 1990s, in disappointment. And, had he but known it, Bully had only another few weeks of League football in front of him when Billy Wright's name was again in the news early in April, 1999. While the striker was preparing for the last of his comebacks, the great skipper in the sky was named in the FA Cup Final Hall Of Fame by the country's leading sports writers and broadcasters.

Billy played in only one Cup final – Wolves' appearances at Wembley in 1939 and 1960 came just before and after his monumental first-team service – and that was enough. His widow Joy Beverley travelled to Molineux to receive the award on his behalf and said: "Of all the things he achieved, he always said that when Wolves beat Leicester in 1949, it was one of his very happiest days. If he was here today to see this award, he would have said: 'I'm chuffed.'"

Meanwhile, the final stirring of the latter-day colossus that was Stephen George Bull was under way. He was making his mark again, even if only in the reserves. Was there one more dramatic curtain call in him? Was that famous first-team goal tally, stuck for seven months on 306, going to click on towards 310 and maybe even past it? He held off the marking of his former Wolves pal Chris Brindley and the effects of a cold to score in the Birmingham Senior Cup semi-final at Hednesford, where Joleon Lescott was also among the marksmen, then netted one and made another in the reserves' win at Burnley. Goals were coming again from those golden boots.

Wolves had come with a rush in their chase for a play-off place, winning eight and drawing six of their 15 League matches in 1999 in the striker's continued absence, their only defeat coming in the last minute at leaders Sunderland. And, when Bull made his celebrated comeback as substitute for the last five minutes of the derby at Birmingham, the impetus was maintained thanks to an early Steve Corica winner.

Bully was itching to play one of the main roles but had to be content with another brief outing from the bench in the Sunday home draw against Albion. The eight-minute appearance in Haavard Flo's place left him fresh enough to play and score against Barnsley reserves the following night but it was senior action he craved as he peered out of the window of Last Chance Saloon.

Lee again named him as a substitute for the live TV game at Bolton the following Friday. The big striker did go on – alas for his legions of fans, it was centre-forward Flo who was preferred as replacement for Keane in the side's fourth draw in five games. Not that it was for any lack of trying that Bull didn't get on at the Reebok Stadium. "I spent the whole of the 90 minutes warming up and thinking I should be out there," he told us afterwards. "I think four goals in six reserve games is enough to get back in the first team but I can't tell the manager how to pick the side. I'm impatient and a terrible watcher and he is putting out a team to do a job. But, when the time comes, I'll be ready."

While Wolves were handling one of their strikers with care, they asked for the same when handing Keane over to his country for a late-season friendly. McCarthy was three years into his job as Irish boss and was urged to be mindful of the fact the teenager was not long back from Nigeria and the World Youth Championships. McCarthy obliged by fielding him for only ten minutes.

## The Final Curtain

Bully's frustration at being unable to gatecrash the starting line-up at club level did not stop him championing the claims of Lee and Ward to the jobs they had filled for more than half the season. He thought the duo were right for the roles on a permanent basis and was handed 32 minutes in which to directly further help their cause when he was sent on at Grimsby in the club's penultimate League match. Another draw, this time 0-0, underlined the fact, though, that Wolves had run out of goals when they most needed them.

They had scored only three in four games since Bully had returned to the squad compared with six in the previous four. And the identity of the two teams barring their path to the play-off places made their plight no easier to bear despite an unbeaten run now stretching to 13 games.

Wolves fans had had no great love for Bolton ever since the play-off collision between the two in 1995 had ended with Bully, beaten and bruised, sitting in the middle of Burnden Park. Nor had by any means all of them shed tears for Taylor when he was ousted from Molineux less than six months later. But the manager was now riding the crest of a wave back at Watford, who won six games out of seven, and drew the other, to leave Wolves as outsiders for the play-offs in the slipstream of them and Bolton going into the final day. Surely he, the man at the centre of the aborted sale of Steve Bull to Coventry, wasn't going to have the last laugh on them?

More irony, potential misery – call it what you will – was added to the mix when Paul Jewell's Bradford City headed to Molineux needing a victory to secure their unlikely elevation to the top flight. Bradford, the side against whom Bully had scored his 300th Wolves goal, had been a Third Division club throughout Billy Wright's playing career and dropped to the Fourth soon after his retirement. Now they were prospering enormously, with Lee Mills, a striker Billy had seen fail to chisel out a lasting career with Wolves, making hay.

Mills had scored against Wolves in December and did so again in the return while Bully was once more gathering splinters. Despite Flo's early opener, the Yorkshire side were 3-1 up and cruising when only Mike Stowell's outstanding penalty save kept Wolves sufficiently in touch to make Paul Simpson's goal significant in an exciting finish. Bully went on for Flo with 28 minutes left but Bradford held on and so, almost unbelievably, did what Barnsley had done two years earlier by beating Wolves to the top flight. The likes of Oldham, Swindon and Charlton had also gone up while Wolves had been trying and failing, the promotion formula remaining as unfathomable as ever at Molineux.

# Billy & Bully

Billy Wright had bowed out by helping Wolves beat Leicester 3-0 and so lift the League Championship for the second year running and the third time in six seasons. Steve Bull's retreat into retirement was preceded by the painful sight of him, his colleagues and frustrated Molineux regulars having to stomach another team's promotion celebrations.

Wouldn't you just guess it but Taylor's Watford also went up. Having beaten Wolves to a play-off place, they then overcame Birmingham over two legs and Bolton in the final, the manager taking a pop at the questionable priorities he believed had been prevalent at Molineux during his time there – an observation Bully later made more gently. "The difference between Watford and Wolves is that we are a team," said Taylor, pointing out that his Molineux tenure had been ended by 'a rich man's son.' "I could never get that team ethos at Wolves. I inherited a dressing room in which all they could talk about was what they were on. Too many players were on too much money. It was hard to get the team ethos and that's the important thing."

Amazingly, it was the seventh time Taylor had taken a team up and, by first going down to the third grade in his second spell at Vicarage Road, he had effectively given Wolves a division start in the race for Premier League membership and still beaten them to it. Promotions peppered his CV, from Lincoln to Watford to Villa and back to Watford. Only the box marked Wolverhampton remained unticked. He had even iced this latest success by winning at Wembley, his home 'patch' at a time when tabloid sports desks thought it funny to portray his head as a turnip. The man who failed with England and paid the price at Wolves for inviting Steve Bull to leave was all smiles as he descended the Royal Box steps with the play-off winners' trophy.

As Watford feted Taylor all over again on that last afternoon of the club season, we were well aware that Bull, the magnificent creaking warrior, would never play for Wolves in the Premier League. With only one year left on his contract and all kinds of doubts over his fitness, there just wasn't time. What we didn't know was that he had already played for the last time for the club so close to his heart.

May 17, 1999, wasn't only the date on which Robbie Williams left the pitch in just his underpants after scoring a goal for his beloved Port Vale. It was also the day Steve Bull, properly attired, walked off a Football League ground for the last time as a professional footballer. Even for experts in the field, it may be a tester to recall where the Superstar – that's Bully, not Robbie – played his

## The Final Curtain

final game before retirement. It wasn't Molineux as another promotion bid finally ran out of steam on the last day of 1998-99. Nor was it Grimsby, where he had gone as a substitute five nights earlier. It was Vale Park.

As an unofficial messenger, I can vouch for the fact the player left it late in obtaining Colin Lee's permission – early afternoon on match-day no less – to keep a date with Neil Aspin by playing in the balding defender's testimonial. Typical Bully! At a time when his team-mates were once more reduced to the role of play-off observers rather than participants, he wanted to be playing.

Down the years, he had scored 13 times against the Potteries side, including a hat-trick in the 1988-89 Sherpa Van Trophy, so it may seem surprising that Aspin, who had just been released on a free transfer following ten years' loyal service and around 400 games, wanted him anywhere near him on his big night. But he had a strong professional admiration for him – and no doubt an inkling that his presence might put a few more on the gate.

"Of all the players I faced in my career, I rate Bully up near the very top," Aspin said. "Certainly he was the best I played against from the lower divisions. His workrate was phenomenal, so much so that you could hold him up as an example to anyone trying to make their way in the game. Graft like he did and young players could go a long way in their careers."

'Aspin For England' had become a popular chant among adoring Vale fans in the 1990s, though much more tongue-in-cheek than when Wolves supporters had started to sing 'Bully For England' during their rampage through the lower divisions. They were two down-to-earth lads who made the most of what they had and who developed a grudging regard for each other during their earthy battles across almost a decade. "I used to try to kick him off the park but he's a tough lad who used to kick me back," Aspin added. "We developed a mutual respect, so we stopped the kicking and just played. There was no-one better than Bully at sitting on your shoulder when the midfielders picked up the ball. He was so keen to steal a yard and he was so hungry for goals. We were never mates but we've both managed at the same level as well, me at Harrogate Town, and he's someone I happily speak to and speak well of. And it was certainly nice when he was able to play in my testimonial."

Vale's long-time boss John Rudge, in recent years an important cog in the Tony Pulis success story at Stoke, has no bigger professional regret than the fact he never managed Wolves. As a former forward, he is well placed to judge the merits of the man who took such heavy toll on his defenders – on one occasion via an early effort that had him pulling out what was left of his hair.

"Bully and Andy Mutch were a formidable partnership for any defence and we seemed to face Wolves a lot in the late 1980s and 1990s," he said. "There were a couple of cup games as well as all the League matches and I remember telling Neil and Phil Sproson before one game at Molineux that we all knew what to expect. There wouldn't be any need to worry about Bull and Mutch dropping off and looking for the ball to be played into their feet. Everything would be knocked into the channels for them to run on to, so we had to be ready. That was the message in our team meeting: Just be ready for those balls into the channels. Then, in the first few minutes, Sproey switched off and Bully banged one in. You just couldn't relax when he was around."

The striker didn't pull up any trees the night he appeared as a guest for Aspin, lining up alongside the likes of Mark Bright, Tony Naylor and Robbie Earle. He didn't score, although it probably wasn't for the want of trying, and didn't go the distance, being replaced by Steve Guppy in a Vale side who won 5-3 against Martin O'Neill's Leicester in front of almost 6,000.

The fact Aspin netted twice and saw another of Vale's goals pinged in by Robbie Williams's left foot underlined the fact that this was not football at its most serious. The showman in Williams couldn't prevent him from peeling off the various items of his kit at the end and throwing them into the crowd. As for Bull, one last restrained, waistline-watching close season lay ahead before making his own exit from the stage.

## Chapter Twenty-Three

# All Over

Billy Wright had called it a day while counting down in stamina training to the 1959-60 campaign. Forty summers later, Steve Bull arrived at the same decision. He, too, decided – in his case under the overwhelming weight of medical advice – that this unusual time of year was the one in which he would remove his sweat-soaked Wolves shirt for the last time.

There was to be no golden swansong for the striker in the form of goals, success and adulation on the Premier League stage. The diving close-range header he powered past Bury's Dean Kiely late the previous September was to prove the last of his magical 306. That match-winner from Kevin Muscat's cross was also his 250th in the League for Wolves while the goal he scored in a 3-3 draw with Barnsley Reserves at Molineux on Monday, April 26 was the last he would ever manage for the club. His last appearance in gold and black was even less conspicuous – a 4-1 defeat against Birmingham at St Andrew's in the final of the Birmingham Senior Cup on May 11.

The dressing rooms Billy and Bully left behind could hardly have presented a greater contrast. Billy, in August of 1959, was the figurehead of a team of back-to-back League champions, he having returned with England from Brazil, Peru, Mexico and the USA a few weeks earlier, still blessed by a sound physique. Bully, creaking under ever-increasing injury handicaps, was part of a Wolves squad stuck in the quicksand of the First Division.

In hindsight, maybe the striker shouldn't have gone away at all on tour in preparation for 1999-2000, the club's 11th successive season in the second tier. He had had fluid drained from his left knee shortly before but, with a hefty pay-as-you-play element to the year left on his contract, he was desperate to go at a time when he was no longer the most talked-about striker at Molineux. Robbie Keane, near the rear of the Stansted-bound coach with Muscat and Carl Robinson while Bully opted for a seat right at the front, was the name on everyone's lips as Aston Villa and Middlesbrough remained engaged in a £6m race for his signature. All that changed, though, on only the squad's second day at Solvesborg, Southern Sweden.

"Hang around a few minutes, we might have something to say about Bully," Colin Lee told me as he departed to his room after lunch. I warned the Express & Star sports desk that a big story was brewing, mindful as everyone on the trip was that the player hadn't been able to join in training.

I paced the corridor anxiously, longing for news before the last of the paper's deadlines that Tuesday afternoon. A few minutes turned into half an hour, the manager making the necessary calls to his MD John Richards at Molineux and club president and chairman Sir Jack Hayward. Then he emerged to announce: "Steve Bull is calling it a day. He's finished." The story led the front page under the banner 'Bully – The End' and the back page under the slightly smaller heading of 'What's Next For The Legend?' Time at last for those battered knees to be spared.......

At the time, the E&S were caught up in a spat with their sister paper, the Shropshire Star. Stories that would routinely be unearthed by one paper and passed to the other for the collective benefit were being withheld. As a result, my stories were not undergoing their normal duplication in editions coming out of Ketley in Telford, where the regime of the day had their own staff man chasing Wolves news from a distance. That all ended, though, on that July day, which, typically, just happened to be the 13th. So alarmed were the Shropshire powers-that-be at going to press without this massive announcement that a truce was hastily called. To football fans within an hour or so of Molineux, there was no bigger story than this to have missed out on.

A few minutes after my report had dropped on the desk in Wolverhampton, Lee and Bull were at the foot of the Stadt Hotel's outside steps to take questions and pose for photographs for the benefit of the small media contingent. The first picture used back home, taken by Nick Potts, the husband of the club's then Press officer, showed Bully in deeply reflective, even morose, mood.

While most of Wolves' players rested in their rooms for that night's game against Olofstrom, though, he soon put on a brave face and got through the session cheerfully enough, the only note of melancholy I could detect coming a few hours later when, looking for small talk, I reminded him that he had scored heavily when Wolves had visited this same town during their tour under Graham Taylor in 1994. "Aarh, those were the days, eh?" he said.

# All Over

It became evident that Bully had consulted Wolves' long-serving physio Barry Holmes before choosing not to go under the surgeon's knife once more and into yet another round of rehabilitation. No longer was the player's decision to say 'no' to Coventry in 1995 the hardest of his life. This was. He made it clear it was going to be a clean break, with no drawn-out descent down the divisions, not even into non-League football. "I'm not interested in trying to go part-time," he said. "It isn't worth the risk of further damage. I hope to find another career in football." But he did promise his long-time pal Mike Stowell he would turn out in his testimonial game 12 months later.

Unlike Billy, who accepted that time had taken its toll and left him vulnerable to the claims of younger players to his shirt, Bull had no immediate chance to say an emotional farewell. There was no looming Whites v Colours match at which he could take his much-deserved guard of honour. Instead, he began a long series of goodbyes by staying in Sweden for the week, signing countless 'last' autographs and posing for endless 'final' photos for fans.

He certainly had a drink or two more than he would have done and he would have been embarrassed by the publicity his retirement generated back home. Commons Speaker Betty Boothroyd expressed her sorrow at his demise and described him as 'one of Tipton's most famous sons,' even if she did slightly stretch a point on behalf of her West Bromwich West constituents by adding: "His goal-scoring ability first dominated the headlines when he played for West Bromwich Albion." At the game Wolves played within hours of his bombshell decision, a 3-2 win over Olofstrom, one Swedish-based fan said: "We should all be wearing black armbands tonight." Bully was snapped by the club's photographer again and had his usual smile for the supporters, even if his outward appearance hid some personal anguish.

While he spent a night or two letting down his greying hair, tributes were being penned. The Express & Star, inviting fans to write in with memories, were inundated as fans all over the globe used the still revolutionary means that was electronic mail to contact Queen Street and declare undying love and admiration. "I always knew Bully's glittering career would end some time but I dreaded this moment," wrote Jason Butler, from Bangkok. Detroit-based David Hipwood said: "He made me proud again to hold my head high and say I was a Wolves fan." From Columbia, USA, Clive Hardy urged Wolves to retire the no 9 jersey while, in Wolverhampton itself, David 'Noka' Powell eulogised: "You made me proud to support the babbies among a sea of Liverpool and

Manchester United shirts at school. A true local lad, you understand the worth of that old gold shirt."

For three days, the paper's columns carried messages of appreciation, among them some from councillors, MPs and Euro MPs as well as heads of supporters clubs and groups, and local industry leaders. Even Lisa Potts, the nursery nurse who protected toddlers in her charge from a knife-wielding attacker in 1996, called him 'a real hero.' A whole page was devoted to Bully in the E&S's Thursday edition. "When it comes to commitment, selflessness, loyalty and ability, Steve stands alone," said the White family from Abingdon, their tribute ending in terms that underlined how his retirement felt like a bereavement: "God bless you mate. It's been a great privilege to 'know' you."

The Rev Robert Blackhall called him 'simply the best centre-forward ever to play for the Wanderers' and thanked him for saving the club. Anthony Parker referred to him as the reason for him making five-hour round trips to matches from Cambridge and Dane Per Dyrholm drew similarities to Wolves' all-time greatest great. "He's one of the most loyal players in the Football League," he said. "Bully can be compared to our legend, Billy Wright, which says it all."

The Express & Star quoted Ron Flowers as calling Bully 'Wolverhampton's own idol' and spoke to Billy's widow Joy Beverley, who said: "I'm devastated. We were all dreading this day. Billy was a great fan of Steve's and admired him very much. We all thought it was so sad he never got to play in the Premiership. He has been a great crowd pleaser and a great servant to the club."

Wolves fans recognised how he had effectively cut short his international career through his loyalty to them and treasured the magical memories of his goals and celebrations, even the chants paying homage to him. He always seemed widely admired by the football community as a whole and one fan, Chris Deeley from Leeds, said Bully's statue should be erected outside Molineux alongside Billy's.

Charles Ross, the long-time editor of the fanzine named in the player's honour, had longer to compose his thoughts – a task he performed with much poignancy in the special 60-page 'Steve Bull – Our Tribute' edition that made up issue 66. "Bully had a truly unique bond with the fans, the like of which no other modern-day player has," he wrote. "He was one of us and he never forgot it. But for an accident of ability, he could have been stood on the terraces with us. As it was, when he took to the field, thousands of Wolves fans took to the field with him. He played the game the way we would like to imagine we would, given the ability and the chance. Giving it his all, each game, all game, no matter what the scoreline, the venue, the opposition. He could play only one way. A Bully goal mattered more than any other. A tap-in from him was worth more than a 25-yard screamer from someone else…….each of those 306 goals was that little bit special; his goals were our goals…….Steve Bull deserved to play in the Premiership more than anyone but I'm not sure the Premiership, all hype and blind greed, deserved Steve Bull."

The player still had a year left on his contract and many fans believed the famous no 9 shirt that his puffed-out chest had filled for almost a decade and a half should be stood down for a year both as a mark of respect and to shield its next occupant from an unfair burden. Certainly, it seemed highly inappropriate that the most inspiring of the 11 gold jerseys had Flo on it rather than Bull when Wolves players' names adorned their shirts for the first time in 1999-2000.

Others demanded that a stand be named after Bully while there were even suggestions that the striker be allowed to kick off Wolves' first game in the Premier League, whenever that might be, as he had done everything humanly possible to try to take them there. It somehow summed up the unfortunate 1990s knack Wolves had of being caught and overtaken (even temporarily) by clubs possessing a mere fraction of their tradition, fan base and resources, that Bully's last senior game should be the one at Molineux which confirmed Bradford's promotion. And the feeling of opposites around the retreat from the playing arena of two of Molineux's very finest did not end with the fact that Billy Wright had stood down while a champion.

Bully, worn down by countless hours of rehab, had not started any of the last 37 matches Wolves had played while he was registered with them. He had been in the starting side only 21 times in 88 games and come off in five of those, so it had been a long, painful descent, especially as he had started 106 of 109 prior to that, his only absence in that time coming through suspension.

Billy, by enormous contrast, wore the no 5 shirt in 81 of the last 88 League or cup games Wolves played while he was with them. In the days when there were no substitutes as protection, he also played some high-profile friendlies during that period, as well as 20 out of 20 games for England. Remarkably untainted by injury worries, he simply went from full fitness and full throttle to full retirement.

MD John Richards, who popped out to Sweden for a couple of days at the end of the week of Bully's big announcement, asked for patience from fans eager to know what he was going to do next. For now, it was probably enough that everyone just came to terms with some uncomfortable home truths. There would be no more aeroplane celebrations, no more pauses for breath with hands on hips and mouth open, no more lung-busting runs with those powerful arms pumping furiously and, above all, no more goals. All gone thanks to a wonky bloody knee.

Stephen George Bull was 34, the same age as Richards had been when he retired as a player, and had scored 306 times in 561 competitive Wolves matches – exactly 100 goals more than Geordie Messiah Alan Shearer managed for Newcastle. He was leaving behind a hole the size of a lunar crater.

Bully played in an era that was starting to become infiltrated by agents who had cash tills ringing between their ears, so the temptation for him to move was much greater than it must have been for Billy. Especially as, for so long, he was part of a Wolves side striving to take their place at the top table – the only one Billy ever feasted at while he was part of the Molineux furniture.

Bully had no designs on following Billy into a media career, although he was by now a much more confident individual at a microphone. Initially awkward and even shy when confronted by reporters' questions, he had learned how to play an audience even of hundreds. But his excursion into punditry was restricted to very occasional radio summarising or TV studio duties. He did, however, have every intention of watching plenty of Wolves matches in a professional capacity. He wanted to manage them. "Hopefully, if my name is put forward one day and, with a bit more experience behind me, I will be there," he said when interviewed for *'The Official Steve Bull Story'* video that was released a few weeks after his retirement.

It's another ironic twist in the Billy and Bully story that the one who was told there was employment at Molineux virtually for life ultimately chose not to take it – while the one who so desired a major role at the club at the end of his on-field service couldn't have it. Bully was not offered a full-time post by the 1999 Wolves, although his legions of fans had demanded it. I understand something was on the table for the striker but it was a role working with teenagers in the academy and not of a status he considered to be as helpful to his career as a carrot dangled in front of his nose by an old ally.

Long-serving Hereford boss Graham Turner succeeded in tempting Bully into a coaching post at a venue at which he had rarely struggled to score goals on his lower-division visits a decade earlier. Working with the Bulls, the manager reasoned, would be a useful breaking-in process for the man with whom he had worked so successfully at Molineux. There was even the potential for some crowd-pulling because Turner also registered him as a player.

Bull made his Hereford debut at Northwich and played a further 11 times for them, usually from the bench. He showed that the goal touch had not deserted him as he scored against Nuneaton and Morecambe in the Nationwide Conference in the second half of 2000-01, on the second occasion with a 16 on his shirt – the same number he had worn on his goal-scoring England introduction. Twelve Norwegian-based Wolves fans dropped in for one game and he nearly made it back to Wembley as Hereford reached the semi-final of the FA Trophy.

Others of a Wolverhampton Wanderers persuasion, meanwhile, were pulling in a different direction for him, a small group of fans striving on his behalf for a royal seal of approval. For months, they bombarded MPs, Government offices and even Prime Minister Tony Blair with letters extolling the player's virtues; not just about his goals and appearances, not just his superhuman achievements in leading one of England's most famous clubs away from the threat of extinction, but also by detailing his work outside football.

They wrote at length about charity work that was above and beyond the call of duty – the unpublicised personal appearances to see sick or needy kids, the unpaid visits to support various worthy causes and the permanent ability to raise a smile and adopt a cheery disposition that was guaranteed to put those around him at ease. For a man who is, or at least was, basically shy, he was in some ways a very good mixer.

The idea to seek the ultimate recognition grew out of a letter in *'A Load Of Bull'*. Why, a reader asked, when numerous sportsmen or women had been honoured, could an accolade not be given to a fabulously loyal record-breaking icon like him? Among those to seize on the challenge were Glyne Wetton, a Staffordshire-based Wolves fan with a handsome record in charity work, and Molineux match-day stewardess and self-confessed Bully 'nut' Evelyn Baker. Thanks to their efforts, 2,000 letters of support flooded into Downing Street but what made their mission all the tougher was that they knew their toils would be in vain if the press got as much as a whiff of the campaign.

Ok, I fib and own up……we were in on it but agreed not to use the story until it came to a successful conclusion. Then came the big announcement in the New Year Honours List of 2000. Six months after his retirement and 41 years after Billy Wright received a CBE, backstreet international Steve Bull, alias Tipton Terror or Tipton Skin, had been made a Member of the Order of the British Empire – and showed off the paperwork as proof.

"I knew a month ago that this was probably on the way and was very surprised," he told me at the time in an exclusive interview. "I had an inkling some supporters were mounting a campaign on my behalf and my reaction was: 'What have I done to deserve it?' I couldn't have achieved this honour without the fantastic help of Wolves fans and I hope they take some pleasure from it, too. I'm a very proud man."

As the recipient of an award from The Queen, Bully was in distinguished company. As well as Billy's 1959 CBE, Bill Slater, the skipper when Wolves lifted the FA Cup a year later, followed his receipt of the OBE by also becoming a CBE. Emlyn Hughes, who raised the League Cup for Wolves in 1980, was also decorated with an OBE while Wolverhampton-born Jack Hayward had become an OBE and a Sir and Rachael Heyhoe Flint's award of the MBE left her well placed to pass some protocol-related tips on to Bully.

When the striker emerged outside Buckingham Palace several weeks later, he was unrecognisable as the beast who had ravaged opposition defences for a decade and a half. There was no hint of that famous stubble beneath his relaxed, glowing smile and he looked a picture in his top hat, jacket, waistcoat and pinstripes when greeted by Willenhall sisters Margaret and Jean Stokes waving gold and black balloons. Sons Jack and Joe were in outfits that matched their dad's as they prepared for an hour or two in the company of their mother Julie in the ballroom seats that overlooked the investiture area. "They have obviously been looking forward to this day," Bully said. "They have been letting everyone know they were going to the Queen's house."

My surprise was not restricted to the fact I was able to walk round the Palace unescorted before the ceremony. I was also shocked to be the only reporter in attendance in the ornate ballroom, complete with chandeliers and red carpets – a lifetime away from the ramshackle Fourth and Third Division grounds at which I'd seen him first make his name in the goal-filled late 1980s.

"Mr Stephen George Bull, for services to Association Football," announced the Lord Steward, The Viscount Ridley, to a room of some 400 people. Around a third of the gathering were fellow recipients with surnames beginning with A, B or C in the first batch of honours winners in the new Millennium. Also in the long queue were Sue Barker MBE and Sir Henry Cooper but there were a lot of civil servants, voluntary workers, armed forces folk and general unsung heroes in between.

Against a melodic background provided by the Orchestra Of The Life Guards, Bully's turn came a few minutes after midday. A bow, a few words, a handshake and it was all over. But what memories, even if three-year-old Joe slept through the best bit on his mom's lap! Bully had once met Prime Minister John Major at Goodyear but such encounters were more the preserve of Billy Wright. The scorer of 306 Wolves goals had certainly never met The Queen, not even in his England career. "I was a bit nervous when I went in but it went very quickly and smoothly," he said while posing afterwards for Express & Star photographer David Bagnall, a shining medal and piece of red ribbon by now on his left lapel.

"The Queen said: 'It's for services to football, isn't it?' and I told her I'd spent 13 years at one club. She asked how many years that made altogether in my career and I said 16." There had been wonderful highlights – twice scoring 50 goals a season, late winners against Albion, netting on his England debut, the run to the World Cup semi-final and blowing other Wolves greats' records out of the water – but no-one could begrudge him calling this his proudest day.

The Bulls made the most of their time in the capital by also taking in Madame Tussaud's and London Zoo, the head of the family revealing that the MBE wasn't the only award coming his way. He had also broadened his professional horizons by passing his UEFA B coaching badges despite delaying his final assessment for some weeks because of discomfort from his knee.

"I've had it in my mind for a long time to go into coaching and these results can only help me," he said. "Now I'm going to test the water." Bully had, of course, already expressed a burning desire to one day manage Wolves but finding a way in at an advanced level wouldn't be easy. His good Molineux buddy Keith Curle had seen his coaching of Wolves' reserves curtailed by Colin Lee's recruitment of Terry Connor as a permanent third-in-command.

The events of subsequent years reminded Bully that there were more employment-seeking ex-players than there were club jobs and, despite being strongly linked with Telford, it was as a PR ambassador for Wolves that he became known, rather than as a manager-in-waiting. Independent public appearances, events and a clothing range bearing his name have remained more reliable earners than his preferred route.

# Billy & Bully

Whereas Billy and Ron Flowers were the only members of the club's 1959 title-winning squad to turn the experiences of playing careers into a spell of management, Bully has seen countless former team-mates given coaching opportunities – or better – while he has waited for the phone to ring.

Curle, Andy Mutch, Keith Downing, Robert Kelly, Phil Robinson, Nigel Vaughan, Mark Venus, Mick Gooding, Mike Stowell, Paul Cook, Shane Westley, Derek Mountfield, David Kelly, Kevin Keen, Darren Ferguson, Peter Shirtliff and Paul Simpson have all had more chance in the dug-out; even Mixu Paatelainen, Adrian Williams, Steve Claridge and Chris Brindley.

Opportunity eventually dawned at Stafford Rangers in 2008. He didn't know the non-League scene but knew a man who did and so recruited Brindley as his no 2, the ex-Molineux reserve having spent almost two decades at that level as a player, coach or manager with the likes of Telford, Hednesford and Kidderminster. "Bully was always enthusiastic and passionate at Stafford and didn't do a bad job," he said. "But the money just wasn't there to give him a real chance of success. It was different for me. I'd been in non-League virtually all my football life but he had had a fabulous reputation for many years and I suppose he wasn't prepared to be dragged down."

Managing the Blue Square club before and after their relegation from the premier division proved a thankless task in trying circumstances and Bully was gone in ten months. "In one way, I'd have felt happier if I'd resigned with him but I'd never earned the money he had and I'd left a job at Rushall Olympic to work with him, so I stayed and was named as his successor," Brindley added. "I found out how difficult it was, though, and realise it was probably a case of right club, wrong time for him."

From former Wolves midfielder and coach Barry Powell, a team-mate of both in the late 1980s and then briefly the co-handler of Bully's commercial interests, comes a suggestion that communication might be the stumbling block. "His passion for getting out on the training ground would not be a problem but whether he would be able to demonstrate his ideas, I don't know," he said. "I've no doubt he'd be a players' manager and organise an occasional night out but there's a technical side as well and he might struggle a bit with that. He was great fun to play with and a great success but I'd be lying if I said I could understand what he was saying to me! He speaks that quickly and, with any sort of crowd noise, it was very difficult picking things up from him."

Bully nevertheless remains a big draw, as we were reminded when he shared the spotlight with the master orator Sir Jack Hayward late in Wolves' successful 2002-03 promotion challenge . The decision to remove John Ireland's name from Molineux's oldest stand did not win the approval of all but the fact it was to be replaced by Bully's drew acclaim from the modern-day masses.

The announcement came at the launch of the player's *'My Memories Of Wolves'* book and he said: "I thought you had to be dead to be honoured like this." It was a view echoed by his England colleague Tony Cottee, who said: "At my club West Ham, we've seen Bobby Moore have a stand named after him well after he died, so it's a great tribute for Bully – and lovely for him – to be honoured at this time of his life. I'm so pleased for him."

Further acclaim has followed. He was given a hero's ovation when stepping on and off the field in a five-minute appearance at the start of the home friendly with Aston Villa in 2006 that the club turned into a 20th anniversary celebration of his signing. Having honoured his pledge to play in Stowell's testimonial and scored a couple in an old boys' game against Albion, he said that was quite definitely that.

With Billy, Jackery Jones, Stan Cullis, Flowers and Derek Parkin, he was then named as an inaugural inductee in Wolves' new Hall of Fame in early 2009, club owner Steve Morgan adding his own tribute to the sextet following his predecessor's oft-stated insistence that no-one could thank Steve Bull enough. "He has been a tremendously loyal servant and a great, great player," Sir Jack once said.

A whole generation of fans had latched on to Wolves thanks to Bully......561 games and a stunning 306 goals, without a single set-piece finish among them. Not bad for someone who once glued bits of beds together for £27 a week.

And what, in 2009, of Billy Wright? Ron Atkinson has been a staunch supporter of the campaign launched this year to try to secure a posthumous knighthood for a man he grew up idolising. "To win 105 caps in an era when they play half the internationals they do now is phenomenal," he said. "His total is probably worth 150 today. When they talk about truly great players, he was right up there and he was an absolutely blinding bloke."

Can two players ever have done so much to achieve superstar status and change the lives of those around them, yet, as individuals, changed so little?

# Subscribers

## A

David Adams
Annie Allman
Peter J Armfield
Mark Astbury

## B

Connor Bainbridge
Evelyn Baker and Jess
Ross Baker
Matt Bakewell
Jock, Charlie, Peter and
Aidan Bamforth
Neil and Sheila Barnes
Tommy and Pat Barratt
Christopher Bayley
Margaret and Victor Bicknell
Malcolm Black
Robert Blackhall
Michael Blakey
Pam and Peter Blakey
Vic Boffey
Lewis and Monica Brayne
Ulf Brennmo
James Paul Broomer
Martin Paul Broomer
David Paul Burrows
Roy Burrows

## C

Alfred Camilleri (Malta)
Martin Carroll
William Robert Cartwright
Jeff Clark
John Clarke
David Cleveland
David Collett
Ian Collett
Steven Cox

## D

Brian N Daniels
Harry Davenhill
Roy S Davies
The Davies Family
Roy Deakin
Sharon Dimmer
The Dungars

## E

David Edwards
Steve English
MKMGC Everiss

## F

Stuart and Paul Ferguson 2009
Cliff Fletcher

## G

Zachary Daniel Galbraith
Brian Gilbert
Erroll Grant
Joseph Grant-Bicknell

# Subscribers

Robert H Green
Brian Grey
Robert and Craig Gubbins

### H
Graham Harridence
Daniel Harrison
Jim Heath
Ann and Paul Hewkin
Josh Hewkin
Steve Hewkin
William John Hickman
Victor Hodges
Douglas Robert Hooper
Andrew Howe
Alfred Hughes
Anthony Hughes
Noel Hughes
Quentin Hughes

### J
Kenneth Jones

### K
John Kedward
David Keeling

### L
John Lalley
George Langford
Mark Langford
Ben Lewis

Olivia Lewis
Simon Lucas

### M
Tony Mallam Forever Wolves
Hayley McDonnell
Terry McIntyre
Per Magnar Meyer
Jean-Pierre Micallef (Malta)
Taila Miller
Richard Moffat
Becci Morgan
Chris and Dianne Morgan
James Morgan
Dave Morris

### N
Geoff Narraway
Chris Neoh
Antony D J Nicholls
Isaac S Nicholls

### O
Dennis Oliver
Keith Alexander Owen

### P
Terry Palmer
Matthew Partridge
Tom Partridge
Ron Peacock
Douglas John Pearl

# Subscribers

Brett Pearson
John B Pearson
David Phillips
Mark Povey
Martyn Pritchard
Terry Prosser

### R

Craig Roberts
Darren Roberts
Wayne Roberts
John Rogers
John Rowding

### S

Chris Salmon
Charles Sammut (Malta)
Jason Shaw
Ben and Tim Sherriff
Terry Shinton
Jim Sibley
George Sinagra (Malta)
Rod Skinner
Steven David Smith
Dave Snow
Dave Stallard
Ron Stevens
Sue (Mutchy)
George Swain
Christopher Swatman
Claire Swarbrick
Valerie Swinton

### T

John Edward Tilley
David Allen Tomlinson
Peter H Turner
Tony Turpin

### W

John T Walker MBE
Graham Terence Walters
Mr D H Weatherill
Steven Wells
Brian West
Colin Westbrook
Kenneth Westwood
Mike Westwood
Glyne Wetton
John Wetton
Charles White
Tony White
Adrian Whitehurst
Dave Wilkins
Judith A Williams
Peter and Joan Williams
John Withers
David Wright
Michael J Wright
Tony Wright